Public Morality and Liberal Society

I do not doubt that the social and political constitution of a people predisposes them to adopt certain doctrines and tastes, which afterwards flourish without difficulty amongst them; whilst the same causes may divert them from certain other opinions and propensities, without any voluntary effort, and, as it were, without any distinct consciousness, on their part. The whole art of the legislator is correctly to discern beforehand these natural inclinations of communities of men, in order to know whether they should be fostered, or whether it may not be necessary to check them.

—Alexis de Tocqueville, *Democracy in America*

Public Morality and Liberal Society

Essays on Decency, Law, and Pornography

HARRY M. CLOR

University of Notre Dame Press
Notre Dame and London

Library of Congress Cataloging-in-Publication Data

Clor, Harry M., 1929
    Public morality and liberal society : essays on decency, law, and
pornography / Harry Clor.
        p.   cm.
    Includes bibliographical references (p.   ) and index.
    ISBN 0-268-03813-9 (alk. paper)
    1. Moral conditions.   2. Social norms.   3. Crimes without victims.
4. Civil rights.   5. Law and ethics.   I. Title.
    HM216.C59   1996   95-50808
303.3'72—dc20   CIP

*The paper used in this publication meets the minimum requirements of the
American National Standard for Information Sciences—Permanence of
Paper for Printed Library Materials, ANSI Z39.48-1984.*

For Margaret, Kate, and Laura

Contents

Acknowledgments   ix

Introduction   1

1. The Problem of Public Morality   9
   NOTES   37

2. The Case for Public Morality   45
   NOTES   94

3. Reflections on the Offensive, the Harmful, and the Good   103
   NOTES   127

4. Choice, Equality, Dignity: Contemporary Liberal Perspectives   133
   NOTES   178

5. Pornography: Feminism, Sexuality, and Freedom of Expression   185
   NOTES   227

Index   233

Acknowledgments

It is not an easy matter to identify for appropriate recognition everyone who has contributed to a six -year writing project—and all the rumination and semirumination leading up to it. I will acknowledge here the most direct or prominent contributors.

My colleague Fred Baumann read and critically analyzed much of this manuscript in its first draft. His candid and incisive criticism saved me from many a platitudinous evasion of the central issues—evasions to which I was all too prone. If any traces of this vice remain they can't be Fred's fault. I am also happy to recognize the more general yet vital assistance provided by the Political Science Department of Kenyon College. My colleagues have not only supported this enterprise with encouragement and released time, they have, over the years, provided endless opportunities for the exchange of ideas in an atmosphere conducive to reflection on basic questions of moral and political life. In these regards I am especially indebted to my colleagues Kirk Emmert and Pamela Jensen.

It is also important to acknowledge the fundamental influence upon this project, and much else in my life, of my teacher and mentor, the late Herbert Storing. As all of his students know, Herb represents a model of intellectual integrity it is hard to live up to. Moreover, he was the original stimulator of my interest in the subject of public morality; he was the source of the inspiration requisite for an undertaking whose conclusions were likely to be something less than popular in academic circles. To my wife, Margaret, who prepared the manuscript, raised the useful questions of form and substance, and put up with me (no small thing), I am more appreciative than it is possible to express here.

In addition, I'm very grateful to the two foundations that have supported this project financially. An Earhart Foundation grant gave me a summer to get the enterprise launched. A grant from the Lynde and Harry Bradley Foundation allowed me, indispensably, to devote a whole semester to its completion. Finally, my appreciation to Kenyon College for faculty development assistance and, more profoundly, for being a place where liberal education matters.

Introduction

This inquiry into moral character and the public good is necessarily concerned with ideas about ethical life and ideas about the social welfare. Exploration of these ideas entails confrontation with many issues, some quite basic. For instance, what, if any, is the legitimate interest of the community in standards of decency and indecency; does our collective well-being depend in some vital respects upon promotion of the former and restriction of the latter? And insofar as such an interest exists, what is our civil society and its law entitled to do on behalf of that interest?

As readers are no doubt aware, the appropriate posture of the civic community toward virtue and vice is a perennial and intensely debated topic. A matter of enduring and philosophic (as well as current and practical) concern, the subject is addressed by almost every major political philosopher from Plato to John Stuart Mill. In twentieth-century liberal societies this grand theme reappears as controversy over morals legislation, "victimless crimes," and, in particular, pornography. Recently a number of commentators have come to view and discuss the subject in terms of cultural conflict or the so-called culture wars. (And there are some who speak more ominously of moral crisis and social disintegration.) To say the least, a considerable body of literature and argumentation exists on this topic. What is my excuse for adding to all that by revisiting this battleground?

Apart from the general truth that the great questions of human affairs are never entirely settled (hence, there is often room for another perspective), the excuse is my special focus on the idea of public morality. This idea has been insufficiently considered as such in the modern debates and yet, I believe, is at the root of the whole controversy. Unlike so many contemporary discussions of this topic, which start from premises of liberal

philosophy and are oriented by an overriding concern with personal liberty
or rights, this analysis begins with the moral interests and the claims of
community. The basic effort is to explicate, in a systematic way, the ethic
traditionally called public morality, explore its vicissitudes, and consider
how far it can be justified in theory and accommodated in practice in
the kind of society we call liberal.

To put it most concisely: by public morality I understand an ethic of
the community as such (not merely a collection of private opinions that
a majority of individuals happen to hold), which is concerned with decency
or civility (not simply personal rights and security from material injury),
which is recognized in public policy and is, at least sometimes, supported
by law. Historically the existence and presumed legitimacy of such a
communal ethic has been most obviously reflected in constitutionally
sanctioned legal policies against pornography, prostitution, polygamy,
incest, narcotics, gambling, suicide, public indecency, vulgarity and drunkenness, and certain violent or degrading entertainments. Nowadays public
morality is the object of so many doctrinal assaults and practical challenges
that it is thought by some serious observers to be doomed or on its last
legs. And some say good riddance; after all, most of the offenses listed
are not among our most urgent public problems. But, as I hope to show,
more is at stake than an aggregate of so-called victimless crimes; ultimately
at stake is our collective self-understanding, our view of what a liberal
community is really about. Is public morality susceptible to philosophic
justification—in itself and for a society whose presumed business is not
virtue but "life, liberty, and property?" I will be arguing that it is. And
can it survive in the face of what look like increasingly libertarian attitudes
and community-weakening tendencies of modernity? Can a society as
diverse as ours be really capable of sustaining any substantive common
ethos? I am less sure of that but will make a case for a cautious yes.

Why undertake such a project that will be regarded in certain quarters
as the pursuit of a lost cause or a misguided preoccupation with the
obsolete? One reason is that this subject gives rise to large controversial
questions about human affairs that are intrinsically interesting. There is,
however, another and less theoretical reason. It is important, I believe,
to keep alive a coherent general rationale for public morality—even if
many of its particulars cannot be substantially implemented under present
conditions. In other words, it is of practical importance that libertarian
doctrines and community-weakening tendencies do not go unchallenged,
and that a rational case for public morality be available when and if the

cultural situation becomes more hospitable. (Unless I'm mistaken, public opinion is a bit more hospitable to discussions of moral character and principles of civility than it was when I started this book six years ago. Yet this probably can't be said of academic opinion and certainly isn't true of avant-garde theories and attitudes.) Perhaps with the Cold War at an end, and the threat of international totalitarianism in abeyance, more reflective attention can be given to the ingredients of a good life: the kind of people we want to be and what we mean or want to mean by *freedom*. The subject of public morality lends itself to this kind of inquiry.

Consider the following exchange (fabricated yet typical enough) between two partisan citizens whom we may wish to call "libertarian" and "traditionalist."

LIBERTARIAN: You are always talking about communal moral values and the need for government and law to support them. That idea has no place in a liberal society; what a liberal society stands for is freedom of personal choice and toleration of diversity—not legislated conformity! And, as a matter of empirical fact, we don't and can't have an ethical consensus in a society as pluralistic and multicultural as ours. These are the reasons morality and immorality are private matters.

TRADITIONALIST: Certainly there is such a thing as public decency! Do we really want to live in a society where "anything goes"—even dehumanizing sexual cruelty in mass entertainment—as long as some people happen to like it? Obviously the great majority of us don't want to live in such a place; that's why we have traditionally maintained legal and institutional restraints against certain manifestations of vice.

LIBERTARIAN: Yes, we do retain some atavistic state policies of interference with the individual freedom of consenting adults, but that is deplorable. How shall it be decided what conception of virtue (and whose) should have public endorsement? You don't seem to realize that your policy invites a moralistic intolerance and censorship more dangerous than any of the "vices" you want to restrict! Why are you so insensitive to the lifestyle preferences of the minority and the individual?

TRADITIONALIST: Why are you so insensitive to the deeply held ethical convictions and traditions of the people? In a democracy the majority are entitled to some influence over the cultural environment in which they must live and raise families! Furthermore, you don't seem to understand that any community needs a decent moral order; we can't live on toleration alone. And we don't have to accept things utterly degrading—grossly sadistic films, for example—in deference to an exaggerated notion of personal autonomy.

LIBERTARIAN: Your conception of what is degrading is a subjective opinion; all such opinions are culturally relative.

TRADITIONALIST: Your moral relativism is wrong and incompatible with social life. Civilized living requires some ethical imperatives.

LIBERTARIAN: It is imperative that personal individuality and choice be respected; that is what free society is all about.

TRADITIONALIST: It is imperative that the human need for community be respected; meaningful freedom is impossible without standards of decency and restraint.

This artificial debate—a reconstructed composite of many real ones—is offered to illustrate the two claims I'm making for the importance of the issues with which public morality is concerned. It's easy to see how the controversy between our libertarian and traditionalist characters points to larger and larger questions not only about liberty and morality but also about society, human nature, and well-being. (Some of the more ultimate questions are beyond the cognizance of such partisan citizens yet are implicit in the subject.) These matters are interesting in themselves and worthy of exploration for their own sake, which, as a lifelong teacher of political theory and law in the context of a liberal education, leads me to them. One can also see how this debate generates certain broad issues of practical concern—practical yet more far-reaching than the debaters usually recognize. These are issues about what constitutes a liberal society and the bonds or standards of value that (might) serve to unite us. Much of what I have thought and written over the years—on censorship of obscenity, on John Stuart Mill's doctrine of liberty, on the rule of law and constitutional interpretation—has been animated by a preoccupation, from one angle or another, with the moral basis of liberal society. This volume is an effort to pursue these themes on a deeper conceptual level. The following is an outline of what each of the five chapters of this book contains.

Chapter 1 (in some respects another introduction) provides an overview of the various controversies and ambiguities about public morality in American life and opinion. Its purpose is not to probe very deeply but to indicate the scope of the subject—the broad range of issues it encompasses—and to consider why it has been both a persistent and a problematic phenomenon among us. I also want to show here that, despite recent erosion, the necessary condition for a public morality—a degree of ethical consensus—still obtains in this country.

Chapter 2, more theoretical and argumentative, presents the case for public morality in a comprehensively systematic way, and defends it against some of the better-known objections (such as those advanced by Mill and H. L. A. Hart). Substantial attention is given to the reasons society needs an ethic of decency, that is, the social and human interests served by it. Having explored these considerations, I then explicate the role of law and its limitations. This chapter brings together the necessary components of the case while taking account of its vulnerabilities, real or alleged.

Chapter 3 picks up on certain themes prominent in recent (especially liberal) approaches to the subject, which could not be dealt with adequately in the previous chapter. It begins with some illustration of what is wrong with the idea that the state must be neutral about morality or ways of life, and goes on to examine critically certain associated ideas, particularly the (usual) liberal view of what is and isn't "harmful." Central to my thesis here is the concept of "moral harm." Hence, the core of the chapter is an argument that there is such a thing as human good(s), despite the claims of radical ethical pluralists or relativists such as Isaiah Berlin, Jean-Paul Sartre, and Clifford Geertz.

Chapter 4 critically analyzes the two predominant orientations in contemporary liberal theory: the libertarian view that stands for the primacy of individual freedom of choice, and a strongly egalitarian view resting on a conception of what human dignity means. Several distinct rationales for the primacy of free choice (and therefore against public morality) are explored, with some emphasis upon the concept of personal individuality (Mill) and social progress (F. A. Hayek). To explicate the egalitarian theory—the concept of "equal dignity" or the equal civic status of lifestyles—and its defects, I analyze doctrines of Ronald Dworkin and John Rawls. There follows a comparison of contemporary liberalism with classical liberalism as represented by John Locke, with a view of showing why the latter is less hostile to public morality than the former. The chapter concludes with a section on "liberal virtues" arguing that, while liberalism by itself does tend to generate some virtues, these are not enough to provide the moral basis that society needs.

Chapter 5 contrasts (more or less favorably) the traditional ethical indictment of pornography with the current feminist indictment. Also confronted are two libertarian claims: that pornography is "free speech" in the constitutional sense and that "pornography is good for you," in other words, liberating. The pornographic treatment of sexuality (and Supreme Court pronouncements on the matter) is a theme periodically appearing in the earlier chapters as especially illustrative of the general subject of public morality, and questions concerning freedom of expression necessarily arise in every chapter. In this chapter, however, the conflict between classical moralist and radical feminist views of what is wrong with pornography is at the center of attention, along with First Amendment argumentation. I have postponed until this chapter any systematic confrontation with free speech doctrine per se.

This collection of sizeable, semi-independent essays (each one designed to stand more or less on its own) directed to a common thesis seems to be the most promising format for this enterprise. The format allows for a degree of flexibility in the pursuit of interesting topics arising from the main line of inquiry (for example, topics about sexuality and morality, liberalism and moderation). It also lends itself to another objective I've had much in mind—to reach with these issues an audience of thoughtful citizens as well as professional scholars. While I do want this work to be relevant to the scholarly inquiry and disputation in this area, I've written the essays with at least one eye on the well-educated citizen. The subject is after all a matter of considerable public interest. Therefore, in chapters 1 and 2 I've tried to formulate the case and discuss the issues in ordinary, nontechnical terms as much as possible (and to rely largely on authors who do so, such as Mill, Patrick Devlin, H. L. A. Hart). And that, primarily, is why I've put off until chapter 4 any extended analysis of the more abstract contemporary theories, such as Rawlsian theory. The intention is to move gradually from elementary and, hence, generally accessible formulations of the topic toward the more intricate (or abstract) ones. Chapter 4 involves some concepts and modes of argumentation unfamiliar to many, but even there I've tried to avoid the most highly recondite of the conceptualizations employed by authors under consideration. And, or course, the concluding chapter on pornography should be as accessible as chapter 1. (Readers with an interest in pursuing scholarly literature or analysis that I've slighted in the text will find periodic help in explanatory notes and bibliographical citations at the end of each chapter.)

As to the substantive orientation of these essays, the reader will discern that some prominence is given to ideas or perspectives derived from the classics of political and moral philosophy (those "Great Books" that have recently become the object of no small amount of controversy in our higher academia). I consult the enduring works of Western thought as well as contemporary writings and outlooks. This approach reflects my professional training and the intellectual enthusiasms of a liberal educator. Yet, such references also reflect my judgment that the current debates, both academic and civic, are in need of a kind of illumination that the classical perspectives can provide and that is hard to acquire without them. What they can provide is not necessarily The Truth but an enlargement of horizons—serious reflections about what is good and bad for us as human and social beings without which the finespun analytic exercises characteristic of much recent academic theorizing may seem unduly narrow, even arid. Consequently, I cite Plato and Aristotle, Locke and Rousseau, about as often as writers and schools of thought from our own time. And, therefore, you will encounter in these essays, as one of the most prominent themes, the traditional concept of *moderation*, of which Aristotle is probably the most renowned exponent. It might be thought that this recourse to classical works contradicts the stated intention to address the intelligent citizen who is not regularly in the business of advanced scholarly inquiry. On the contrary, one thing I hope to illustrate is how the classical perspectives (appropriately reflected upon) can speak quite meaningfully to our real concerns about moral community and liberty. Moreover, it is a well-known function of Great Books to help us distance ourselves (if only temporarily) from the partisan passions and orthodoxies of our own time and place.

This is largely a book of arguments and counterarguments and reflections thereon. While I wish to present a case for public morality, I do not presume that the analysis and argument offered here amounts to a conclusive proof and resolves the problems I've referred to as enduring. It seems to me that the human and social problems under consideration here are of the kind that don't lend themselves to conclusive, once-and-for-all resolutions having the character of proof. Neither, however, are they mere matters of subjective opinion unamenable to reasoned judgment. The history of ethical and political philosophy teaches us, on the one hand, that moral and social truths are hard to come by and, on the other hand, that some ideas are better—rationally more defensible and more appropriate for the kind of beings we are—than others. To state the point very simply for now, neither "absolutism" nor "relativism" is warranted. When categorical principles of right are affirmed with the claim of certitude, skepticism is warranted. Every principle of right (whether advanced on behalf of morality or liberty, the community or the individual!) is inevitably susceptible of reasonable doubt from some perspective or plausible exceptions in some context. Yet none of this justifies a posture of total skepticism or the sort of nihilism that rears its head nowadays in some segments of the academy, often under the name of post modernism. In a sense nihilism (like unjustified certainty) is an easy way out. What is hard is that we are, as Plato's Socrates regularly suggested, intermediate beings—living always somewhere between knowledge and ignorance, truth and falsehood.

A number of our contemporaries seems to believe that the only authentic way to acknowledge this human condition is to be "nonjudgmental." But abandoning judgment is not the only way, even if it were (in any rigorous sense) really possible. People can hardly help having opinions and trying to justify them. The appropriate response to this situation, I think, is reasoned dialogue, involvement in the give-and-take of argument, especially, where possible, the most articulate arguments. And that is why this book is arranged as it is. I have sought to present the major lines of argument against public morality, as well as my own position, in such a way that readers can grapple with the issues. This requires that the positions taken by the leading adversaries be presented in their own terms and at sufficient length (and that my response to those positions be sufficiently pointed) to enable a reader to appreciate what is at stake. It is a result of this procedure that difficulties in the case for public morality are periodically exposed, but I'm not interested in concealing the difficulties. And these essays are every bit as interested in stimulating reflection about the civic importance of moral character as they are in advancing a policy. Here, as in other areas of public affairs, it is at least as important to grasp what is at stake as it is to have a particular solution.

I

The Problem of Public Morality

I

The concept of public morality presents a significant problem to modern liberal, especially American, society. Understanding the intricacies of this problem requires first a relatively concrete definition of what it means to have a public morality and a survey of the various implications and controversies thereof—sufficiently to counteract unduly narrow or dismissive conceptions of what this subject is about. With its meaning adequately articulated, one can more easily show why public morality is not something obsolete or inevitably doomed to dissolution; one can show, on the contrary, how it is both a persistent reality and a persistent dilemma in American life.

Some people believe that we need not have any such problem as the one to be explored here; there is, they think, an easy solution: laissez-faire and to-each-his-own. A vision of society is offered in which each and every adult individual chooses his or her own "values" or "lifestyle" under the protection of a political order whose posture toward the diverse moralities and ways of life is one of strict neutrality. That vision is depicted and extolled as the free society or the open society or, in more recent terminology, "the republic of choice"[1]—a republic in which maximal individual freedom of choice is the primary desideratum, the overriding concern. The issues of liberty and community involved are too far-reaching to be amenable to such a simple resolution.

Whatever else might need to be said of it, a public morality is a communal ethic—an ethic upon which the social well-being is (somehow) supposed to depend and that is therefore regarded as a matter of public, not merely private, interest. On this point American opinion seems to be infected with ambiguities or obscurities. Some of these have been with us for a long time; others are of relatively recent origin.

We Americans are periodically accused of being a moralistic, even puritanical people. Yet we are the inheritors of a political theory and system of government notorious for its hard-boiled, unsentimental realism about human nature and human beings in society. Speaking of evils threatened by the pervasive agitation of self-interested and unjust political factions, *The Federalist Papers* asserted: "[W]e well know that neither moral nor religious motives can be relied upon as an adequate control."[2] Freely acknowledging the prominence in human nature of dangerous inclinations and passions, our Founders sought for adequate control largely through various institutional and economic arrangements—structural checks and balances and a multiplicity of economic interests operating to constrain and moderate each other. James Madison and his associates are renowned for having adopted and recommended "a policy of supplying, by opposite and rival interests, the defect of better motives."[3] And they are almost as renowned for having emphasized the frequent derivation of moral attitudes from material interests. Their policy, with its sober reluctance to rely upon virtue and its candid acknowledgment that human affairs are usually determined by materialistic self-interest, has shaped us, its beneficiaries, in important ways. Carrying this outlook to its utmost conclusion (as the American Founders never quite did), one is inclined to discount the significance of ethical considerations in favor of organizational and economic ones. The attitude generated is that, as far as the public affairs are concerned, what really counts and needs attention is not moral standards but effective institutional structures; what is decisive is not the moral character of citizens but their material security and satisfaction. It is, therefore, to material security and satisfaction rather than moral standards and character that laws and policies need to be addressed. This is one form of American realism, deeply rooted in the modernistic outlook.

From time to time, however, we do explicitly recognize another aspect of reality: institutions are composed of persons, and even the most structurally effective institutions governed by the most carefully devised rules will degenerate if the persons involved are sufficiently defective. That presumably is what Thomas Jefferson had in mind in his famous remark that "it is the manners and spirit of a people that preserves a republic in vigor. A degeneracy in these is a canker which soon eats at the heart of its laws and Constitution."[4] The point is more precisely articulated by John Stuart Mill in his work *Representative Government*. To illustrate his argument that "the qualities of the human agents" is a factor more important than the machinery and procedures of government, Mill asks: "Of what efficacy are rules of procedure in serving the ends of justice if the moral condition of the people is such that witnesses generally lie and the judges and their subordinates take bribes?" And more broadly: "Whenever the general disposition of the people is such that each individual regards only those of his interests that are selfish, and does not dwell on or concern himself for his share of the general interest, in such a state of things good government is impossible."[5] On this view ethics would be a factor at least as weighty as economic condition, and moral character (of a sort) would be a matter of concern for society as a whole, for "the republic."

It is on such premises as these (isn't it?) that the promotion of ethical "values" is generally recognized as a function of public education, and we seek by other modes of civic education—exhortation, patriotic ritual, inspirational symbolism, and the like—to mold attitudes or feelings conducive to public spirited citizenship. And it is on such premises that a (perceived) decline of "moral values" is treated, in media, schools, and other civic forums as a condition harmful or threatening to the well-being of the country.[6] And all this notwithstanding the contrary opinion, also notable among us, that a person's moral commitments and loyalties are one's own business, probably subjective, and, in any event, beyond the reach of the community or the state.

Apparently Americans are quite interested in questions of morality and immorality, especially when public officials or other prominent persons are suspected of vice. But here too a kind of ambivalence in our opinions is observable. In the case of political leaders accused of gross sexual misconduct, many of us are heard to say that this is a private matter: "What does his personal life have to do with the performance of his governmental function?" Often enough, however, we will not support that leader with our votes; in the end the people frequently act as if somehow a public interest is involved. (Or, at least, the leaders act as if such behavior is problematic enough to require efforts to conceal or deny it.) As for prominent persons—sports figures or celebrities, for example—we frequently seem to think that their decency or indecency is, in one way or another, our business. Yet there is considerable uncertainty or vagueness about the reasons and therefore about the legitimate ground of public judgment in such affairs. What exactly is wrong with eminent sports figures gambling or taking drugs? Is it only the danger of direct injury to the integrity and functioning of the sport? Or is it a larger question of "bad role models"? As to these alternative grounds for complaint, the citizenry seems unclear or unsure of itself. But insofar as the latter is our concern, a notion of public morality is presupposed. After all, what do we mean when we say someone is a "bad role model"? Normally we mean someone whose character defects make him or her an unfit (perhaps dangerous) object of lionization and emulation by impressionable members of the community. Concerning the status of this evaluation, some people might be willing to admit that, for them, it only expresses a subjective, private preference, as if "bad role model" were to be translated simply as "I happen to prefer a different lifestyle." But surely that is not what most of us intend to express. The complaint or the apprehension is (putatively at least) about an objective social evil—the moral miseducation or corruption of fellow citizens and future citizens.

One could offer many additional illustrations of this preliminary point— that much of our public discourse is about standards of good and bad, and that some of the discourse assumes that good and bad *character* is of civic import. Of course, by itself this point hardly proves anything. It is also true that a great deal of our public discourse is about personal liberty and toleration of difference. Consequently, our concern for moral values is periodically offset by uncertainty about standards of value and doubts about our entitlement to pronounce on the way individuals wish to live; we are loathe to appear dogmatic or intolerant. Sometimes we vacillate between expressions of moral outrage and libertarian permissiveness. (As might be illustrated by variable public and legal reactions to violent or degrading rock music productions.) The very term *values,* in such frequent use among us, suggests an ambiguity. While often employed, as I've indicated, to denote socially important norms (albeit with no small degree of vagueness), in other contexts it is employed in a manner implying the subjectivity of normative judgments as mere expressions of personal preference. The language of values, it would seem, both reflects and obscures our concern with moral character; it might well constitute a way of talking about that subject indirectly and without quite recognizing that we do so.

II

Do we Americans and inhabitants of modern liberal society have a public morality? The reader who has been with me so far will not be surprised by an answer involving some combination of yes and no. But before such an answer can be fully meaningful, the basic concept needs more definition and certain distinctions must be made explicit.

One might wish for some preliminary clarification of the terms *public* and *morality*. The former does not refer essentially to an ethic about things occurring in public places (although that becomes important in certain contexts). Rather, what is envisioned is a morality with public status, recognized as an ethos of the community per se; a body of norms inherent in the traditions and supportive of or presupposed by major institutions of the society. This understanding must be distinguished from an alternative view (pervasive on the libertarian side of controversies over morals legislation) that what is called public morality is nothing more than an aggregate of opinions that happen to be held by a majority of individuals or social groups at the moment. As against ephemeral attitudes of that sort, what is referred to here is a body of norms rooted in long-range civic interests and generally recognized as such. This factor of recognition is not unproblematic. It is not a necessary condition for the existence of a public morality that the average citizen can clearly articulate or justify its tenets or always obeys them. What we are talking about is a body of presuppositions implicit in a way of life, periodically acknowledged in civic discourse by institutional or opinion leaders and sanctioned, more or less, by the legal order.

The other preliminary consideration—what in this context is meant by *morality*—is one of greater perplexity. This question can hardly be resolved in advance as a matter of formal definition; it is, after all, one of the underlying substantive issues of the inquiry. But to orient the inquiry, some initial observations are necessary. If we were to employ the term *public morality* in its broadest conceivable sense, there could be little doubt that the United States and every other polity that has appeared on earth has had a public morality. Every human community affirms some standards of action and ways of living as normative for its members (and gets angry when they are disobeyed). It's hard to envision how a collection of people without any common principles or convictions at all could have the character of a society; what would constitute the social bond? Even the strongest liberal devotees of individuality and cultural pluralism must come to acknowledge in the end that the society they envision cannot do without some commonly accepted or authoritative norms. In fact, those devotees do affirm certain personal rights or equal liberties, and the ethical imperatives associated therewith, as civically authoritative principles (for example, freedom of expression and proscription of social or religious intolerance). That affirmation, however, is often accompanied by the claim, explicit or implicit, that such an "ethic of rights" (as we may call it) is all the public morality that a liberal society needs. It is against that claim and its variants that much of this book is contending.

There is no doubt that in the ethic of equal individual rights our society has an established public morality with some of its tenets enforceable by law. (The Civil Rights Acts of the 1960s undoubtedly enforce moral norms, and the propriety of their doing so is now virtually uncontested.) The fundamental questions are about the sufficiency or insufficiency of that morality. Is a shared ethical commitment to principles of personal liberty enough of a common ethical commitment to hold together a society as individualistic as our own? Or does our kind of society also require a different kind of morality, functioning to counterbalance or moderate its libertarian impulses? At any rate, our controversies, current and perennial, about society's investment in morality are usually controversies over a morality that is something more than an ethic of rights and liberties. What is it then; how should it be characterized? For introductory purposes here let us call it an ethic of decency or civility. An ethic of decency reflects notions of what is humanly respectable (or degrading) conduct and what is a civilized mode of life. It is associated (as the concept of right or rights is not) with judgments about the worthy and the unworthy—and ultimately ideas of the good and the appropriate for human beings.

Much of the contemporary controversy focuses on the entitlement of a liberal society to promote or endorse the kind of morality mentioned above by law (or by compulsion of pubic opinion). Most simply, may the liberal state ever employ its legal agencies to enforce concepts of decency? According to John Stuart Mill's famous and much-referred-to principle of liberty, the answer is apparently an emphatic NO. Mill's principle is that an adult person's liberty of action may be restricted (whether by law or social pressure) *only* "to prevent harm to others," never for that person's own good (paternalism) and never because of mere public distaste for the action (moral populism).[7] It's obvious that quite a lot depends upon what one understands by "harm to others." Elsewhere I have maintained that what Mill means (and has to mean) is conduct directly and palpably injurious to the life, health, liberty, or material possessions of identifiable and nonconsenting persons.[8] In other words, society is disabled from proscribing any actions that do not substantially and imminently threaten these elemental interests, no matter how indecent or vicious it thinks the actions are. And this includes an absolute prohibition on legal "paternalism" and "moralism."

It is a fact of some interest that modern liberal democracies do not embrace and live by Mill's doctrine in its entirety. Regarding the idea of "individuality" underlying Mill's principle—that "[o]ver himself, over his own mind and body, the individual is sovereign"[9]—we may say that American democracy is impressed with the idea yet compromises with it. A number of legal enactments against "vices," which we retain, must be viewed as deviations from Mill's doctrine of liberty. In matters of sexual conduct there are prohibitions concerning prostitution, pornography, live sex shows, public indecency, polygamy and bigamy, incest, sodomy, bestiality, and the like. A list of nonsexual "morals offenses" would normally include narcotics (mere possession as well as trafficking), some forms of gambling, suicide and assisting in suicide, euthanasia, duelling, abortion of a viable fetus, public drunkenness (when it can be characterized as disorderly conduct), desecration of the dead bodies of human beings, and certain violent entertainments such as bullfights, dog or cock fights, "dwarf tossing," and bare-fist prizefighting. In principle the restrictions apply to the voluntary conduct of "consenting adults." Moreover, in many instances the applicability of restrictions is not contingent upon a showing that the persons involved are likely to suffer physical or material injury.[10]

While these are not among our most prominent or relentlessly enforced laws, we do maintain them—even in "the republic of choice." Why? Why have the lawmaking representatives of the people sought to proscribe such activities? Some critics have a ready answer: since "morals offenses" are not protections against involuntary exposure to real material harm, they must be cases of political responsiveness to deeply felt popular revulsions, traceable ultimately to religious or other nonrational sources. So why not just sweep away all these illiberal and anachronistic legal taboos? As a matter of fact, these various proscriptions are no doubt attributable to a variety of motives and reasons, some less credible or consciously deliberated than others. But the critic's sharply dichotomized picture of the possible grounds for such laws is too simple. The legislator may argue that some deeply felt popular revulsions actually reflect socially valuable attitudes and are unfairly characterized as mere taboos. Perhaps not every restraint that isn't a protection against material injury is irrational. In any event, it's safe to say that, while we have relaxed or liberalized some of these restrictions, we are very unlikely to abolish all of them outright on sheer

Millian principle. It is highly probable that liberal society will continue to prohibit duelling—no matter that the duels are scrupulously confined to consenting adults in circumstances utterly private. And we are unlikely to abolish all restrictions on drug possession or polygamous marriage on the uncompromisable premise that each individual is sovereign over his own body and mind.

As to the status of legislation concerning sexual propriety, a recent Supreme Court case, *Barnes* v. *Glen Theatre* (1991)[11], is sufficiently illustrative to warrant extended attention. Like many localities, the city of South Bend, Indiana, has had a policy against nude dancing in public establishments. Applying Indiana's public indecency law, the city prohibited totally nude "dancing" in a nightclub (The Kitty-Kat Lounge) and a pornography shop. The Supreme Court upheld the law against First Amendment challenges, noting that "public indecency statutes such as the one before us reflect moral disapproval of people appearing in the nude among strangers in public places."[12] Though acknowledging that performances of this sort may be considered, marginally, as "expressive conduct," Chief Justice Rehnquist's plurality opinion found "the statute's purpose in protecting societal order and morality" both legitimate and sufficient to justify the restriction.[13] The four dissenting Justices challenged the Court's apparent reliance upon "societal morality" as a rationale. In the dissenters' view the only legitimate objection to, and reason for preventing, public nudity is to protect other people from involuntary confrontation with something they find very offensive. And of course there is no such problem in the Kitty-Kat Lounge or in the backroom of the pornography shop. Therefore freedom for "expressive conduct" must prevail.[14] In his separate opinion supporting the plurality, Justice Scalia observed: "The purpose of Indiana's nudity law would be violated, I think, if 60,000 fully consenting adults crowded into the Hoosierdome to display their genitalia to one another, even if there were not one offended innocent in the crowd. Our society prohibits, and all human societies have prohibited, certain activities not because they harm others but because they are considered, in the traditional phrase, 'contra bonos mores', i.e., immoral."[15] That traditional phrase, which the Justice saw fit to use approvingly, is one of the several legal formulae by which the idea of public morality has been represented in Anglo-American law. Justice Scalia's colorful remark was addressed not only to the dissenters but also to Justice Souter, who found it possible to join the Court plurality (thereby establishing a majority) on the basis of a public interest in social order but *not* social morality. Justice Souter found South Bend's prohibition legitimate only because of certain "secondary effects" to which adult entertainment establishments like Kitty-Kat give rise, such as encouragement of prostitution, sexual assault, and other criminal activity.[16]

This case serves to illustrate the current situation of public morality in the courts rather dramatically. The principle that the law may be used to restrict some (possibly "expressive") activities *because* the community finds them grossly immoral or indecent is upheld but not very firmly. Four Justices subscribe to the principle (allowing legislators to continue subscribing to it for the time being); four Justices dissent from it on libertarian grounds. The Justice who tilts the scales in favor of the prohibition does so on suppositions about materially harmful effects rather than indecency. (Sauter's position doesn't exactly apply John Stuart Mill's stringent test for permissable restraints upon personal liberty, but it seems to have more in common with that test than with the plurality's traditionalist position). And considering that the statute proscribed only *total* nudity, the 5-4 majority in its favor does seem rather slender. Furthermore, the opinions of the Chief Justice and Justice Scalia offer no suggestion as to *why* society is entitled to enforce its moral disapproval of nakedness among strangers in public places (other than references to the fact that such a power has long been assumed in the law). That is, the case provides us with little explicit guidance as to the rational grounds of public morality.

What, rationally speaking, could be the matter with a wholly voluntary congregation of 60,000 (or 600 or 60) people in the Hoosierdome for the mutual display of genitalia? Presumably the Millian principle, strictly applied, would resolutely preclude any restrictions imposed for the reason that the public, which constitutes a large majority, finds such an activity disgusting; Mill teaches emphatically that the mere "likings and dislikings" of society are no legitimate basis for coercion. What if our Hoosierdome revelers would also choose to engage in group sexual intercourse? And if the group intercourse they happen to enjoy is sadomasochism or bestiality—would that make any difference? None at all according to strict Millian doctrine; in the absence of palpable injury to nonconsenting persons, the activity belongs in the inviolable domain of personal liberty. Against this libertarian posture one may argue that public decency laws legitimately support certain important human qualities or standards of value that are assaulted by such orgies and would be eroded if the orgies were allowed to occur with impunity. These include standards supportive of monogamous family life and proprieties or sensibilities about erotic privacy which are associated with love and mutual respect. Whether adequate or not, this is an argument about something more than mere arbitrary "likings and dislikings," the irrational taboos of a majority; it derives from a conception of the social good. The underlying question in the *Glen Theatre* case is how far (if at all) the legislator is entitled to act upon such a conception of the social good.

Now suppose that instead of a sex orgy our Hoosierdome enthusiasts would wish to express themselves by systematically desecrating the dead bodies of their relatives. (Perhaps in order to dramatize their emancipation from conventional taboos.) Assuming that the event were so arranged as to avoid any public health hazard, and no children or unconsenting adults were involved, one wonders what, if anything, opponents of the *Glen Theatre* decision could have to say against it. Surely strict libertarian principle would mandate nonintervention; where is the "harm to others"? And, every bit as surely, the community would not stand for this event. Why? The average citizens' answers would no doubt include words like *degrading, inhuman, brutalizing.* A more adequate response would probably have to explicate the (apparent) supposition that some respect for the dead is an indispensable aspect of our humanness. The short answer is that wherever certain things are revered—held in awe or deep respect—flagrant degradations of them will be deemed beyond the outer limits of toleration. Maybe we could live by Millian libertarianism in its entirety if, as a people, we were willing to give up reverence and revered entities altogether. If we could totally accept what Max Weber called "the disenchantment of the world," then dead bodies would have no particular significance (along with much else) and desecration would be no problem. Evidently, we are unwilling to go that far. Though modernism has made much progress among us, our view of the world has not become so thoroughly disenchanted that we find everything tolerable.

The moral attitudes just depicted (and legislation associated therewith) may be offered as evidence that the necessary condition for a public morality—the existence of a societal consensus about decency and indecency—is fulfilled among us. Yet numerous critics will maintain that this could not be the case in a society as pluralistic as ours. They will claim that, even apart from the rights and wrongs of the matter, common beliefs, and hence public morality, cannot survive in our highly dynamic and diversified modern democracies. The point can be made in various ways and at different levels of abstraction or profundity. Let us consider first the relatively simple empirical claim that our country is so heterogeneous as to be without any common beliefs on matters of decency.

Herbert Packer observes that this society "neither has nor wants a unitary set of moral norms. . . . We don't begin to agree about the 'morality' of smoking, drinking, gambling, fornication and drug-taking, for example. . . . Our moral universe is polycentric."[17] It is true enough that on many ethical questions, including those noted by Packer (with drug-taking as a possible exception nowadays), we usually experience as much conflict as consensus. Packer could have added abortion and other subjects to his list.[18] The heterogeneity and variability of viewpoints is a well-known reality of American life that should and does constrain public endorsement of moral norms. But this is a fact susceptible to exaggeration; one can become overly impressed with our diversity at the expense of other aspects of social reality. (All "pluribus" and no "unum"?) It is interesting that Packer's list of subjects that we don't begin to agree about contains no reference to drug peddling, pornography, sadomasochism, incest, abortion of a viable fetus, polygamy, and, in general, the ideals of monogamous marriage. Surely pluralists have some arguing to do if they wish to contend that "the people of the United States" have no shared ethical outlook whatever on these subjects.[19] And the burden of proof is not met simply by noting the absence of unanimity. If it were impermissible to speak of communal ethical norms in the absence of unanimity, then no complex polity could ever be said to stand collectively for anything. (It would be as impermissible to assert that the United States, collectively, stands for principles of equal rights, private property, or capitalism as it would be to claim that we respect monogamy and certain ideas of decency.)

But this kind of response doesn't sufficiently address the more profound type of skepticism about moral consensus in our society. A critic might acknowledge the ethical agreements to which I've just alluded and yet maintain that they represent a rather superficial and unstable phenomenon. Such moral consensus as we have, it will be said, is weak and is being progressively weakened by underlying disagreements—disparities of opinion and ways of life that are deeper and on the increase. Perhaps it is destined for irrelevance if not outright dissolution.

This theme has recently become the subject of some rather high-level theoretical debate. In his prominent work *After Virtue*, Alasdair MacIntyre maintains that modern liberal societies neither have nor can acquire any significant consensus about the human good; what we have are endless disputes among philosophic positions rooted in unresolvable conflict between rival premises or first principles. MacIntyre, no friend of radical polycentricism, concludes with sadness that there is "no rational way of securing moral agreement in our culture."[20] MacIntyre provides us with illuminating insight into the apparently interminable disagreements among contemporary moral philosophies (utilitarians vs. Neo-Kantians, egalitarians such as John Rawls vs. libertarians such as Robert Nozick, etc.). But his deep pessimism is justified only insofar as this deadlock of academic theorists reflects or produces a similar deadlock among the citizens of American society. One might claim that the former condition is not grounds for practical pessimism, since our philosophic world and our practical ethical or social one are two different things. A viewpoint like this can be discovered in Jeffrey Stout's response to MacIntyre that we may summarize as follows: Our society indeed has a shared morality composed of numerous "overlapping platitudes" that are adequate for practical purposes; MacIntyre's mistake is to worry about philosophic conflicts over the sources of those platitudinous beliefs—a societal ethic can function well enough without any philosophically defensible foundations or agreement thereon.[21] Stout surely has a point insofar as he means to suggest that the shared norms that unite the citizens of a community like ours need not be wholly rational or grounded in principles that the citizens could validate as a matter of theoretical analysis. Society is not a seminar in moral philosophy. But do we really think that a human community can be bound together for long by a mere collection of platitudes ("commonplace" observations, as my dictionary has it) that people just happen to agree upon for a variety of (possibly incompatible) "reasons" that no one could ever justify by serious rational inquiry? To claim such a thing, it seems to me, is to make the mistake that is the diametric opposite of the rationalist one MacIntyre is said to have made. MacIntyre responds:

> Against Stout I want to suggest that he is indeed right in thinking that there is a consensus of platitudes in our moral culture, but that this belongs to the rhetorical surface of that culture, and not to its substance. The rhetoric of shared values is of great ideological importance, but it disguises the truth about how action is guided and directed. For what we genuinely share in the way of moral maxim, precepts and principles is insufficiently

determinate to guide action and what is sufficiently determinate to guide action is not shared.[22]

MacIntyre's basic point, apparently, is that we can agree upon nothing but (platitudinous) generalities and these are inadequate for the direction of conduct. For example, we agree upon a general maxim against lying but disagree endlessly about its application in practice, that is, the appropriate modifications or exceptions to the principle (e.g., Lying to help a friend or to serve the national interest).[23] MacIntyre's choice of the example of society's mixed views toward lying is both interesting and problematic. The status and stringency of the norm against lying has been a subject of continuing controversy in moral and political philosophy—from Plato to Kant to the present—and uncertainty and disparity of views are hardly a special condition of contemporary thought. Moreover, one needn't conclude that our uncertainties and disparities about concrete applications means that the general disapproval of falsehood or deception is *merely* platitudinous and wholly inefficacious in our social life. (Politicians and other public figures frequently lie to the people, but don't they take care not to get caught in flagrant instances of it because they fear widespread disapproval?) In this as in other areas of moral life, norms that are too abstract to *determine* conduct might yet be influential in the guidance of judgment about conduct. The mere fact that lying to help a friend or in the name of the public good normally requires a persuasive justification (which may or may not be fulfilled) is evidence that we have, in some measure, an operative social standard on the subject. Consider the question, how many Americans would give their ethical sanction to a practice of deceiving one's friends or betraying the country simply for one's own selfish interest?

The same line of argument may be advanced regarding the matters of decency with which this essay is more directly concerned. How many Americans will give ethical sanction to erotic nudity among strangers in public places, sadistic sexual practices, pornography, polygamy, the "drug culture," and grossly violent or degrading entertainments? (How many would sanction the introduction of bloody gladiator performances among consenting adults?) And, like the disapproval of lying and deception, these popular attitudes seem to be somewhat more deep-rooted among us than MacIntyre (or Stout) is willing to acknowledge. Furthermore, the numerous legislative enactments against those "indecencies" constitute evidence at variance with the claim that our moral universe is (utterly) polycentric. And the persistence of legal proscriptions of this sort is also, I believe, evidence contrary to the claim that our moral consensus belongs merely to "the rhetorical surface" of our culture.

We now come back to the question: Why do the representatives of the people enact and maintain these laws against indecencies? As I've suggested, some of the enactments may be viewed as supportive of attitudes and sensibilities associated with a valued institution, the family. Consider the proscriptions against prostitution, pornography, and polygamy; each of these activities is (in its own special way) antithetical to the idea of a loving and enduring erotic commitment to one person. When the Supreme Court upheld antipolygamy statutes in 1879, it did so partly on the grounds that the institution of monogamy is at the foundation of our kind of society and way of life; "upon it society may be said to be built."[24] But these and other legal prohibitions may also be seen as efforts to discourage practices regarded as degrading or dehumanizing per se (e.g., bestiality, drug addiction, promotion of vicious dog fights). In these matters the legislator need not be paternalistically concerned with the well-being of the individuals directly involved in degrading practices; he might be concerned with the eventual effects of such things upon standards of value deemed important for the well-being of the community. For example, the lawmaker might believe that dehumanizing images of sexuality portrayed by a multibillion-dollar-a-year pornography industry will in the long run erode socially indispensable qualities of mind and character. By acting against long-range, indirect, and subtle effects of that sort, such a policy violates Mill's stricture that compulsion may be used only to prevent direct and palpable injuries to nonconsenting persons. But it is not simply a policy of paternalism—coercing a person for his or her own good. And it is not exactly a policy of "moral populism"—enforcing the tastes and distastes of a majority simply because they are a majority. What it seeks to do is employ the criminal law in support of norms deemed vital to a socially cherished way of life. Some of the farthest reaching issues are about the justification(s) for that endeavor (justifications to be explored more systematically in the next chapter).

Yet morals legislation as such is only a part of our subject. Though applications of the criminal law are often at the cutting edge of controversies over public morality, it is important to see that much more is involved in the subject than that. Also involved are questions about family and education: parental custody of children, criteria for the definition of a family, the fitness of teachers in public (and private) schools, appropriate rules of behavior and disciplinary authority in the schools, and much else. In 1978 the Supreme Court of Illinois refused to award child custody to a divorced woman who was found by the state to be living in "open and notorious cohabitation" of the sort that "debases public morality."[25] Is the court's principle a valid one or should the legal and social definition of family be liberalized so that it comfortably incorporates such cohabitation? Is the state of California entitled to revoke the credentials of an elementary school teacher who has been found guilty of, as the state supreme court put it, "outraging public decency" by participation in the group sex activities of a "swinger's club"?[26] Answering in the affirmative, the court majority noted that such behavior "calls into question plaintiff's fitness to teach moral principles."[27] (The dissenters denounced "atavistic views" about both morality and teaching.) If the state of California's position has any validity, it must be on the assumption that there really are such things as public standards of decency—moral norms in which society has an interest and which, therefore, it is entitled to have taught in its schools. On what other legitimate basis could state educational statutes stipulate (as they often do) that "good moral character" is a prerequisite for the function of an educator? In a society without any public morality, the state could not meaningfully impose such a requirement (there could be no authoritative answer to the critical question, "Whose conception of moral character?" and "Whose business is it?"), and this case could hardly have arisen.

The implications of a public morality are still broader than what is suggested by these illustrations of criminal prohibition, civil law, and educational policy. They extend also to considerations about the kinds of things the state may properly *support*. Should a government-financed agency provide grants for exhibition of artworks that are (putatively) obscene or indecent? What about grants made by the National Endowment for the Arts in support of projects like the Mapplethorpe photography exhibit that some serious critics denounced for featuring "gross images of sexual profligacy, sadomasochism and the bestial treatment of human beings"?[28] And what are we, the citizens, to make of this problem? On the latter question it would seem that there are three basic alternative attitudes: (1) Disapproval and demands that government withdraw its financial aid—on the premise that we shouldn't be subsidizing violations of established standards of decency; (2) Indifference on the premise that the larger society and its interests are in no way affected; (3) Approval of the subsidy on the grounds that inventiveness and freedom of choice are being encouraged. If (1) is strong enough to outweigh (2) and (3), then we have unambiguous evidence of a public morality in existence (apart from any legal sanction); if (2) and (3) easily prevail, one suspects that no such, or at least a very weak, public morality exists. In actuality, the Mapplethorpe imbroglio of 1989–91 presents a mixed picture. Public outcries and various Congressional efforts to ensure against future NEA funding of obscenity are indications that a public morality exists. On the other hand, the partly successful libertarian counterattack and ensuing vacillation and compromises are evidence of this public morality's infirmity or ambiguity.

The immediate point here is that a public morality is much more than a collection of "victimless crimes"; its ramifications extend well beyond the considerations of legal enforcement. They also encompass norms operating in civic education and (periodically) activating public opinion. But that is half the story; the other half is that it makes a difference whether or not there is a structure of law reflecting and supporting opinion (and education) on moral matters. It is most unlikely that opinion alone would sustain a public morality if that opinion were never embodied in and ratified by the legal order. To summarize: a public morality in the full sense is an ethic of decency, socially recognized as a matter of communal concern, generally endorsed by the legal system, and in some instances enforced by the criminal sanction.

I've been claiming that we have such a communal ethic, while acknowledging that it is something problematic among us. This twofold thesis is perhaps most graphically illustrated if one juxtaposes the Supreme Court's jurisprudence in the area of obscenity (or pornography—legally the terms become synonymous) and the area of public vulgarity or profanity.

The Supreme Court has repeatedly upheld the Constitutionality of antipornography regulation (within fairly stringent rules designed to protect literature and art of "serious value"),[29] though it has usually done so without commentary on the public interests served by the regulation. In the *Paris Adult Theatre* case (1973), however, the Court did offer this commentary:

> We hold that there are legitimate state interests at stake in stemming the tide of commercialized obscenity, even assuming it is feasible to enforce effective safeguards against exposure to juveniles and to passersby. . . . These include the interest of the public in the quality of life and the total

community environment, the tone of commerce in the great city centers, and, possibly, the public safety itself.[30]

It is evident that this rationale does not depend upon a showing that exposure to pornography operates as a direct incitement to antisocial conduct ("harm to others" in the Millian sense). The wording of the passage identifies "the quality of life" and the "community environment" as desiderata independent of "the public safety." The first two expressions convey the idea that the character of the moral and cultural environment is a societal interest that government may act to protect (at least against a tide of commercialized obscenity). While the expression "quality of life" might have been chosen to avoid moralistic language, its employment in this context presupposes that we have a conception of decency, more or less established and discernable, by which the quality of life is normally measured. In other words, it assumes a degree of moral consensus such that average persons could be expected to agree in the perception of what constitutes "quality"—and especially its degredation—in their environment.

But Court decisions on the subject of public vulgarity, including decisions virtually contemporary with *Paris,* tell a different story. In 1969 one Paul Robert Cohen was convicted of disturbing the peace by marching up and down the hallways of the Los Angeles County Courthouse wearing a jacket prominently proclaiming "Fuck the Draft!" Reversing the conviction in 1971 in *Cohen* v. *California,* the Supreme Court emphatically denied that "the states, acting as guardians of public morality may properly remove this offensive word from the public vocabulary."[31] Among the reasons for this conclusion was the Court majority's great uncertainty that ascertainable, agreed-upon standards of evaluation exist in such matters. (Or should we say virtual certainty that no such standards exist?) For the majority, Justice Harlan wrote:

How is one to distinguish this from any other offensive word? . . . [W]hile the particular four-letter word being litigated here is perhaps more distasteful than most others of its genre, it is nevertheless often true that one man's vulgarity is another's lyric. Indeed, we think it is largely because government officials cannot make principled distinctions in this area that the Constitution leaves matters of taste and style so largely to the individual.[32]

This Court didn't quite say that there is no principled or rational basis whatever for identifying obnoxiously vulgar expression, but it came close enough. Strictly speaking, "one man's vulgarity is another's lyric" means that judgments in this area are wholly subjective and relative to diverse personal opinions or tastes. It is not surprising, therefore, that a year after *Cohen*, and under its authority, the Court refused to uphold a state conviction for repeated use of the epithet "Motherfucker!" by a member of the audience at a public school board meeting.[33]

How is the Court's relativistic stance in *Cohen* and its progeny compatible with its outlook in obscenity cases like *Paris Adult Theatre*? This juxtaposition of cases is not to suggest that the two sets of conclusions are in outright logical contradiction; cases of public profanity and cases of "literary" obscenity could present the law with considerations sufficiently different to warrant different Constitutional results. But surely there is a sizable tension here on the level of basic outlook and perception. The pronouncement of *Paris* about the quality of life rests on the supposition that some societal consensus exists on what is decent and indecent, while *Cohen's* emphasis on our judgmental uncertainties and variabilities presupposes that we hardly have any shared, agreed-upon standards of decency. And the fact that the former deals with pornography and the latter with vulgarity or profanity does not resolve *this* tension. If it were really true that "one man's vulgarity is another's lyric," why wouldn't it be equally true that one man's (or woman's) degrading pornography is another's uplifting beauty? Does it make any sense to say that when it comes to pornography we have enough of a shared morality to warrant reference to *the community's* quality of life, but when it comes to "Fuck the Draft!" and "Motherfucker!" and the like in public places, all is relativity and subjectivity of opinion? The reason such a distinction wouldn't make sense is that our attitudes toward pornography and toward vulgarity are subdivisions of the same general moral outlook (or category—decency and indecency—in matters of expression). And it is the Supreme Court's perception of that outlook that is confusing.

Paris and *Cohen* are incompatible not so much in specific constitutional conclusions as in their conceptions of the relevant American ethos and way of life. These cases embody two different versions of what our society is like (and, beyond that, about speech and reason and even about the meanings of words).[34] To put it starkly, insofar as the *Paris* version of reality is valid, we have an authentic communal ethic of decency; insofar as *Cohen's* picture of reality is correct, we do not. More broadly, to the extent that the Supreme Court adjudication of recent decades is an indication, public morality is coming to have a rather equivocal or ambiguous status among us.[35]

III

The problem of public morality that I've outlined thus far cannot be adequately grasped without some reflection on its rather deep roots. In the background of our current and practical controversies is a perennial philosophic one about virtue and freedom in political society. A number of the perennial themes have persisted in the American tradition and law, though often in a form rather diluted or obscured. Hence, there are two complex stories to be taken account of—one a matter of political philosophy and the other a matter of American history. (While it is impossible to do justice to these things in a chapter like this, ignoring them runs the greater risk of superficiality.)

If the idea of an enforceable public morality is problematic in contemporary society and opinion, it is worth remembering that this has not always been the case in Western thought. Aristotle taught that "legislators make the citizens good by forming habits in them, and this is the wish of every legislator, and those who do not effect it miss their mark, and it is in this that a good constitution differs from bad one."[36] The good habits that Aristotle had in mind were called—by him and in the classical tradition as a whole—"virtues." In the classical understanding, moral virtues are certain qualities of character that enable a person to restrain or refine the elemental passions and direct them to higher ends. Far from maintaining that the moral life is no business of the political community, Aristotelianism maintains that the formation of character is its primary business. The full development of the distinctively human potentialities is what society is essentially about, and that requires virtuous capabilities such as temperance or moderation and courage. In this sense virtue or, in terminology often used synonymously with it, "human excellence" is an *end* at which political association aims. In another sense, however, virtue (that is, some degree of it) is an indispensable *means* to the social good—a precondition for civic harmony and fraternal bonds without which one cannot have a genuine social life. In any event, since these humanizing and socializing qualities are hardly easy for individuals to acquire on their own, their promotion must be the business of civic institutions. That, in a simple sketch to be sure, is the classical perspective[37] that retained a strong hold on Western political theory until the seventeenth century.

As we know, that was not the political philosophy presiding over the establishment of the American Republic. Our Declaration of Independence proclaims that the end of just government is to secure the inalienable natural rights of individuals to life, liberty, and the pursuit of happiness (as the individuals perceive happiness). Nothing is said in either our Declaration or written Constitution about promotion of virtue or restriction of vices. John Locke, whose influence upon the authors of these documents is hard to deny, taught that human beings form and inhabit organized society "only with an intention in every one the better to preserve himself, his liberty and property."[38] The primary business of civil law and authority is to maintain the conditions under which life and liberty are secure and property can be accumulated successfully in peace. Locke's *Second Treatise of Government* says nothing at all about any public interest or governmental role in the moral development of citizens. And the influential doctrine of his *Letter Concerning Toleration* rigorously separates church and state so as to erect a formidable barrier against any state action concerned with the salvation of souls. It would seem that Lockean liberalism relegates desiderata of moral character, along with those of religion, to the private side of life.

These alternative political philosophies present us with a fundamental debate about the nature of the human community and the social good. From the classical viewpoint, organized society (the "polis") is essentially an arena for the moral education or civilizing cultivation of human nature. From the Lockean viewpoint it is basically an arena for the security of certain elementary natural interests of every individual—summarized by the trilogy "life, liberty, and property"—and the lawful adjudication of inevitable conflicts over these interests. The far-reaching questions about society and human fulfillment raised by these theoretical perspectives (and others developed in reaction to them) have a profound bearing upon any systematic case for public morality or against it.

But we are confronted more immediately with a dilemma about our own national experience. How are we to explain the origins and persistence of a public morality, including legal proscription of vices, in a polity whose official philosophy is, or at least was, profoundly shaped by Lockean (and Madisonian) liberalism?[39] A critic might regard these legal restrictions as mere relics of an outmoded philosophy embodied in atavistic custom, and accepted among us out of unreflective deference to old habits. I hope it is already clear why such a dismissive account won't work. These interventions of the state in the moral life have received deliberate constitutional recognition over and over again. From the beginnings of the Republic, states and localities have legally exercised what came to be known as "police powers"—the authority to regulate on behalf of "the public safety, health and morals." A prominent Supreme Court decision of 1903, upholding the authority of the Federal government to restrict lotteries, affirms in the course of its argument the state's "power to protect public morals."[40] In 1912 the Court found no difficulty in upholding Federal statutes against prostitution as an exercise of governmental powers "to promote the general welfare, material and moral."[41] The Court did not explain or find it necessary to explain how the general welfare comes to have a moral as well as a material component. As late as 1963, Chief Justice Earl Warren, writing in an obscenity case, took for granted as a well-established principle "the right of the Nation and the States to maintain a decent society."[42]

Until quite recently, the legitimacy of a public morality was assumed or accepted in principle by clear consensus of our official constitutional interpreters. Why? On what basis? A hard-line libertarian critic almost has to take the position that they were simply wrong—all of them—about the character of our constitutional polity. For those who find such a proposition rather improbable if not embarrassing, two alternative premises are available. First, it may be argued that our inherited (more or less Lockean) liberalism is actually more accommodating to a public morality than is apparent. In general terms, the line of argument would be that adequate protection for life, liberty, and property is a fairly complex matter, depending, along with other things, upon certain supplementary ethical attitudes and restraints among the public at large. Where that supplementary ethic is in need of legal support it may be supported—not for the sake of virtue but for the sake of preserving the moral environment that liberty and property need. Whether such a policy can be derived logically from Locke's philosophy, or made consistent with it, is a subject needing more attention than I can give it here. For now one might wonder how many of the morals offenses I've mentioned could be encompassed in a genuinely Lockean rationale without considerable stretching. (Perhaps it would be easier to make a Lockean case for restrictions upon gambling than nude dancing!)

Secondly and alternatively, it may be argued that Lockean liberalism, while in itself antithetical to a public morality, has been counteracted or moderated by other historic elements of American life, especially religious elements. In this scenario, a communal ethic of decency was generated in the Colonial period and nurtured from the early years of the Republic to the twentieth century—not at all by liberal philosophy but by a Christian (largely Protestant) consensus. It would seem to follow that public morality has existed in the United States despite, and even in uneasy tension with, the basic liberal ideas. A dualistic account of this sort is illuminating insofar as it indicates that liberalism and public morality, deriving from different sources, may function to check and balance each other (e.g., the latter authorizes a policy of legal control of pornography, while the former imposes stringent constraints on the policy in the interest of personal liberty and literary freedom). And this perspective helps to account for the various ambiguities in law and civic attitudes that we've been noting. But a perspective focusing so heavily upon its religious roots appears to leave public morality without any grounding in the secular interests of society, thereby calling into question its civic justification.

A somewhat more complex historical analysis is offered by Robert Bellah and his associates in *Habits of the Heart*. Their approach takes account of *three* different traditions; as the authors put it, there are three "central strands of our culture—biblical, republican and modern individualist."[43] By "republican," as distinguished from the other two, they seem to mean a devotion to political self-government and the requisite *virtues* of public spirited citizenship; that is, the recognition that authentic self-government requires citizens with a responsible concern for public affairs and willingness when necessary to subordinate private interests thereto. The basic point is that in the formative years of the Republic and throughout much of the nineteenth century, the biblical and republican strands provided a delimiting moral and cultural context for American liberalism. Because of these two influences upon it, our individualism was constrained by ideas of obligation to community; "both of these traditions placed individual autonomy in a context of moral and religious obligation that in some contexts justified obedience as well as freedom."[44] Though the authors do not focus on the concept of public morality per se (and rather neglect the role of law), their analysis does serve to make sense of its historical presence among us.

The relative status or influence of "biblical" and "republican" elements in the makeup of the American civic ethos is a subject of extended scholarly controversy.[45] For our purposes here what matters is the awareness that our Lockean and Madisonian liberalism has had to make room for opposing influences both civic and religious. Equally important is the insight, for which Alexis de Tocqueville is famous, that the religious influences have served genuine civic interests. Tocqueville credits the Christian heritage of Americans for having promoted "habits of restraint" that are "singularly favorable both to the tranquility of the people and to the durability of the institutions they have established." The earthly and political character of these benefits is emphasized in this notable passage: "I do not know whether all Americans have a sincere faith in their religion—for who can search the human heart?—but I am certain that they hold it to be indispensable to the maintenance of republican institutions."[46] One of the most valuable (and difficult) lessons we may learn from Tocqueville is that the social habits, or the ethics, that democracy needs are not simply those that it spontaneously produces and endorses. The good health of the republic depends also upon what we might call a countervailing ethic that functions to restrain certain harmful inclinations that modern democratic society tends to generate. These include tendencies to inordinate concern with material and physical gratification, restless and fluctuating desires, exaggerated sense of personal autonomy, and that preoccupation with one's private and petty interests that Tocqueville called "individualism."[47] Certain norms and qualities of character that serve to counteract these tendencies are generated (in part) and supported by religious belief, but their validity does not depend upon religious belief. Those habits of restraint are justifiable as significant contributors to political goods and human well-being.

If the view of American society and its problems that I've just summarized has any truth, then classical ideas about "virtue," that is, about the civic importance of moral character, have a continuing significance for us. Perhaps no society could totally neglect such ideas and still flourish. If so, that could be one of the reasons our society and our people traditionally have not neglected them. In America we owe both the liberty we cherish and its moderation to a kind of compromise. Lockean liberalism—with its vision of society as an aggregate of individuals, independent and self-interested, who have contracted for material security—has had to accommodate a countervailing communal morality to some extent.

IV

A new and more aggressive liberalism emerging in recent decades is less accommodating. This outlook generates theories of personal autonomy or freedom of choice extending well beyond the natural rights of "life, liberty, and property" in our classical liberalism. These doctrines advance (or presuppose) as the ideal human being the autonomous individual who freely chooses his or her own "lifestyle," even his or her own "identity," to the greatest extent possible. It follows that the worth of a society is to be measured by how much it removes obstacles and maximizes every individual's opportunities for such choosing. And this seems to entail the conclusion that a worthy society is one that does *not* have an authoritative public morality (that is, a morality of decency or restraint; of course, it would have a sizable ethic of rights). I shall generally refer to this school of thought as libertarian or autonomist.[48] This libertarian movement has been the source of progressive legal doctrines of rights and escalating claims concerning a constitutional right to "privacy." It is also the generator of increasing indictments of morality laws and policies as either "legal paternalism" or "legal moralism." Legal paternalism is that practice of coercing a person for his own good so famously condemned by Mill. Legal moralism is depicted as the enforcement of a society's conventional morality *for its own sake* when violations of it are substantially harmless, the proscription of "harmless immoralities." Thusly understood, public morality is condemned as pointless, oppressive, and counterproductive.[49]

Next door to this libertarian perspective is an egalitarian one, affirming a current conception of equality that extends well beyond the meaning of "all men are created equal" in our original philosophy. On the basis of this new conception, public morality is condemned as a kind of arbitrary and unjust state preference for some people's lifestyles over others. Laws against prostitution, obscenity, polygamy, public vulgarity, even drug use and the like are indicted as violations of the equal dignity or respect that is due to all persons, because such laws operate on the premise that some ways or choices of life are inferior and less worthy than others.[50] (On this view, the state of California is guilty of violating Cohen's right to equal dignity and/or respect when it tries to prevent him from denouncing the draft in the kind of language that reflects his feelings but that the majority finds indecent.)

Though these libertarian and egalitarian positions derive from somewhat different philosophic premises, they lead eventually to the same result: insistence that the liberal state must be neutral toward ways of life. Organized society and its laws are to be confined to a posture of strict neutrality regarding "values" or opinions of what is humanly good and worthy. This means essentially that the community as such may not have a preferred idea of the humanly good or worthy; private individuals will opt for one or another of the multifarious notions of good life that a pluralist society offers—with a view to personal satisfaction and without any guidance from the civic community.

The new liberalism has become a prodigious source of challenges not only to legal proscriptions of "vices" but also to established norms, attitudes, and policies in many areas of our social life. Due in part to the progress of this outlook in our universities and mass media, as well as courts of law,[51] public morality is very much on the defensive, and its existence among us is infected with the anomalies and equivocations observed in this chapter. Indeed, in contemporary social analysis the idea of "culture wars" is periodically offered as a model of our situation.[52]

These effects are reinforced by a pronounced skepticism about things moral and political that often accompanies the new liberalism. As Sanford Levinson, one of its proponents, characterizes this outlook, it is "fundamentally dubious of the existence of a shared moral reality."[53] This statement means not only that our society is radically heterogeneous in moral opinion but also, more pointedly, that there hardly is such a thing as ethical or political truth for anyone to rely on; all ethical claims are profoundly questionable. (Levinson cites favorably the Nietzschean view that "[t]ruths are illusions whose illusionary nature has been forgotten.")[54] The immediate effect of such radical skepticism is to call into question the validity of any norms that society may wish to enforce or support as a matter of public morality. Thus in *Cohen* v. *California* and in similar cases, norms concerning the vulgar and profane are more easily relativized and debunked as mere phenomena of shifting opinion. The same process is evident on the libertarian side in cases of pornography and public indecency. The moral standards by which pornography or indecency are identified and judged are denigrated as mere subjectivity or ethnocentric bias. A similar debunking movement may be expected to occur in opposition to existing standards of propriety in the public schools. Why should an elementary school teacher be penalized by loss of teaching credentials or otherwise simply because, in contravention of some people's (groundless and reactionary) moral attitude, she participates in a group-sex "swingers' club"?[55] As the colloquial expression has it, "who is to say" that there is something wrong with such behavior? And so on. In this way the edifice of public morality is assaulted piece by piece and gradually eroded.

Libertarians often welcome this process, believing that human liberty is expanded as the ethic of decency is undermined. They do not seem to worry that the ultrarelativism they encourage regarding ethics as such will infect their own preferred ethic of rights and liberties. But why confidently assume that the latter will remain comfortably intact? Such sanguinity seems quite unwarranted insofar as ultrarelativism becomes outright nihilism.[56] And it is also unwarranted insofar as a regime of rights and liberties needs the supportive constraints of a moral consensus.

I began this chapter with a reference to the concept of "the republic of choice." The author of that terminology, law professor Lawrence Friedman, has introduced the idea thusly: "[W]e live in what I call 'the republic of choice.' It is a world in which the right 'to be oneself,' to *choose* oneself is placed in a special and privileged position; in which *expression* is favored over *self-control*."[57] The new liberal philosophy surely justifies and encourages this situation, though Friedman deems the situation largely a result of "popular culture." But, as I've been mentioning, it is not entirely true that we live in that "republic." In our law and popular culture, personal choice and self-expression are indeed privileged desiderata, but they are not in such a position of overriding privilege as to take precedence over competing moral considerations all the time. It is still the case that individual freedom of choice and expression must sometimes yield to a public morality favoring self-control. And, as far as one can tell, the most radical forms of moral skepticism are largely confined (thus far) to certain segments of the academic and intellectual classes. The freewheeling republic envisioned by Professors Friedman and Levinson has not yet materialized in its entirety. But it might well do so; we have come a considerable distance toward it and away from the republic envisioned by Jefferson and by Tocqueville. We could quite conceivably go all the rest of the distance.

Is that an outcome that we should welcome and desire to promote? Some observers will say that the question is practically irrelevant, that the progressive removal of communal moral restraints upon personal autonomy is an inevitable development—the product of forces of modernity (capitalistic, technological, etc.) that cannot be altered. When advanced by libertarians, this deterministic position is rather anomalous. It supposes, strangely, that individual human beings have some liberty to determine their destiny but the community has none, that individually we can make significant choices while collectively we are driven by historical forces beyond our control. My question is far from any assumption that we have complete control over our social destiny; it only assumes that we—as a public or community—can have some influence over what happens to us or what we become. One need not hasten to the deterministic conclusion that public morality is altogether doomed by irresistible developments of modernity. The movement toward utmost moral laissez faire might still be modified if we are persuaded that it ought to be.

This could be the appropriate time for our society to confront basic questions about what we stand for, what our civilization means. With the end of the Cold War, which has necessarily preoccupied us for over forty years, perhaps we can look inward. In 1986, with the Cold War still threatening, Leszek Kolakowski wrote: "However distasteful our civilization might be in some of its vulgar aspects, however enfeebled by its hedonistic indifference, greed and the decline of civic virtues, however torn by struggles and teeming with social ills, the most powerful reason for its unconditional defense (and I am ready to emphasize this adjective) is provided by its alternative. It faces a new totalitarian civilization of Sovietism."[58] The passage should make us uneasy. In view of a threatened totalitarian alternative, our libertarianism, our regime of personal rights and liberties, is clearly worthy of unconditional support. Presumably, however, the totalitarian alternative has now been removed as a serious threat to us. What justification remains for wholehearted devotion to a civilization such as Kolakowski depicts? Shall we say that our civilization is worthy of that devotion because it stands for freedom—and freedom means simply the right of every individual to live just as he or she pleases? (This of course would include the inalienable right to sustain, for mass entertainment, a multibillion-dollar-a-year pornography industry and, for the enjoyment of our children, celebrations of orgiastic violence presented by numerous rock music or "heavy metal" groups and the like).[59] Is utmost freedom of choice its own justification regardless of what is chosen? Does it validate the society that maintains it—even if the result is, to use Kolakowski's terms, large scale vulgarity, hedonistic self-absorption, and loss of civic virtue?

This is, in large part, a question of what we mean by freedom or what we value as meaningful freedom. In accordance with a powerful element in our historic experience, which generally goes by the name of individualism, Americans have always wanted to think of themselves as beings independent and free. But historically a public ethos has served to temper that spirit of independence, placing limits around it and sometimes even informing it with civic interests.[60] Now that public ethos is weakened as the influences, civic and religious, sustaining it have weakened. In Bellah's terminology (as good as any on this point, I believe), a new self-expressive individualism has emerged that is no longer confined or informed by the biblical and republican traditions.

While expressive individualism is much endorsed in current libertarian doctrine, we do find a growing number of scholars and social diagnosticians warning against the ill effects of its excesses. Bellah and his associates doubt that "an individualism in which the self has become the main form of reality can really be sustained . . . [that] such individuals are capable of sustaining either a public or a private life."[61] Others worry about a libertarian ideology so heavily focused upon *rights*—the rights of individuals—that it precludes even recognition and discussions of communal interests (which cannot be formulated in terms of personal rights). Law professor Mary Ann Glendon indicts "our [current] American rights dialect" for, among other things, "its penchant for absolute, extravagant formulations, its near aphasia concerning responsibility, its excessive homage to individual independence and self-sufficiency,"[62] along with the corresponding neglect of "the social dimensions of human personhood" and "the sorts of groups within which the human character, competence, and capacity for citizenship are formed."[63] In 1983 sociologists Brigitte and Peter Berger coined the term *hyper-individualism* for what they saw as "an increasing emphasis on the individual over against every collective entity, including the family itself, which has been the historical matrix of modern individuation."[64] It is a fact of some importance that the new liberalism, with its calls for more and more personal autonomy, is encountering scholarly reaction of this sort on behalf of sociality and our collective affairs.

Among the critics is a school of thought which often goes nowadays by the name of "communitarianism."[65] These thinkers deplore the lack of civic identity or public spiritedness in our society; they seek policies, institutions, and a way of life considerably more cooperative (and less self-oriented) than ours has been. Some of their formulations seem to call for a rather far-reaching restructuring of liberal fundamentals. If a *predominantly* communalistic or fraternal society is what these critics envision, that appears to be an unrealistic expectation as long as we are in "Lockeland"—a commercial society devoted to facilitating the individual pursuit of happiness as individually perceived. To be sure, public morality (often ignored or slighted by the more radical communitarians) is, in some degree, a communitarian policy. But the policy, as it has existed in this country and as it is understood in this book, is hardly an aspiration to thoroughgoing social solidarity; it is less ambitious than that. What it envisions is not the transformation of American liberalism into a self-subordinating fraternalism (like the ideal Kibbutz), but rather the maintenance of certain common bonds and standards of value for the checking and balancing of our libertarian inclinations. As such, public morality is far from being an answer to all the problems that our kind of society generates (and it would be dangerous to think of it that way); in practice it can never be more than a partial amelioration.

Yet, systematic reflection, including theoretical reflection, upon the subject of public morality can help to illuminate our larger problems and concerns. And that is one reason it is a fact of importance that the new liberalism has not gone unopposed. The objections and reservations, articulated by respected thinkers, may make it easier for us to entertain basic ideas and suppositions substantially at variance with the predominant individualistic ones. Perhaps it is not naive to think that now there might be fewer obstacles to serious consideration of the case for public morality.

NOTES

1. See Lawrence M. Friedman, *The Republic of Choice* (Cambridge, Mass.: Harvard Univ. Press, 1990).

2. Alexander Hamilton, James Madison, and John Jay, *The Federalist Papers* (New York: New American Library, 1961), p. 81.

3. Ibid., p. 322.

4. John Dewey, ed., *The Living Thoughts of Thomas Jefferson* (Greenwich, Conn.: Fawcett, 1963), p. 88.

5. John Stuart Mill, *Representative Government,* in *Utilitarianism, On Liberty and Representative Government* (New York: E. P. Dutton, 1951), pp. 257–58.

6. A case in point is the report of a Federal advisory panel, The National Commission on Children, just publicized at the time of this writing. According to the *New York Times,* the report "emphasizes . . . the importance of moral values, and says that schools are 'too often silent on critical moral and ethical issues.'" Also the panel "laments what it describes as 'a steady onslaught of advertising, violence and sex' that pours forth from the family television" (*New York Times,* June 24, 1991, p. 1). Obviously, the report's criticism and lamentations presuppose that moral education belongs in the public schools not only with the private family and that "a steady onslaught of violence and sex" on television represents a national problem not just a familial and personal one.

7. *On Liberty* (Indianapolis: Bobbs-Merrill, 1976), p. 13.

8. See Harry M. Clor, "Mill and Millians on Liberty and Moral Character," *The Review of Politics,* 47, University of Notre Dame, (January 1985), pp. 4–5.

9. *On Liberty*, p. 13.

10. It would seem that Mill's principle is also violated by a number of regulations calculated to protect consenting persons from sheer physical injury, such as the legal requirement that drivers wear seatbelts. These are interesting but peripheral to the topic of public morality.

11. *Barnes* v. *Glen Theatre, Official Reports of the Supreme Court*, vol. 501, part 2, 560. (June 1991).

12. Ibid., 568.

13. Ibid.

14. Ibid., dissenting opinion of Justice White et al., at 590–93.

15. Ibid., concurring opinion of Justice Scalia, at 575.

16. Ibid., concurring opinion of Justice Souter, at 582.

17. Herbert L. Packer, *The Limits of the Criminal Sanction* (Stanford, Calif.: Stanford Univ. Press, 1968), p. 265.

18. Perhaps by now cohabitation can be added to the list. Lawrence Friedman claims that cohabitation has lost its social stigma in Western countries. See Friedman, *The Republic of Choice*, p. 157.

19. Summarizing the results of a 1985 *Newsweek* poll on public attitudes toward pornography, Richard Randall observes that "73 percent said they would 'totally ban' magazines depicting sexual violence . . . 68 percent would bar theaters from showing movies that portrayed sexual violence and . . . [l]arge majorities would ban or in some other way restrict magazines showing adults having sexual relations." Moreover, "the same poll showed a majority of respondents offended by the 'sexual content' in mainstream mass media" (Richard S. Randall, *Freedom and Taboo: Pornography and the Politics of a Self Divided* [Berkeley: Univ. of California Press, 1992], p. 206). Randall also examined six surveys of the National Opinion Research Center from 1973–83 in which "[t]he percentage of respondents believing that 'sexual materials' (which, subjectively, might include much more than socially designated pornography) 'lead to a breakdown of morals' ranged from 51 percent to more than 60 percent" (Ibid., pp. 207–8).

20. Alasdair MacIntyre, *After Virtue* (Notre Dame, Ind.: Univ. of Notre Dame Press, 1984), p. 6.

21. Jeffrey Stout, *Ethics After Babel* (Boston: Beacon Press, 1988), pp. 210–14.

22. "The Privatization of Good: Inaugural Lecture," *The Review of Politics* 52, (summer, 1990): p. 349.

23. Ibid., pp. 349–51.

24. *Reynolds* v. *United States*, 98 US 145 (1878).

25. *Jarrett* v. *Jarrett*, 400 NE 421 (1979).

26. *Petit* v. *State Board of Education*, 10 Col. 3rd 29 (1973).

27. Ibid. This case is presented almost in its entirety in Thomas C. Grey, *The Legal Enforcement of Morality* (New York: Alfred A. Knopf, 1983), pp. 86–92.

28. See Samuel Lippman, "Say No to Trash," "Dialogue: Art and the Taxpayer's Money," *New York Times*, June 23, 1989, p. 23. The now famous (NEA supported) Mapplethorpe exhibit included a graphic photograph of one person urinating into another person's mouth, one of the artist with a bullwhip inserted in his anus, and some pictures of children in erotic poses.

29. *Miller* v. *California*, 413 US 15 (1973).

30. *Paris Adult Theatre* v. *Slaton*, 413 US 49 (1973), at 57–58.

31. *Cohen* v. *California*, 403 US 15 (1971), at 25.

32. Ibid.

33. *Rosenfeld* v. *New Jersey*, 408 US 901 (1972).

34. An emphasis upon the nonrational components and functions of speech pervades the *Cohen* decision. *Cohen* declares that the Constitution is every bit as solicitous of "the emotional function" of speech as it is of the "cognitive function"; indeed, the former "may often be the more important element of the overall message to be communicated" (*Cohen* v. *California*, at 26). This ruling is at variance with the Court's insistence in its decisions on obscenity that what the First Amendment is primarily solicitous of is "the unfettered exchange of *ideas*" (*Miller* v. *California*, at 35—emphasis in original) and expressions of "reason and the intellect" (*Paris Adult Theatre*, at 67).

35. Though I'm suggesting that the work of the Supreme Court is an important indicator, this factor can be exaggerated. Arguably, the Court has been less friendly to public morality than the legislature that enacts morality laws and the citizenry that supports them (at least more often than the Court does). See Donald P. Kommers, "Comment on MacIntyre," *The Review of Politics*, 52 (summer 1990): pp. 364–66.

Illustrative of this point are Supreme Court cases on "indecency" in broadcasting media. *FCC* v. *Pacifica Foundation*, 438 US 726 (1978), concerns an FCC "complaint" against a New York radio station for airing George Carlin's monologue "Filthy words" at two o'clock in the afternoon, a time when children might well be in the audience. By a margin of (*only*) 5–4, the Supreme Court upheld the employment of this rather mild sanction for violation of the statutory prohibition against "indecent" utterances on the radio. Dissenters, accusing the Court majority of "ethnic myopia," denounced the standards of decency employed as mere cultural prejudice of the majority in violation of "cultural pluralism." In 1989 Congress passed a law banning indecency in broadcasting at all times; in 1991 the law was struck down by the Court of Appeals for the District of Columbia.

36. Aristotle, *Nicomachean Ethics, Introduction to Aristotle*, ed. Richard McKeon, (New York: Modern Library, 1947), pp. 331–32.

37. What my sketch particularly oversimplifies is the universality of virtue (and problems associated therewith) in classical thought. Suffice it to say here that Aristotle takes full account of the fact that different societies define virtue

quite differently. And his ethical philosophy is well known for its sensitivity to the variability of the human situations in which moral judgments must be made.

38. John Locke, *Second Treatise on Government* (Indianapolis: Bobbs-Merrill, 1952), p. 73.

39. While the predominance of Lockean philosophy at the beginnings and in the early years of our polity is, as I've said, hard to deny, there are some who have tried to deny it or call it into question. In one of the most thoughtful (and least extreme) presentations of the argument that ideas of "republican virtue" presided over the American Founding, Hadley Arkes says: "The Founders did indeed speak in the language of Locke and Hobbes, but their minds were furnished also from other sources. They drew upon a tradition of writing that ran back from Locke to Hooker to Aquinas to Aristotle" (Hadley Arkes, *The Philosopher in the City* [Princeton, N.J.: Princeton Univ. Press, 1981], p. 15). This is quite true and in some contexts quite important. But finally one must ask the question about degrees of influence: How much Locke and how much Aristotle; how much of the early modern "materialism," how much of the classical virtue? On the predominance of the Lockean outlook, see these two interestingly different, yet in my opinion rather persuasive, statements: John P. Diggins, *Lost Soul of American Politics: Virtue, Self-Interest and the Foundation of Liberalism* (Chicago: Univ. of Chicago Press, 1986) and Thomas C. Pangle, *The Spirit of Modern Republicanism: The Moral Vision of the American Founders and the Philosophy of Locke* (Chicago: Univ. of Chicago Press, 1988). A valuable overview of the differences between Aristotelian and Lockean perspectives is provided in Martin Diamond, "Ethics and Politics: The American Way," in *The Moral Foundations of the American Republic,* ed. Robert H. Horwitz, (Charlottesville: Univ. of Virginia Press, 1986).

40. *Champion* v. *Ames,* 188 US 321 (1903), at 323.

41. *Hoke* v. *U.S.,* 227 US 308 (1912), at 322.

42. *Jacobellis* v. *Ohio,* 378 US 184 (1963), at 199.

43. Robert N. Bellah et al., *Habits of the Heart: Individualism and Commitment in American Life* (New York: Harper & Row, 1985), p. 28.

44. Ibid., 142–43.

45. For a strong statement on the importance of biblical influence in our origins and early history, see Richard J. Neuhaus, *The Naked Public Square: Religion and Democracy in America* (Grand Rapids, Mich.: Eerdmans, 1986). For a somewhat different view, see Irving Kristol, "Republican Virtue vs. Servile Institutions" (Bloomington, Ind.: The Poynter Center, 1974). Kristol says: "Our idea of 'republican virtue' derives from the Romans, and it is a political conception rather than a religious one" (Ibid., p. 6). In *The Spirit of Modern Republicanism,* Thomas Pangle provides an excellent critical analysis of the alternative views and claims on this subject. Pangle acknowledges the significance of religious and civic republican influences but regards these as subordinate to the Lockean-Madisonian emphasis upon material self-interest. While I have always been persuaded by the

evidence for that view, perhaps one should acknowledge that these questions about the relative historic weight of diverse ideas are not subject to absolutely precise resolutions.

46. Alexis de Tocqueville, *Democracy in America*, vol. 1 (New York: Vintage Books, 1945), p. 316.

47. See Tocqueville, *Democracy in America*, vol. 2, second book, especially chapters 2, 10, and 13.

48. The term *Millian* is tempting, since the new liberalism often features the arguments of *On Liberty*. But the term is not entirely accurate in view of some of Mill's other writings and his concern with moral character that I alluded to at the beginning of this chapter.

49. The literature of autonomism is very extensive. Two typical works are Joel Feinberg, *Rights, Justice and the Bounds of Liberty* (Princeton, N.J.: Princeton Univ. Press, 1980) and David A. J. Richards, *Toleration and the Constitution* (New York: Oxford Univ. Press, 1986). Also see H. L. A. Hart, *Law, Liberty and Morality* (New York: Vintage Books, 1966). While I do not wish to identify Professor Hart simply with libertarian autonomism, his work has provided it with both stimulus and some basic concepts.

50. See Ronald Dworkin, *Taking Rights Seriously* (Cambridge, Mass.: Harvard Univ. Press, 1977), especially ch. 12.

51. For a critical documentation of this trend, see Richard E. Morgan, *Disabling America* (New York: Basic Books, 1984) and Rogers M. Smith, "The Constitution and Autonomy," *Texas Law Review* 60 (February 1982). A typical example of it applied to constitutional law can be found in Lawrence Tribe, *American Constitutional Law* (Mineola, N.Y.: Foundation Press, 1978), ch. 15, "Rights of Privacy and Personhood."

52. While that model illuminates some aspects of the situation, I have not adopted it because it suggests that what we have is virtually all conflict and no consensus. See James Davidson Hunter, *Culture Wars: The Struggle to Control the Family, Art, Education, Law and Politics in America* (New York: Basic Books, 1992). Hunter sees the situation primarily as one of intense conflict between two (more or less) religious outlooks, the "orthodox" and the "progressive." And he finds this warfare to be so pervasive as to render almost impossible any "common agreement as to what constitutes the 'good' or the 'right'" (Ibid., pp. 312–13 and 318). But Hunter also acknowledges that these intense partisans do not constitute a majority of the population (for example, see p. 159). It is therefore too early to give up on the concept of a substantive public morality as Hunter seems to do and is implied in the "culture wars" model.

53. Sanford Levinson, *Constitutional Faith* (Princeton, N.J.: Princeton Univ. Press, 1990), p. 78.

54. Ibid., p. 175.

55. *Petit v. State Board of Education*, pp. 33–34.

56. Levinson says: "[T]hose of us who are classified as nihilists have drunk deeply at the well of those branches of modern thought most skeptical of concepts like truth, neutrality or disinterestedness. . . . At the very least there are, from this perspective, no self-evident, immutable, or eternal truths. And the more local, socially constituted truths of our cultures and everyday lives are, in important ways, up for grabs" (*Constitutional Faith,* p. 175). Levinson is a teacher of constitutional law devoted to principles of personal and civil liberty. But how can Levinson's favorite principles entirely escape the acids of his ultramodernism? Surely a rigorous nihilism puts libertarian "truths" up for grabs along with everything else.

57. *The Republic of Choice,* p. 3.

58. Leszek Kolakowski, *Modernity on Endless Trial* (Chicago: Univ. of Chicago Press, 1990), p. 149.

59. If illustration on this point is necessary, here is a brief sampling of lyrics from the now famous group 2 Live Crew. "I won't tell your momma if you don't tell your dad. I know he'll be disgusted when he sees your pussy busted. Won't your momma be so mad if she knew I got that ass?" (cited in Christopher Hitchen, "Minority Report," *The Nation,* July 30, 1990, p. 120). Other examples include, "so we try real hard just to bust the walls," and "He'll tear the p---y open cause it's satisfaction" and "Suck my d--k, bitch, it makes you puke" (cited in George F. Will, *Newsweek,* July 30, 1990, p. 64.) A broader range of examples is provided in Hunter, *Culture Wars,* ch. 9, "Media and the Arts."

60. It is of some import that the great American celebrators of individual independence, such as Thoreau in *Walden,* Emerson in "Self-Reliance," and H. L. Mencken, have intensely decried the debilitating "conformity" of their fellow citizens. But arguably they didn't get it exactly right. Probably not all of what they decried is fairly describable as mere conformity—mechanical and empty. Some of it might well be attributable to a spirit of community of which the authors are unappreciative.

61. Bellah et al., *Habits of the Heart,* p. 143.

62. Mary Ann Glendon, *Rights Talk: The Impoverishment of Political Discourse* (New York: The Free Press, 1991), p. 14.

63. Ibid., p. 109.

64. Brigitte Berger and Peter Berger, *The War Over The Family* (Garden City, N.Y.: Doubleday, 1983), p. 120. Also see the recent writings of Christopher Lasch, beginning with *The Culture of Narcissism: American Life in the Age of Diminishing Expectations* (New York: W.W. Norton, 1978). A pioneering work in this genre (though a rather extreme statement of the case) is Sebastian De Grazia, *The Political Community: A Study of Anomy* (Chicago: Univ. of Chicago Press, 1948). Said De Grazia: "[T]he earth is parched with the aridity of the Individual. . . . The world . . . needs the ideal of the Citizen, a man of duties and responsibilities . . . of religious and political beliefs," Ibid., p. xi.

65. See Michael Sandel, *Liberalism and the Limits of Justice* (Cambridge: Cambridge Univ. Press, 1982) and Wilson Carey McWilliams, *The Idea of Fraternity in America* (Berkeley: Univ. of California Press, 1973) and "On Equality as the Moral Foundation for Community," in *The Moral Foundations of the American Republic,* ed. Robert H. Horwitz. Also see Benjamin R. Barber, "The Compromised Republic: Public Purposelessness in America," in Horwitz, *The Moral Foundations.*

The Case for Public Morality

The previous chapter identifies, without systematic analysis, several rationales that may be said to inform the historic practice of public morality in the United States. The task here is to explore the basic rationales more systematically or philosophically and with a view to their theoretical justification. As "public morality," properly understood, does not mean just any ethos that happens to be prominent in some time and place but one upon which the long-term well-being of the community is supposed to depend, the central questions are about the social interests at stake. Why does society need a public morality; what are the goods to be promoted or problems to be resolved by it? And, as public morality is not something that occurs automatically, but something that requires more or less deliberate cultivation by institutions, questions about its maintenance (and the difficulties or limits thereof) are also important.

To anticipate, in a simple way, the inquiries to follow, there are ultimately two analytically different lines of argument for public morality. One rationale focuses upon what can be called (somewhat loosely) communitarian considerations; the other concentrates on considerations of virtue. The former is concerned with a society's need for some common ethos or moral consensus to unite or harmonize its members. The latter is concerned with certain qualities of character. I'm not suggesting that these rationales are either monolithic or wholly separable; each has its interesting variations and *dependence* on the other. Taken together, these rationales provide the major reasons the polity neither can nor should be neutral about ways of life. Yet given this understanding, I do suggest that the distinction between the two rationales is important enough to warrant more attention than it usually gets.

The enterprise of this chapter is susceptible to various misunderstandings. Some of these are due to the relative complexity of the subject and the consequence that certain appropriate qualifications must often be postponed while the most general features of the argument are in focus. It's impossible to preclude misunderstandings altogether, especially with regard to the case for a societal ethic of restraint. But in an effort to reduce them, I offer the following preliminary observations about the nature of the subject and the inquiry.

1. Any theory of public morality (and for that matter, any theory against it) is obliged to give an account of the relevant communal interests, ethical norms or virtues, and functions of law. These are the major (though not the only) components of the case. For most of the chapter I'll be focusing on these three components one by one for the sake of thoroughness. Of course, the procedure is imperfect; the three components cannot be discussed in total separation from each other. But I do want especially to postpone extensive consideration of the moral role of the law, and issues of enforcement generally, until questions about the bonds of community and ethical standards have been addressed on their own terms.

2. Claims on behalf of public morality often involve the conjunction of two propositions: (A) that any civic populace is entitled to maintain ethical norms central to its collective way of life, and (B) that such norms need not (or cannot) be subjected to rational evaluation or defended philosophically. It is important to state in advance that I believe the rationale for public morality must go further. While the communitarian claim represented by the first proposition is to be taken seriously as a necessary part of the case, it cannot constitute the sufficient justification for a public morality. Such justification requires some confrontation with issues of ethical philosophy, that is, judgment about the character and worth of the moral norms whose civic endorsement is at issue.

3. Also calling for some advanced notice here (though hardly susceptible to full resolution) are certain perplexing methodological problems of theory and practice or universality and particularity. Edmund Burke maintained that our well-being in society mandates not only liberties but also "sufficient restraint upon [our] passions." But he went on to say that "as the liberties and restrictions vary with times and circumstances, and admit of infinite modifications, they cannot be settled upon any abstract rule."[1] Burke's point is that the appropriate balance of liberties and restraints can never be decided conclusively by theoretical principles to be applied universally, or in the same way, to all societies; exactly what proportion is desirable must be determined by practical wisdom. The importance of

recognizing and accommodating the variability of human affairs has been acknowledged in almost every philosophic justification for a public morality. But this sensible caveat exposes a difficulty: if it be taken literally or to its utmost conclusion, there could be no theoretical or general justification for public morality at all; the only judgments possible would be utterly circumstantialist ones tailored to the particular (and changing?) conditions of our society here and now. As Richard Rorty (an apparent proponent of such a view) suggests, the standards and concepts that moral philosophy can reasonably employ are those reflecting "how we live now."[2] Even Burke doesn't reject "abstract principle" to that extent; if he did so, he would have to admit that virtually nothing could be asserted about human or social good as such, including his general claim that a worthy polity requires some balancing of restraints and liberties. Whatever philosophic conclusions one might finally reach on the epistemological problem, practically it would seem highly advisable to steer clear of this (particularist or cultural relativist) precipice as well as the opposite (doctrinaire universalist) one.

4. An Aristotelian approach offers a more attractive alternative to the perennial dilemma I've just sketched. The variability of human affairs is too great to allow for rigorously universalistic prescriptions of specific norms, but elements of constancy in human nature do allow for certain general observations that are "for the most part true"—at least about the conditions of well-being in civil or civilized society.[3] A theoretical justification of public morality must rely upon some ideas of that sort— propositions about human conduct or social life purporting to be usually (though not always) valid. And it is a significant part of my task to articulate those ideas. Yet an Aristotelian approach would remind us that even such qualified universals will need more modification as they are applied to more specific circumstances. For us the relevant circumstantial factors are of two different kinds: the needs and concerns characteristic of liberal society *and* developments of recent decades in our American society.

In the following analysis, the endeavor is, insofar as possible, to move from the more abstract or theoretical to the more practical aspects of the case. For each of its major components, I explore and develop the fundamental general idea first—pointedly enough for clarity—and then introduce the appropriate qualifications or modifications. Ideas about what is good (please remember that this means *usually*) for human beings in society must often be adjusted in view of the good and beliefs characteristic of liberal society. And conclusions or principles derivable from these inquiries are no doubt in need of further modification if they are to have practical application under our current conditions. Pragmatically minded readers might wonder why these latter practical constraints are not made more central to the analysis. I don't make them central because the inquiry is more concerned with what is optimal for a liberal society than with the concessions that might have to be made to contemporary realities. It would be a mistake to allow current pragmatic exigencies to dominate thinking about the fundamental questions. In other words, it is important to have the basic case for public morality coherently in mind—even if present circumstances would preclude any but a highly compromised or attenuated actual realization of it in the near future.

5. Finally, in the concluding section I summarize and respond to certain persistent objections from libertarian and other sources, the aim being to put the case as a whole in philosophic perspective. Still, it's hardly to be expected that everyone will be persuaded by the arguments advanced here. It will be sufficient if reflection is promoted on the underlying reasons why decency isn't simply a private matter and why a morally neutral political society would not be a desirable one.

I. Community

We are concerned in this section with justifications for public morality that emphasize the conditions of social unity or solidarity. There are variations among possible justifications of this sort because there are various possible reasons for valuing social unity or solidarity. Probably the best-known and most intensely debated rationale for public morality in recent times is that offered by Sir Patrick Devlin. Libertarian critics have relentlessly targeted Devlin's position, perhaps on the assumption that its refutation would be decisive for the whole controversy. This debate exposes several of the underlying issues and is a good place to begin.

The crux of Devlin's position is that every society must have some sort of common morality to bind its members together. For example, no social order can accommodate the profoundly conflicting ethical orientations of monogamy and polygamy; society must make a choice. In the absence of shared beliefs, not only about politics but also about ethics and family, Devlin argues that "the society will disintegrate," that it will not survive. Therefore, he concludes, "society may use the law to preserve morality in the same way as it uses it to safeguard anything else that is essential to its existence."[4]

To formulate the case as Devlin does is to invite the response, made by H. L. A. Hart and others, that a society can survive (as many have) despite great changes and much diversity in moral beliefs. Hart maintains that the moral consensus necessary for sheer survival is quite minimal: "The survival of any society" requires rules "forbidding, or at least restricting, the free use of violence, rules requiring certain forms of honesty and truthfulness in dealings with each other, and rules forbidding the destruction of tangible things or their seizure from others."[5] These, he suggests, are essentially all the collective norms and beliefs that we need; on all other matters we can live with "moral pluralism." A burden of proof is thrust upon Devlinites to demonstrate, empirically, that societies without a broader moral consensus must disintegrate. Hart challenges them to prove by sociological evidence that extensive moral pluralism isn't viable.[6]

Insofar as the issue is made to turn only on the minimal prerequisites for the mere existence of *any* social order, Professor Hart is in a strong position. But suppose Devlin had formulated his thesis on the claim that a *communal life* is impossible without a widely shared ethos. Suppose he had said that civic harmony—a mutual trust or respect and a measure of affection among citizens—cannot prevail without a relatively broad consensus on moral fundamentals. Then the debate could take place on more even terms.

Let us first try to imagine concretely a society among whose members no standards of value are widely shared except the desirability of abstention from violence, theft, and gross deception. Regarding family, sexuality, love, decency, education, human development, the admirable, and the base—and such attitudes or aspirations as are related thereto—the members of this society do not agree at all. Not only do they live differently in these regards, they have no common authoritative norms whatever by which to judge of such matters. (Playfully, we could imagine that one-third are devoted monogamists, one-third polygamists, and the remainder promiscuous hedonists of various sorts—devotees of sadomasochism or of a drug culture or whatever.) It probably cannot be proven that this aggregation of persons would fail to survive as a social system of some sort, that it would inevitably disintegrate altogether. But what kind of society would exist? How much would Hart or anyone else wish to claim, with or without sociological evidence, that such a society could have the character of a community, with relatively strong social bonds and a meaningful collective life?

Devlin's rationale is still of value because it serves to remind us, at a time when cultural diversity is often unqualifiedly celebrated, that there is something to be said for the unifying and socializing functions of common moral beliefs. Yet the deeper questions raised here are not about the requisites of sheer survival; they are about the grounds of a community's entitlement to maintain norms constitutive of its distinctive way of life. Does the civic community per se have a legitimate interest in maintaining a preferred way of life, or must one concede, as libertarian and ultrapluralist arguments often imply, that only the individual or the ethnic group can assert such an interest? This far-reaching question about social unity and plurality is, I believe, the first issue of large theoretical import arising out of the Hart–Devlin debate. We need to confront this question on its own terms.

Hart labels the (putative) communal interest as "the conservative thesis," which he proceeds, rather dismissively, to define as the claim that "the majority have the right to follow their own moral conviction that their moral environment is a thing of value to be defended from change!"[7] Thusly formulated, this is simply a claim on behalf of the will or feelings of those who happen to be the larger number, and one that Hart seems to regard as easily refutable. While Hart's formulation is hardly all there is to the "conservative thesis" (if we should agree to call it that), the majoritarian concern is worth initial attention. Of course, few would argue that the majority, simply because it is a majority and a large one, is entitled to have and preserve from any change exactly the kind of moral environment they want, imposing their preferences wholesale on everyone else. But what about a qualified entitlement to public surroundings relatively free of things outrageous to their deep-rooted sensibilities? In the total absence of even that entitlement, a great number of people could find social life quite distasteful. Is it desirable, even safe, for society to make no concession whatsoever to intense beliefs and feelings of multitudes of its citizens? As a matter of fact, such concession is reflected in ordinary legal and social policies like "public decency" requirements against nakedness or extreme vulgarity in public places. I do not believe (as does Hart) that the only justifying reason for such policy is the protection of individuals from involuntary exposure to things they happen to find offensive,[8] but insofar as that is one prominent reason, the policy obviously favors the sensibilities of the majority over divergent ones. (After all, there are persons who would prefer much more freedom and "openness" about bodily things in public; some libertarians are even offended by the prudishness of the conventional constraints.) At any rate, a fixed principle denying the general populace any control whatever over their cultural environment can be challenged, on the basis of both a democratic and a utilitarian concept, as inconducive to "the greatest happiness of the greatest number."

But the case cannot rest very heavily upon these majoritarian grounds or on a simple aggregation of subjective satisfactions and dissatisfactions. Moreover, whatever may be said for and against the moral claims or cultural interests of the majority of individuals in a democracy, the communitarian case cannot be reduced to those claims. Libertarians who engage in such dismissive reduction seem to suppose that society is basically a collection of private individuals, most of whom just happen to agree (for the time being) on certain values. Such a supposition ignores the role of tradition and institutions, that is, the heritage of a people, in shaping beliefs and giving to society its distinctive cohesive form. Inherited institutions like the monogamous family hardly represent a mere aggregation of preferences or tastes that a large number of persons *happen* to have. Along with certain other established practices and standards (private property, for example), monogamy has shaped a way of life that gives our society its defining character, providing norms and orientation even for many of those who don't (or think they don't) value it. Its dissolution would have ramifications of such magnitude in virtually every area of our lives as to bring about an essentially different kind of society and culture.[9] Seen from this vantage point, public morality is an agency in the preservation and transmission of a people's tradition, and tradition is a prime requisite for the cohesiveness or unification of society. So we are back to the basic question: Why should we value cohesion? More precisely, why value bonds of union beyond the bare minimum necessary for the sheer existence (as distinguished from the characteristic form or ethos) of a society?

The following is a summary of the argument more or less in its classical mode and beginning with the virtually obvious. The fundamental import of civic unity or harmony as a social desideratum is in fact (commonsensically) presupposed by almost everyone who has a responsibility for the public good. Isn't a condition of pervasive mistrust, discord, or antagonistic factionalism universally recognized as political pathology, even where life and property are not threatened? Hence, the prevention or amelioration of such discord is generally acknowledged as a function of statesmanship (indeed of leadership in any association) and civic education. This is not to say that the bond of unity among citizens is the whole of the social good, or is always the overriding desideratum (there are necessary and desirable diversities); in the long run, however, it is the precondition of all but the most rudimentary social goods. Now the strongest promoter and preserver of bonds is that relationship among citizens that in classical political thought is called "civic friendship" or "fraternity"—a feeling of solidarity compounded of respect, affection, and public spiritedness. And, among ordinary people, fraternal feeling of this sort depends upon shared convictions or presuppositions about what is worthy and unworthy, admirable and disreputable in human life. People sharply differing on things of this magnitude seldom like or care about each other very much; commitments important to them preclude friendship. To make the point in more positive terms, the sense that one belongs to a community that has a certain character—that "stands for something"—seems to be an indispensable ingredient of personal devotion to the public good. Moreover, on the assumption that we are beings with social as well as individualistic needs; this condition of relative solidarity with others is also an ingredient of personal well-being. In other words, civic fraternity or communal spirit may be valued as instrumental to important interests of society and as an end in itself because it is an aspect of human fulfillment.

The perception that there is a collective "we" who have a way of life together (rooted in traditional practices and symbols that unite us)[10] can be, at best, a powerful promoter of devoted citizenship and, at least, an inhibitor of the grosser forms of antisocial exploitation or selfish indifference to the public well-being. As this perception—this identification of individuals with a larger social whole—declines, one's horizon becomes progressively narrower; eventually one can even lose all concern for the future of the country and any willingness to make sacrifices for the next generation. And, as the bonds of community unravel, individuals will often experience forms of disorientation or unhappiness resulting from the frustration of wants belonging to the social side of human nature. The extremity of this condition is depicted by some modern thinkers as *anomie* "a painful uneasiness or anxiety, . . . a feeling of separation . . . a feeling of pointlessness" resulting from the disintegration of common norms and beliefs.[11] But one need not adopt in its entirety that psychological version of the communitarian case to appreciate the considerations involved in the classical concern with (to borrow Rousseauian language) "the concord of the citizens" and "the public fraternity."[12]

A reader might be inclined to say that these are rather elementary realities that couldn't be conclusive as to the larger issue. Perhaps. But the import of these realities is rarely acknowledged in discussions of public morality, especially on the libertarian side. The effect of actually admitting these considerations into the discussion is to readjust the burden of proof between proponents of extensive moral pluralism and proponents of moral consensus. When pressed by these concerns, the former will be impelled to embrace one of two alternative positions. They can maintain that a spirit of community, including the qualities just mentioned as associated therewith, is not an important desideratum (at least not when it comes into any conflict with claims for personal autonomy). Alternatively, they can argue that communal spirit, acknowledged as an important desideratum, is entirely compatible with a thoroughgoing pluralism, and that its flourishing is not dependent upon a deliberately cultivated public morality. The first position is more often presupposed than directly or systematically argued. When articulated, its ultimate thesis would be that, after all, civic solidarity is not such a good thing because personal individuality is the good thing. The claims usually made for the priority of individuality and personal autonomy will be explored critically in chapter 4. It is best to focus now upon the second position, which acknowledges the value of community but, in one way or another, takes its actualization for granted.

It is sometimes suggested that a genuine communal unity can exist on the basis, simply, of tolerance. At least, enthusiasts for utmost moral and cultural diversity periodically speak as if that is what they believe. Yet, isn't it evident that sharp moral disagreements on things deemed fundamental to a worthy human life impose heavy strains on the capacity of ordinary people for toleration? And this seems evident even where tolerance is considered a major virtue. Suppose a group of polygamists were to move into your (fairly liberal) neighborhood, not only practicing their polygamy openly but also publicly advocating and promoting it. No doubt you and your liberal neighbors will abstain from acting forcibly to eject these people or subjecting them to conspicuously coercive measures. But how will you feel about them and their way of life? How will you interact with them as fellow citizens (and they with you) when vital questions of civic or educational policy are at issue? Now suppose that these neighbors are also practitioners of clitorectomy (for clarity let's say upon willing adult women). You might take the view that as long as the activity is wholly voluntary, it's nobody's business but the participants. But is that a likely reaction? Aren't you and your neighbors more likely to regard this practice as an abomination and, at the very least, feel more hostile than friendly toward those engaged in it? In any event, such is the reaction one would expect from people who have a real attachment to the norms (familial, humanitarian, romantic, etc.) that these practices violate. Indeed, this sort of response is much more to be expected than the libertarian one wherever there are common norms that matter to people and a communal identity of any strength.[13]

Of course tolerance can be taught and must be taught in a liberal society. And its scope can be fairly extensive—where underlying it there is solid agreement on some substantive fundamentals.[14] But one may wonder how powerful a tolerationist ethic would have to be to sustain real communal ties in a society characterized by radical moral pluralism. It would be contrary to much experience to assume that a strong ethic of tolerance comes easily to most human beings, hence promotion of it amidst utmost diversity would require efforts well beyond mere admonition. A powerful religion of universal love (above all else) could possibly do the job for a population sufficiently pious. In the absence of that kind of religious disposition, however, the conclusion is hard to avoid that an ethic of toleration as demanding as the one required would have to be systematically instilled and enforced by institutions of the state. Perhaps doctrinal sympathizers with far-reaching cultural or moral diversity would agree, in which case they are committed to a rather stringent public morality of their own.[15] If they do not have such measures of enforcement in mind, we may appropriately ask why not; on what basis do they assume that they can do without these measures?

In a somewhat different version of the position under consideration, it will be said that, while toleration alone might be insufficient to sustain enduring bonds of community, a thoroughly pluralist liberal society naturally generates other unifying commitments that are sufficient. One could claim that in the absence of common ethical beliefs, common material interests will produce a body of citizens who care about each other's well-being. Thomas Paine was apparently confident that economic factors in a free society—"the mutual dependence and reciprocal interests which man has upon man"—tend naturally to "create [a] great chain of connection which holds it together."[16] Surely we have good reasons for doubting this sanguine faith. There is much more evidence for the contrary Madisonian view that "the latent causes of faction are . . . sown in the nature of man" and that modern economic life tends to divide us into diverse groups "activated by different sentiments and views."[17]

THE CASE FOR PUBLIC MORALITY 55

In response some will argue that authentic liberal community needn't rely entirely upon either economic interest or an ethic of simple tolerance. Great differences of lifestyle notwithstanding, citizens can be warmly bound together in their positive allegiance to the civic principles of personal liberty and equal individual rights. In other words, there is no need for a public morality beyond the liberal ethic of rights and liberties (and norms instrumental thereto). Perhaps the most interesting recent statement of that perspective is to be found in Stephen Macedo's work, *Liberal Virtues: Citizenship, Virtue and Community in Liberal Constitutionalism.* Writes Macedo: "An appreciation of the values and ideas grounded in liberal justice could help debunk the notion that liberal regimes are incapable of generating a common ethos capable of unifying society."[18] Macedo isn't always very clear about what exactly is at the core of that ethos, but often enough he identifies it as follows: "Liberalism stands, above all, for the positive value of freedom, freedom to devise, criticize, revise and pursue a plan of life, and it calls upon people to respect the rights of others whether or not they share the same goals and ideals."[19] That is, the self-determination or free choice of each individual is the chief good, and the rights that serve to promote that self-determination constitute the unifying social ethos. This is a familiar theme, but how much sense does it really make? Isn't it rather counterintuitive that people can be truly bound together in anything approaching a fraternal association on the basis of a principle of personal autonomism—the sovereign right of each individual to choose independently his own goals or ideals and go his own way? A celebration of individuality above all else, and a policy of maximizing it, might have some valuable results, but it's hard to see how communal consensus or identity could be one of them. Macedo correctly points out that liberalism calls upon people to respect the rights of others regardless of differences (even vast differences?) in goals and ideals. But calling upon them to do so is not exactly the same as actually inducing them to do so on a regular basis; for that outcome, something more than exhortation is apparently needed. And even supposing a reliable consensus on elementary rights, it remains questionable that such a minimalist consensus is sufficient to produce anything more than a bare modicum of mutual identification and attachment to the polity among highly diverse citizens. (Perhaps that is all thinkers like Macedo have in mind when they speak confidently of social unity, but they seldom say so). We may doubt that much civic friendship is promoted by an agreement upon what persons have a right to do but not at all upon what it is humanly respectable to do or what is a decent life. (You can "respect" someone's right to devote his life to gambling or the brothel without having any actual respect for, or fraternal interest in, the person who lives that way.)

These considerations can be directed more pointedly to the need for public morality in a liberal society. For the sake of the argument, let us accept provisionally the minimalist definition of a liberal citizenry, as one collectively devoted only to each member's physical security, personal liberty, and material possessions (everything else being relegated to the "private sphere"). It is probable that such limited collective purpose is what Hart is presupposing when he asserts that a society can exist on an ethical agreement encompassing no more than a commitment to abstain from violence, theft, and fraud. We can accept that assertion in the abstract (as I have) while continuing to wonder *how well* a consensus thusly limited would serve even the interests it is meant to serve. To put it in perhaps a more interesting way, are "life, liberty, and property" likely to enjoy a high degree of security among an aggregate of individuals who agree *only* on the value of life, liberty, and property? It's not so hard to envision the formal acceptance of rules for the protection of these desiderata by people who otherwise differ profoundly about the good life and human decency. What is harder to envision is the willingness of those people to endure substantial personal sacrifices for the sake of each others' liberty and property. And what about the ethic of promise-keeping that is impera- tive for a Lockean commonwealth, or that "honesty and truthfulness in dealings with others" that Hart acknowledges to be a requisite of any social existence?[20] Is a scrupulous honesty and truthfulness much to be expected among groups of people whose ways of life are alien, and maybe distasteful, to each other? Aren't effective norms of honesty, like other cooperative dispositions, more to be expected among those with shared beliefs and common substantive standards of value? It would seem that an ethical consensus confined to the values of life, liberty, and property is bound to be insufficient, that the maintenance of these liberal principles in good condition depends upon social bonds that, in turn, are shaped by a moral outlook encompassing more than those principles. And, as I've suggested, an ethic of toleration alone cannot be relied upon to create that larger moral outlook. On the contrary, no matter how much tolerance might be celebrated as a "liberal virtue," the extent of its actual practice is dependent in some degree upon the existence of a prior moral community.

There is another reason for thinking that a shared moral outlook performs a supportive function for liberal democracy. If it is true that human beings need some form of social identity, some sense of belonging to a communal life transcending our individuality, then eventually many people will become disaffected from a political regime that fails to provide any satisfaction for this need. In positive terms, a liberal regime that facilitates or accommodates a tradition-based ethos is in a position to benefit from allegiances deriving from the social side of human nature. And, given its tendency to fragmentation, our kind of regime can use that support. Arguably this and the aforementioned consideration are among the reasons every historical liberal society has had a public morality extending well beyond the proscription of violence, theft, and fraud. (If Hart's contrary formulation is meant to depict a type of society, it is one that nobody has ever lived in and for which, consequently, there is no sociological evidence.)

I have written at some length about the importance of the communal bond and its linkage to moral consensus because there is an exaggerated ideological and cultural pluralism to be counteracted. Remaining to be discussed (briefly here and more thoroughly later) is the sustaining role of civic institutions, including the law. The following three observations can serve, temporarily, as an outline of that part of the argument.

1. While as social animals human beings may be said to have a natural need for bonds of civic union or friendship, it cannot be said that the moral consensus, which is a condition of such union, is a natural necessity. There are also powerful centrifugal tendencies in human relations (noted by thinkers as diverse as Aristotle, Madison, and Freud) that tend to divide us. Hence, moral consensus is something not usually developed or maintained automatically; it is something that must be cultivated by institutional and educational or "socializing" agencies. Almost necessarily, these agencies include various pressures to recognize and abide by established norms.

2. The law is one of the more prominent pressure-applying and socializing agencies. Without the ultimate support of the legal order, other institutions will be hard put to accomplish their task of inculcating, maintaining, and transmitting norms. And where standards of value are cherished, or believed to be indispensable to a way of life, citizens are naturally inclined to call upon constituted authority to protect them from blatant violation.

3. A communal life involves not only a measure of common allegiance to cherished norms but also a social environment that is congenial because it reflects those norms. Public morality endorsed by law

provides support for the endeavor of citizens to sustain that kind of environment; for example, it sanctions efforts of local governments and neighborhoods to prevent the proliferation of adult theaters, sex shops, prostitution, drug dealing, and the like in their midst. The law cannot really remain neutral in the conflict between those citizens and the pornography, prostitution and drug interests; it must take a side with the ethos of the former or the (putative) liberty of the latter. A legal order that regularly frustrates the moral interests of the many—because it always favors individual autonomy and cultural diversity over the conditions of social unity—is promoting the alienation of citizens who feel themselves compelled to live in a milieu they find ugly and degrading.[21]

Before leaving the theme of community, it is important to confront and engage a powerful counterargument against the communal spirit. Surely, the argument might go, communal spirit can produce at least as many evils as goods. Devotion to our own ways and beliefs, collective devotion to ways and beliefs because they are "ours," is a frequent source of narrow parochialism. It is often the source of a deleterious hostility to others who are different from us. And at its worst, this disposition promotes a dangerous nationalistic or ideological idolatry; many people have been persecuted and slaughtered on behalf of patriotism or some form of tribalism. Therefore, one must conclude that patriotism and civic fraternity per se are not desirable; indeed, aren't we better off and safer with as little of them as possible?

Most thoughtful people are unlikely to find this extreme conclusion acceptable—even when the dangers noted are taken seriously. Why? Isn't it because we can hardly conceive of a good society without any of the ties and loyalties that a spirit of community sustains? We suppose (don't we?) that in the absence of social bonds of that sort, significant human needs and aspirations remain unfulfilled. On this account, I believe, one is constrained to reject boundless moral pluralism as undesirable. What may be called "love of one's own"—a human inclination at the root of unifying tradition—is widespread and powerful in most if not all of us. To ignore its wants altogether (or always to subordinate it to "moral pluralism") could not be the height of wisdom in social philosophy.

On the other hand, it surely isn't wisdom to sanction on these grounds any consensus or ethos that a people might happen to embrace, regardless of its character or content. The public spirited enthusiasm of John Calvin's

Geneva, Robespierre's revolutionary nationalism, and the regime of the Iranian Mullahs are quite unattractive to anyone under the influence of the modern Enlightenment or the liberal outlook. A communitarian might respond that oppressive zealotry of such extremity is most unlikely to prevail in our society (and that we ought not to be driven by exaggerated fears of it to embrace all the evils of excessive individualism). That is, I believe, true enough. But why? Why exactly is it that we don't have to worry very much about the triumph of fanatical doctrines in our society as a whole? That must be largely on account of our liberalism—especially the longstanding institutions and attitudes nurtured by our original ("Madisonian") liberalism. Indeed, the avoidance or containment of fanatical movements is one of the primary reasons for the system of governmental checks and balances, freedom of speech, and economic multiplicity that the Constitution promotes. One is well advised, therefore, to avoid policies that could undermine our constitutional liberal regime.

The aforegoing lines of argument resemble a dialogue because they represent two different and sometimes competing interests of our polity. The purpose of this dialogue format is to indicate the difficulty of embracing either side to the total exclusion of the other. Of course, we value our multiplicity, but that isn't all that we value and all that we are. Insofar as a kind of *liberal community* is what is wanted, our respect for diversity and need for unity have to be accommodated in some sort of balance. Consequently, the expectations and demands of both radical pluralists and radical communitarians will be frustrated, and appropriately so, in favor of the search for a middle ground. A liberal community, especially a large commercial one, cannot aspire to a full-scale Rousseauian fraternalism (or the kind of deep, warm, and semi-familial solidarity that sociologists have called *gemeinschaft*). As Rousseau well understood, such fraternalism requires a small, culturally homogenous, and relatively noncommercial society. But this general truth doesn't force us to settle for the opposite, atomistic vision of ourselves as only a collection of independent individuals (and groups) loosely bound together by elemental interests in material security and committed to autonomy on everything else. Of course we could be compelled to such a view by sheer practical exigency—if our cultural or moral diversity were so extensive and intractable as to preclude any but the most minimal terms of union. (There are countries in the world that are in that unenviable position; the old Yugoslavia and the newly envisioned Bosnia come to mind.) But liberal societies still have traditions and ethical bonds extending beyond the bare minimum and sufficient to sustain a degree of civic friendship—if they are recognized and nurtured. We are not faced with a simple either/or, one extreme or the other—either totalitarian unity or a society of moral strangers.[22] To summarize the two-sided point I've been making: the communitarian case for public morality encompasses a part of the social good that we need to recognize and accommodate; yet in our kind of polity it encounters vital competing considerations with which it must compromise.[23]

Another way to identify the basic limitation of the communalist rationale is to note that it shares with Devlin's "survivalist" rationale a certain philosophic anomaly. Taken by itself, it could require us to endorse, as socially desirable, very divergent systems of belief and practices that we find to be cherished in diverse countries. After all, people in Saudi Arabia might be unified by devotion to polygamy every bit as much as Americans are by devotion to monogamy. Viewed strictly, the rationale seems to be neutral as to the substance of the norms and institutions that promote communal bonds; what counts is that the bonds are promoted. A theory sanctioning on this basis sharply conflicting moral practices and commitments could possibly be a coherent one, but only for those willing to embrace a rather thoroughgoing ethical relativism. And then it is questionable how far such relativism is compatible with a real devotion to monogamous (or any other) standards of value.

The communitarian component in the case for public morality should not be dismissed as libertarian pluralists tend to dismiss it. But neither can it serve as the sufficient condition for legitimation of a public morality. Public spiritedness or civic fraternity is a social good but not equally so in all situations; we want to evaluate the different forms and sources of fraternal association, don't we? At some point in the inquiry, questions of what makes for community have to give way to questions about better and worse (not merely strong and weak) bonds of community. In other words, one cannot avoid thinking about the value of the ethos that is serving the associative function. It is time to confront more directly the question "What morality?" and related issues concerning the basis of morality.

II. Character

As a starting point it is useful to identify the substantive ethos that is implicit in the proscriptions of our traditional public morality. Then we can proceed to the broader and more positive consideration of what is good character and society's interest in it.

When one thinks of the three probably most notorious sex-related "morals offenses"—prostitution, pornography, and polygamy—a connection to the ethos of the monogamous family is apparent. The point is a commonplace one that those practices are inimical to the ideal of a binding erotic devotion between two persons. To put it a bit differently, prostitution, pornography, and polygamy assault principles of fidelity and sensibilities about sexual relations whose function it is (or was) to protect the valued institution of monogamy. Hence, traditional public morality has condemned those practices in support of these principles and sensibilities. The valued institution is assaulted in a different way by incest among parents and children (whether the latter are minors or consenting adults): for parents and children to view each other as sex objects is profoundly destructive of the kind of nurturing affection by which the family is essentially constituted. Even the condemnation of bestiality might be understood, in part, as an extension of the familial ethic. Perhaps this rationale could be stretched to encompass some nonsexual offenses as well. It could be argued that the deliberate desecration of dead bodies somehow strikes at feelings grounded in beliefs about the honor due to departed loved ones. Stretching still further, it comes to mind that practices like gambling might well have been censured as destructive of family stability and responsibility. And, of course, the monogamous family has been the beneficiary of more direct support from a variety of public policies.

Does it make sense to have a public morality supportive of monogamy? "Of course," a communitarian might say; "it is *our* institution!" But the argument required here is one about the *value* of that institution, apart from the simple fact that it is ours. We need not stop to explore at length the sizable body of evidence concerning particular social and human costs of "family breakdown."[24] Suffice it to say that the monogamous family (at its best) has long been recognized as a locus of mutual affection and devoted nurture that is virtually irreplaceable by anything available in the vast and impersonal societies of the modern world. This institution seems to be the best agency we have for the development of personalities who can be self-directing individuals capable of taking responsibility for their own lives *and* social beings with larger human sympathies and capability for public responsibility.[25] These are qualities of character that a liberal democracy needs in its citizens; how could it do without them? Also, the family connects the generations, providing continuity (social, cultural, ethical) in a world where so much is in flux. This too is a factor not without import for the well-being of the polity. On these and similar grounds, monogamy has a social value that makes it something more than one among several lifestyles that private individuals may choose, and a public policy of supporting it has at least a prima facie justification.

Yet society's interest in the family does not suffice to explain public morality in its entirety. Among other things, the monogamous ethic cannot account for all the morals offenses (drugs, suicide, duelling, brutal entertainments, gross public vulgarities, or incivilities having nothing to do with sexuality). And even the core sexual offenses are insufficiently accounted for on that basis; underlying those proscriptions is a larger moral perspective. As suggested in chapter 1, we seem to condemn some things on the premise that they are uncivilized or beneath the dignity of human beings or destructive of qualities important to our humanity. This is the perspective that I've called an "ethic of decency." More explicit attention can now be given to what *decency* means in this context. For illustrative purposes a brief focus on the subject of pornography should be useful.

Productions (stories, films, magazines, performances, advertisements, etc.) deserving to be called pornographic are characterized by graphic and detailed portrayal of sexual acts—in the absence of love or affection and with the effect that the erotic life is reduced to its grosser physical or animal elements. The passion depicted and stimulated is a thoroughly depersonalized sexuality, the desire for the possession of bodies without any regard for the personalities who inhabit them. (Strictly speaking, in hard-core representations no personalities inhabit them.) Human beings, women especially, are vividly portrayed as objects to be used and manipulated for one's gratification, that is, as pleasure-producing tools. The life explicitly depicted and graphically promoted in the pornographic world is a life devoted to the uninhibited accumulation of a mass of pleasurable sensations, with an interest in other people simply as instruments to that end. And in the sadistic variety, which, arguably, is the logical outcome of the manipulative pornographic perspective, viewers are invited to find sensual enjoyment in scenes of domination, cruelty, and violence.[26]

The traditional communal morality that condemns pornography is part of an ethos associating sexuality with love or affection; it considers the erotic relation as a relation among persons not merely between bodies. Hence, it proscribes as indecent the treatment of sexual intimacy as a commodity and any strong association of erotic feelings with hostile, destructive, or violent ones. And, as it regards bodily functions involved in the sexual act as intimately private matters that are degraded when put on public display, it views as indecent any detailed exhibition of them. More broadly, this is apparently an antihedonistic morality, directing us to aspirations deemed higher than the gratification of primal impulses and, to that end, mandating the control of sexual appetites or pleasures. In this sense, it is an ethic of self-restraint (distinguished from, as we may put it, an ethos of personal liberation and self-expression).[27]

Hence our traditional ethic of decency, when pressed for its implications, can be seen as reflecting or representing two fundamental desiderata: *self-control* and a kind of *civility*. The former has, in part, a view to human ends or goods more elevated than sensual and material gratification. The latter involves a degree of respect for other people that precludes their treatment (at least in an erotic or physical way) as mere interchangeable objects of one's self-centered desires. And it is in the service of these two desiderata that certain conventional proprieties—called "decencies"— have been generated.

You might want to ask why this ethos is so interested in sexuality. One answer periodically offered by adversaries of public morality is that "the Judeo-Christian tradition," which they say often dominates our morality, is deeply hostile to sexuality and pleasure.[28] While this claim probably has some validity as to aspects of our nineteenth-century moral code, it seems decreasingly relevant to the predominant national milieu and opinion in this century. Does it really make sense to maintain that we have an ethic of sexual decency because modern (urbanized and liberalized) society is strongly infected with Puritanism or that the United States is in some significant respects a "Victorian" regime? (This kind of claim calls to mind the expression "beating an old dead horse.") Demonstrably, the prevailing modern opinion tolerates much of the erotic in art and literature. And our law tries hard to draw a firm distinction between the pornographic treatment of sex and treatments of it that have serious literary, artistic, or educational value, however offensive they might be to the majority.[29] It is at best an oversimplification to attribute contemporary public morality on sexual matters to the lingering influence of an ultraconservative religiosity.

A more serious answer to our question is implied in the Supreme Court's opinion in the *Paris Adult Theatre* case. Said the Court:

The sum of experience, including that of the past two decades, affords an ample basis for legislators to conclude that a sensitive, key relationship of human existence, central to family life, communal welfare and the development of the human personality, can be debased and distorted by crass commercial exploitation of sex.[30]

The passage makes two interesting observations about human sexuality: that it is something of fundamental import for the well-being of the community (not just the individual) and that it is something vulnerable—subject to distortion and debasement. And the Court majority, along with their supporters among the citizenry, would no doubt agree that the thoroughgoing depersonalization of sexuality is a distortion of it.

The vulnerability or relative fragility of sexual feelings and relations is the subject of a considerable portion of the world's literature, is it not? While to attempt a conclusive explanation of this phenomenon would be hazardous, one can make sense of it on the basis of a certain fairly prominent understanding of what is involved in the erotic life. The erotic life combines, in a way never entirely free of the mysterious, some of the most sublime and some of the least sublime of human inclinations. Eros is the arena for a unique interaction of compelling animal impulses and delicate, distinctively human sensibilities. Frequently it is an arena in which primitive or powerfully self-centered urges and elevated aspirations are in competition for predominance. Therefore this is, as we often say, "a sensitive subject"; it can be the inspiration for a sustained intimacy and affection with another person—and it can be the occasion for possessiveness, hostilities, and humiliation. If we believe that the desirable end, for society and individuals as well, is a communion responsibly maintained, we ought to be aware that there are obstacles and vicissitudes on the way to that end.

A well-known modern view of the subject argues that the obstacles and vicissitudes are nothing but the results of conventionally imposed constraints; if society would only desist from imposing various artificial proprieties upon it, the sexual impulse would be unproblematic. This viewpoint comes to us in two versions. The Kinseyite or "scientific—behavioral" version supposes that by nature the impulse is really only a harmless, pleasure-seeking biological function (like eating and sleeping). A more romantic variation of the thesis assumes that left alone (that is, by nature) the sexual inclination is spontaneously affectionate or wholly loving, hence entirely benign. All that is needed is its liberation. Our traditional public morality is informed by a different, rather more complex and less sanguine, understanding of what is natural. Therefore, according to the traditional view, the healthy development of the sexual passion always requires some constraint and refinement of its more animalistic or self-aggrandizing urges. And in that process of refinement we need the guidance of communal norms.

This point about natural inclinations can be generalized well beyond the area of sexuality. The ethic of self-restraint rests, ultimately, upon two presuppositions about the human condition. First, there is the insight that we are creatures whose natural endowment includes certain irrational and unsocial passions that are originally powerful in all of us. Developing the capacity to deal with these is a matter of vital importance for every person and every society. The other perception is that there are more elevated or more social possibilities to which we can direct these crude impulses—but only by first submitting them to some rational control. It's hard to envision a greater disparity in moral philosophy and psychology than the division between outlooks that recognize the centrality of this problem for human well-being and those that do not. The problem may be viewed in the light of a Freudian psychology,[31] but one need not be a Freudian to take it seriously. Its centrality is attested to by many great thinkers of various times and places, including some such as Locke and Aristotle, whose moral and political philosophies are otherwise quite different.

In his treatise on education, John Locke says:

> He that has not a mastery over his inclinations, he that knows not how to resist the importunity of present pleasure and pain for the sake of what reason tells him is fit to be done, wants the true principle of virtue and industry, and is in danger of never being good for anything. This temper, so contrary to unguided nature, is to be got betimes; and this habit, as the true foundation of future ability and happiness, is to be wrought into the mind as early as may be.[32]

We are not now concerned with the largest questions about the meaning of virtue and happiness in the Lockean view. The point here is a relatively simple and limited one: Locke recognized (probably more than many of his liberal descendants do) that we have inclinations much in need of a discipline, the acquisition of which is the first condition of successful living, whatever the other conditions might be. Notice that such a discipline must be "wrought into the mind," that is, made habitual so that it will constitute one's normal behavior.

This habituated capacity for self-mastery—an ability to say *no* to the the demands of present passion so that one can make a judgment about the propriety of satisfying it—is the foundation of what we ordinarily call "character." Of course that isn't the whole story about character; we must consider other important elements. But this capacity is the foundation in the sense that without it the other elements are most unlikely to be acquired.

Beyond this elementary formulation, the subject can be developed in a variety of ways. In Aristotle's more elaborate account, good character is an ensemble of acquired dispositions or virtuous habits, each of which constitutes the moderation of a particular set of passions. Bad character is an ensemble of the opposite, immoderate habits or vices. A virtue of particular interest to us here is the one he calls *temperance*, which is concerned with the control of sensual appetites (especially the pleasures of touch and taste). The vice to be worried about in this case is *self-indulgence*; the self-indulgent person is unable to resist the demands of sensual appetite. Why is self-indulgence something to be avoided and criticized? In an illuminating passage from his *Nicomachean Ethics*, Aristotle provides two reasons. First, "the sense with which self-indulgence is connected is the most widely shared of the senses, and self-indulgence would seem to be justly a matter of reproach, because it attaches to us not as men but as animals. . . . To delight in such things then, and to love them above all others, is brutish."[33] Second, "In an irrational being the desire for pleasure is insatiable . . . and the exercise of appetite increases its innate force, and if appetites are strong and violent, they even expel the power of calculation."[34] According to the first line of argument, what is wrong with the self-indulgent person is that he pursues, above all other things, the gratification of impulses that belong to us as animals and not as distinctively human beings. And that, the argument suggests, is beneath our dignity. The second consideration has to do with reason and freedom. If overindulged, the sensual desires can become insatiable, undermining, even expelling, the rational element in us. And we ought to avoid getting into that shape because, thereby, the thinking and choosing part of us will be enslaved to the irrational. In that shape we cannot be self-governing.[35]

Another relevant dimension of Aristotelian ethics must be noted here. Self-indulgence is not the only kind of intemperance; there is an opposite form of intemperance that Aristotle refers to as "insensibility." This vice

can be depicted as an unwillingness or inability to be involved in any
sensual enjoyments. While Aristotle makes it clear enough that self-indulgence is the vice most of us must worry about, it's important to see that
the insensible person is also intemperate. The virtue called *temperance* is
an intermediate condition lying between two extremes—one an excessive
and the other a defective participation in the sensual side of life. And this
is the structure of every Aristotelian virtue. To illustrate: courage is a
mean between excessive fear (cowardice) and total fearlessness (rashness);
good temper is a condition intermediate between too much and too little
disposition to feel or express anger. And it is likewise with friendliness,
truthfulness, justice, and the rest of the virtues that, according to Aristotle,
make up good character. Every virtue therefore is a kind of moderation.
The aim of character development is not to obliterate the passions or
simply to suppress them; they are, after all, the raw materials of action
and fulfillment. The aim is to regulate and direct them.

The classical principle that the extremes are to be avoided has much
political import and relevance to our subject of public morality. On this
basis a fanatical moralism could not be regarded as virtuous any more
than an overriding zeal for physical gratification could. Zealotry of any
kind, including the moralistic kind, is suspect. Human development and
fulfillment, to which virtue is ministerial, is largely a matter of balance.

Ethical orientations that regard character-building as crucial are almost
inevitably rooted in, or associated with, a certain conception of the elementary passions—that they aren't entirely benign or naturally tame. Some
passions can become insatiable and all-consuming, demanding gratification at the expense of everything else. Hence, much is at stake, for both
individual and society, in the development of "habits of restraint."[36]

Yet the capacity for self-restraint is the groundwork of character, not
the whole of it. A number of the self-restraining capabilities that Aristotle
calls virtues are in the service of sociability or civility in the broad sense
of the terms. Insofar as temperance, courage, good temper, friendliness,
truthfulness, justice, and the like are habitually observed, a rational and
harmonious society is possible—one in which civic union derives (to a
large extent) from reasonable and lawful deliberation. We might not
entirely agree with Aristotle's list of approximately thirteen virtues; one
can take issue with some of the things on the list or the omission of some
things. (Courage is very prominent, while compassion is not a distinct
virtue at all, and "undue humility" is a vice).[37] But surely it's hard to
deny to many of these qualities the status of virtues necessary for a desirable

communal life. Any society needs personalities who can be depended upon to form and fulfill obligations. And, beyond obligations, a decent community must have members who can respect or care about others enough to take an interest in their well-being and sometimes make sacrifices of personal interest for a public good. Imagine a society of thoroughly self-indulgent, unreliable, and uncivil characters; what would be the quality of life for these incessantly self-seeking and isolated "citizens"? However one may choose to conceptualize the several attributes defining character, there is wide practical agreement that the possessor of it is, at least, someone able to resist present gratification for the sake of deliberation about future consequences, someone who can be relied upon by friends or associates, and someone with larger aspirations than a self-centered pleasure seeker has. Indeed, don't we ordinarily encounter fewer disputes and more consensus about the major ingredients of good character than we do about moral codes or theories? It is a most interesting phenomenon that, often enough, people who differ as to particular ethical rules can agree, basically, on what or who is an admirable human being.[38]

Perhaps it will be evident to many readers how these considerations concerning moral decency and character are applicable to the needs of a *liberal society*. Yet for the sake of comprehensiveness it is worthwhile to formulate the point more explicitly.

While the cultivation of virtue is not its end or chief good, liberal democracy can be said, broadly speaking, to depend upon moral character in the following two ways. First, precisely because, in many matters of social consequence, that regime must leave its members free to govern themselves, it needs reasonable assurance that most people most of the time will be capable of self-control and prepared to desist from, at least, the grosser forms of incivility. The second consideration is more directly political. Our kind of polity depends substantially upon mutual respect among citizens; persons who view each other pornographically, or as mere objects and opportunities for self-gratification, are unfit for any sustained cooperation in the conduct of civic affairs. In general terms, a republican polity needs citizens of respectable character because vital public policies affecting everyone will be determined by the consent of those citizens. Hence, the observation so often found in the historic literature on this subject that "a licentious people cannot [for long] be a free people."

But this general rationale can't resolve all the questions that arise regarding the substance of a legitimate public morality in a liberal regime. Indeed, implicit in this rationale is a far-reaching question of political philosophy. Functionally, the self-restraining virtues, and society's interest in them, can be conceived of in two rather different ways. Virtue may be seen primarily as a requisite and component of human development, as the major contributor to a worthy and highly fulfilled life. Alternatively, it can be seen as a useful instrument preservative of the rudimentary conditions of our well-being, that is, requisite for the satisfaction of our elementary needs. To put it in stark terms, ethics can be associated with achievement and excellence *or* with the security of one's life, liberty, and property.

The former perspective will be recognized as the classical one, exemplified in Aristotelian ethical philosophy. "We may remark," says Aristotle, "that every virtue or excellence both brings into good condition the thing of which it is the excellence and makes the work of that thing to be done well."[39] Virtues in this sense are powers or abilities that develop—bring into optimal condition—the potentialities that are distinctively human and enable us to maximize the kinds of activities of which our species is uniquely capable. Hence, the function of temperance is not simply to preclude grave disorder in personal and social life (though it would have that effect) but to facilitate the full maturation of the qualities that enable us to live fully as rational animals. From this perspective the virtues have a certain nobility or loftiness; their essential goal is to elevate us. And, correspondingly, their acquisition, to the high degree that excellence involves, is a demanding enterprise.

But suppose that one is most doubtful about standards of excellence and about any higher human fulfillments. Suppose one believes that the wants or aspirations that characterize human beings, and conclusively govern us all, are the urge for self-preservation and the craving for pleasures, along with a need for security in the pursuit of preservation and pleasure. Believing these things, the seventeenth century philosopher Thomas Hobbes found it necessary to subject the concept of virtue to a fundamental redefinition. The moral virtues, Hobbes said, are simply "the means of peaceable, sociable and comfortable living," means necessary for avoiding the miserable conflict and warfare to which egoistic human nature gives rise when unrestrained.[40] Morality then, is to be understood as a collection of rules conducive to the public peace, and thereby the survival of life in security and comfort, a body of precepts supportive of law and order.

Which of these alternative perspectives is most appropriate for a liberal society? In much of liberal thought, that question almost answers itself. Insofar as Lockean philosophy identifies the foundation of modern liberalism, we must conclude that this is the kind of society that makes liberty and security, not good character, its central concern. To the extent that morality has a role to play in Lockean society, it would have to be as a means to the preservation of those goods that are of central concern there. And that is what Locke does seem to have in mind in his prescriptions for an education conducive to mastery over one's inclinations. Apropos of his educatee, Locke remarks: "As years increase liberty must come with them, and in a great many things he must be trusted to his own conduct, since there cannot always be a guard upon him, except what you put into is own mind by good principles and established habits."[41] Apparently Locke envisions here a person who will be living in a more or less liberal regime that leaves many things to the choices of individuals. Persons unable to control their impulses cannot be trusted to their own conduct without serious danger to the lives, liberties, and material goods of others. Furthermore, utterly self-indulgent hedonists are unlikely to be industrious and productive contributors to a commercial society. Therefore, certain restraining principles must be instilled by habituation.

The Lockean view of what morality amounts to, and its role in society, would seem to be rather more Hobbesian than Aristotelian. It's true that the prominence of liberty in Locke's view of the social good differentiates him from the former, yet his omission of the enobling or elevating function in ethical life differentiates him still more from the latter.[42] That omission cannot fail to affect one's conception of what are the important virtues or components of good character. Hobbes and Locke both advance to the central position those qualities that make for mutual accommodation and social peace. Hobbes lists among the most important moral virtues the following principle: "*complaisance*—that is to say, that every man strive to accommodate himself to the rest."[43] And in almost the same language, Locke gives high priority to an educational regime that, under the name of civility, ensures "that they may bend to a compliance, and accommodate themselves to those they have to do with."[44] Neither thinker includes courage among the moral virtues. Hobbes says nothing about sexual morality: he advances no ethical norms addressed to the sensual side of life per se. Locke says almost nothing explicitly about sexual morality (though he treats the family as important and presupposes monogamy). What we have here is an ethos heavily emphasizing the reduction of conflict and hence narrower in scope than the ethos advanced by the ancient philosophers.

When we carry this outlook to its utmost conclusion, we arrive at the position that morality is a set of rules for the prevention of "antisocial conduct." The immoral or unethical, then, would consist (only) of conduct palpably or materially "harmful to others." This limited view of the moral domain is the one that John Stuart Mill tends to adopt in *On Liberty*. And, more obviously, this is the position of H. L. A. Hart; that is, insofar as Hart means to endorse any public morality, it is this minimal ethic of violence prevention, material security, and order maintenance.[45] It would follow that most of the standards of decency we've identified as belonging to our traditional public morality are not really moral principles at all, since the activities they censure are not direct or palpable injuries to (nonconsenting) others. The interesting question is whether a liberal society is well served by this trend in liberal thinking that, precisely considered, removes much of human life and character formation from the domain of ethical concern. Is it a good thing that the ethic remaining is one that doesn't ask very much of us?

Even John Stuart Mill, in some of his writings, departs (inconsistently?) from the narrow view. In his *A System of Logic* Mill says: "Ideal nobleness of character, or . . . a near approach to it in any abundance, would go further than all things else toward making human life happy."[46] In the expression "ideal nobleness of character" something like the classical conception of the virtuous life is surely implied. Yet, as we've seen, the incorporation of that conception into the public morality of a liberal society is quite problematic. Liberal ideology does not endorse and liberal society will not submit to civically mandated standards of excellence.

Insofar as this is a dilemma, it need not be wholly intractable, either in theory or in practice. In theory one can envision alternatives to a minimalist or survivalist ethic of material security on the one hand, and a demanding ethic of nobility on the other. We can envision between these poles a spectrum of moralities involving varying degrees of each.[47] In this way the theorist can consider where on that spectrum the public morality of a liberal society is best located.

Why undertake such a quest? Why not settle for the minimalist public ethic that, in effect, says the following to the citizen: "Be sure to abstain from violence, theft, and fraud (and pay your taxes); after that you can live just any way you please (as long as you let everyone else do so)—the community makes no further moral demands upon you"? To summarize the answer bluntly: this ethic is too low and uninspiring; it doesn't aim high enough nor is it broad enough to facilitate either public spiritedness or character development. Its mandates are compatible with massive social indifference and a pervasive self-indulgent sensualism; conceivably it could preside over a nation of thoroughly self-absorbed hedonists (at least for a time). Under a public morality rigorously confined to proscription of gross antisocial conduct, the legislator or policy maker would be largely disabled from acting with a view to the cultivation of good character or the inhibition of its opposite. In principle public moral judgment would have to be confined to palpable material injuries or "clear and present danger" thereof. And character development even in public education would be suspect and tenuous enterprises at most. A decent liberal society needs an ethic aiming higher than that, with norms devoted to promoting the social side of human nature and norms devoted to moderation of appetites—on behalf of aspirations rising some distance above primitive urges.

More specifically the community needs moral mandates addressing wants and passions having what we may call an addictive potential. Passions unleashed by sexuality, narcotics, and gambling come readily to mind. Sexuality can be all-consuming, especially when the impulse is repeatedly solicited in a pornographic manner that denegrates all moral and aesthetic constraints. And this is no small or isolated phenomenon; students of human nature from Plato to Freud and beyond have shown how sexuality bears extensively upon general character formation and personal identity.[48] But, for the illustration of the basic point, let us focus upon the more obvious case of narcotic drugs like heroin and cocaine, and the compulsive proclivities they unleash.

No one denies that liberal society has a vested interest in prohibiting destructive actions that may result from these proclivities. The more interesting questions concern the legitimacy of public norms and policies designed to produce personalities that do not have or yield to such inclinations. Criminologists James Q. Wilson and John Dilulio write:

> There is an obvious moral reason for attempting to discourage drug use: the heavy consumption of certain drugs ravages human character . . . the pleasure or oblivion they produce leads many users to devote their lives to seeking pleasure or oblivion, and to do so regardless of the cost in ordinary human virtues such as temperance, duty and sympathy. The dignity, autonomy and productivity of the user is at best impaired, at worst destroyed.[49]

Is liberal society well served by the idea that its legitimate collective interest in the moral life begins and ends with the grossly injurious behaviors (murders, assaults, robberies, school disruptions, etc.) to which personalities of this sort give rise? That idea is the logical outcome of a doctrine that the posture of the liberal community toward ways of life must be one of strict neutrality. Taken to its logical conclusion, such moral neutrality would preclude communal or public endorsement of temperance, duty, and sympathy as against the drug-oriented lifestyle. The polity could condemn the palpable material injuries but not the way of life or the personality type associated with them. But is it really a matter of only private concern if large numbers of the country's citizens are regularly devoting themselves to pleasure-seeking or oblivion? Insofar as a negative answer needs illustration, imagine a citizen body with a majority of heavy cocaine users. They could hardly muster the public spiritedness necessary for any subordination of private desire to the public good. And in all probability they will use their personal liberty to make life increasingly miserable for each other. No doubt they will sooner or later vindicate the old proposition that individuals who cannot govern themselves are unsuitable for political self-government. Hence, a republican polity must take steps to ensure that it won't be peopled by large numbers of personalities who live only for immediate pleasure or some form of oblivion.

In other words, to achieve even the limited objective of preventing gross depravities, a liberal community must have accepted standards by which "ravaged character" can be recognized as such and stigmatized. That is, it needs a public morality that functions to discourage the development of certain kinds of undesirable character and encourage the cultivation of virtues like temperance, duty, and sympathy. Moreover, virtues like these are not very well promoted on the basis of a civic ethic narrowly focusing on the prevention of blatantly antisocial conduct. To encompass such virtues one needs an ethic with broader horizons—a more comprehensive view of what character means. It isn't enough for society to say, "Don't do these utterly base things!" It needs to be able to hold up a model of what is worthy.

The problem of drug-induced moral degeneration is but an extreme example of the reality and the social importance of good and bad character. Less extreme but nonetheless significant examples are abundantly evident in ordinary life, both private and public. The effectiveness of education depends substantially upon the character of teachers and students—the devotion, sometimes self-sacrifice, of the former and the self-discipline of the latter. Self-discipline in some degree is also requisite for the liberal virtue of tolerance, for law abidingness, and for that independent pursuit of distant goals that a free and commercial society relies upon in so many ways. And suppose there were no habitual compunction whatever against deception and manipulation of others? (An interesting thought experiment: imagine how you would get along for a single day without being able to assume that most of the things said to you are at least somewhat true.) As to political life, William Galston offers the following insight:

> The greatest vices of popular governments are the propensity to gratify short-term desires at the expense of long-term interests and the inability to act upon unpleasant truths about what must be done. To check these vices liberal citizens must be moderate in their demands and self-disciplined enough to accept painful measures when they are necessary. . . . Constantly unbalanced budgets—the systematic displacement of social costs to future generations—are signs of a citizenry unwilling to moderate its desires or discharge its duties.[50]

These moral realities were as evident to earlier thinkers like Tocqueville[51] as they are to perceptive contemporary observers. James Q. Wilson maintains that "a variety of [current] public problems can only be understood—and perhaps addressed—if they are seen as arising out of a defect in character formation."[52] He includes in this category problems of schooling, welfare and public finance, in addition to crime.[53]

For liberal society to be in a position to discourage the defects and promote the worthier characteristics, an ethic is wanted that, while requiring of us something less than moral excellence in its highest classical reaches, demands of us rather more than abstention from violence, theft, and fraud. As an abbreviated way of connoting such an intermediate morality, I've been using the expression "ethic of decency." (In definition of *decent*, my dictionary uses, among others, the following terms: "respectable, satisfactory, fairly good.") The group of traditional prohibitions summarized at the beginning of this section is such an ethic, or, more exactly, it constitutes part of such an ethic. From that perspective it is indecent to live the kind of life depicted and recommended in pornographic productions, to allow one's higher faculties to be overwhelmed by drug or other addiction, to enjoy as entertainment spectacles involving cruelty to persons or animals, to desecrate the dead bodies of human beings, to urinate in streets and parks, and to express oneself with blatant vulgarity in public places. These tenets and the like represent the negative or proscriptive dimension of a larger ethos whose principles or purposes can be identified, if not with utmost precision and certitude, at least with relative clarity and confidence. While each of the acts proscribed invites its own specific ethical diagnosis, all of them are acts felt to be degrading or ugly. This feeling is rooted in the perception that they are violative of proprieties that have the function of lifting our existence above brutish impulse, proprieties serving, as we say, to "refine" or "sublimate." Some of the norms perform that function by encouraging respect—more exactly, precluding gross disrespect—for the interests and sensibilities of others and, more basically, for man as a being with a mind and "dignity." (To desecrate a dead body and to portray a woman pornographically is to forget what one is obliged to remember about the status of a human being.) And some of the norms act, or can act, in the service of a more rational life by stigmatizing and helping to control certain extreme manifestations of the irrational in us.

I am not arguing that these particular moral proscriptions are universal and categorical imperatives or that all the principles associated with them are philosophically unchallengeable. The common American ethic of decency that they represent isn't flawless. In practice it (like every actual communal ethic) is embedded in social custom and traditional beliefs that are not entirely dictated by reason. On the other hand, it would be a sizable mistake to treat this ethic as a mere collection of rationally indefensible local taboos. A number of its standards—especially those facilitating respect for other persons—are responsive to the Lockean (and Hobbesian) interest in social peace. Other aspects of it are reminiscent of classical ideas of the worthy and unworthy and the aspiration for a community with ends more inspiring (or distinctively human) than security and material satisfaction. The traits of character to which these standards, taken together, contribute represent considerably more than the parochial interest or transient opinion of a particular time and place.

To generalize the point, the capacities for self-restraint and civility are invaluable human virtues that, however, are acquired (usually) in the observance of norms associated with some particular communal ethos or tradition. No historic ethos can claim to be the flawless or the only vehicle for the cultivation of these virtues; they can be promoted in varying degrees by a number of different traditions. But not every ethos is equally conducive to this cultivation; some are more attuned to that end than others. Hence, we may conclude that a particular ethic of decency is eligible for the status of public morality on two conditions: that its content is conducive to the ethos, or the habits, of a reasonable and civil existence *and* that it is supported by a communal consensus of some breadth and depth. Here we are reminded of the communitarian side of the case for public morality—the priority of unity over pluralism on moral fundamentals. And we are reminded of why such priority is necessary but not sufficient for a justifiable public morality. What finally counts the most for our social well-being is *who we are*; that is, our possession in sufficient degree of those moderating and civilizing qualities called character.

III. Law

Society needs a unifying and civilizing ethos. But why, it will be asked, is it ever necessary to bring the law into it? Aren't communal relations and moral values strong enough to prevail by noncoercive means? And, this questioner might continue, if they aren't, why do they deserve to prevail; how valuable, after all, is a morality that needs to call upon the assistance of political authority?

It should be reasonably clear why an ethic of restraint and moderation could stand in need of the law's assistance. That ethic makes claims upon us that are resisted by primal urges and desires. Though its mandates may finally contribute to fulfillment of our higher aspirations as human beings, they are neither self-evident truths nor objects of natural desire. We are not spontaneously attracted to the qualities of moderation; real appreciation of them is the result of a more or less demanding education and habituation. Very often, then, they exist among us (perhaps like civilization itself) in a condition of some fragility.

These realities provide the basis for answers to the claim that a worthy morality should be able to overcome threats to its principles by reliance upon rational persuasion, or, as Professor Hart puts it, "argument, advice and exhortation."[54] Pornographers, pimps, drug peddlers, and those strongly attracted to their services, are notoriously unresponsive to direction by reasoned argument and ethical exhortation. Of course argument, advice, and exhortation are important agencies in the moral life, and, where likely to be sufficient, these are the preferable agencies. But their frequent insufficiency is one of the more prominent factors of human experience.

What is needed ordinarily is an effective social morality, which means one publicly recognized or endorsed by the community as such. And it is through the legal order that the public status of ethical norms is most pointedly affirmed. The enactment of law is, among other things, an authoritative definition and announcement of what the community stands for. This aspect of legal reality is obscured by an opinion about the nature of law that identifies it wholly with coercion, as if to legislate is to say only that certain specific acts shall be penalized. Frequently, if not always, to make a law is to articulate and promulgate a principle, thereby both manifesting and affecting attitudes about what is right and wrong. Law, on this understanding of it, has educative as well as compulsive functions. This is an understanding with ancient roots in Western thought.

The more truncated view of what law is about, which denies it any role in the moral life, is contradicted not only by traditional thinking but also by recent insights. The idea of law as a kind of moral educator receives support from a variety of current sources; one of these (perhaps unexpectedly) is criminology, the legal area in which coercion and punishment are most prominent. Thoughtful criminologists observe that the criminal law performs its function not merely by threatening wrongdoers with painful consequences by also by *stigmatizing* wrongdoing; that is, solemnly condemning it. In this way those ethical standards of the community that have been violated are dramatically reinforced. Herbert Packer notes that the criminal law is one of the institutions by which people are "socialized" and "moral norms are learned"; he refers to "the subtle process of value reinforcement through the process of criminal stigmatization."[55] Here we envision the law operating on the attitudes of citizens—on mind and affect, conscious and unconscious.

Looking beyond criminology to the legal enterprise as a whole, law professor Mary Ann Glendon observes: "There is no escape from the fact that, willy-nilly, law performs a pedagogical role. It contributes in a modest but not a trivial way to that framework of beliefs and feelings within which even our notions of self-interest are conceived."[56] The reason it has this role, according to Glendon, is that the law is inevitably involved in the interpretation of reality. The law cannot do its work without articulating "visions" of what is true or good and thereby exercising an "influence on the manner in which we perceive reality."[57] For example, our legal regulations and decisions concerning family life, divorce, and abortion convey visions, including moral messages, about the family, the individual, and society. For Glendon, it is most important that we give thought to the kind of messages we are sending through the law. This perspective indicates powerfully why a legal system is never simply a collection of utilitarian devices for the prevention or resolution of disputes (another truncated picture of what law is about); it is also a formulator and enunciator of ethical ideas.

The central point can be formulated in a variety of ways. The version of it that I want to stress is that the law teaches by promulgating, in a decisive manner, the message that certain ethical standards have public status—that they are norms *of the civic community* and not merely private opinions. Law is one of the basic instruments by which a society defines itself, by which we determine, through constituted agencies, who we are collectively. You might ask why, on this legal philosophy, it would be necessary to affix penalties; if moral teaching and self-definition is what we're after, why not settle for solemn legislative pronouncements? Obviously the sending of ethical messages is only part of what we're after (as stigmatization is only part of what the criminal law is doing), but to that end penalties are ordinarily necessary to make the pronouncements decisive. By enactments "with teeth in them" the community makes clear that it is serious about the standards it declares. The assumption is that, over time, such authoritative declarations of principle will effect minds and characters. Most people, wishing to identify with their community, and to be well regarded in it, are disposed to take their bearings from what they perceive to be its crucial beliefs and commitments. (Where in the long run this is not the case, one has to doubt that any real community exists.)

American civil rights law of recent decades provides a case in point. It's hard to deny that our public opinion is substantially more opposed to racial segregation and favorable to equal rights than it was prior to the Supreme Court decisions and the legislation of the 1950s and 1960s. The principles affirmed in those enactments did not immediately prevail, but, with time and habituation to living under them, most Americans have come to acknowledge them as our civic standards of right (even when we don't fully live up to them). No doubt social factors other than the law have contributed to this result, but surely the legal enactments and judgments have been a major catalytic contributor (even to the activation of some of those other social factors).

Cognizance of this standard-setting and reinforcing function of law is essential for an understanding of both public morality in general and certain particular legislative policies. To illustrate: carefully devised antiobscenity statutes can serve as an affirmation that "we the people," acting through our constituted deliberative organs, recognize ethical limits regarding commercial exploitation of sexuality. By publicly condemning the more extreme forms of such exploitation we proclaim, in an emphatic way, that a moral community exists that is not neutral about the pornographic treatment of human beings and erotic life. Needless to say, obscenity statutes will never obliterate all pornography (as civil rights laws don't obliterate all prejudicial behavior.) More realistically, the statutes may aim to promote the following desirable consequences. Pornography can be made less plentiful, less obtrusive in the social environment, and more difficult to acquire than it would otherwise be. In this way a social milieu is preserved in which the traditional moral education will have a better chance to be effective. A more subtle consequence is the support provided for the social opinion that disapproves the "values" that pornography represents. Citizens and families endeavoring to maintain decent norms, and educate the young therein, are encouraged by communal endorsement of their beliefs. And the beliefs of some persons could be bolstered, rendered clearer as well as firmer, as a result of the law's deliberation.

We see therefore that, in principle, the law can contribute to the shaping of character in two ways. First, it may function as a device for the removal of obstacles to the conduct of moral education by those most directly involved in the enterprise—families, schools, religious agencies. It's true that these are the primary moral educators, as is so often claimed by opponents of public morality. But it is not true, as some of those opponents seem blithely to assume, that these agencies can always perform their task without the support of the legal order. For the family to teach decency in an environment saturated with drugs, commercialized sex, and the like is a notoriously difficult thing. (And of course the public schools could not teach morality without some legal authorization or sanction.) Second, the law educates in a less-obvious though possibly more far-reaching manner through the endorsement of moral opinion. An ethic of decency may be articulated and strengthened in the public mind by the law's condemnation of specific violations of it and by the validation of norms that such condemnation entails.

Some crucial aspects of the law's educative role are succinctly summarized by Rousseau. "The censorship," he says, "upholds morality by preventing opinion from growing corrupt, by preserving its rectitude by means of wise application, and sometimes even by fixing it when it is uncertain."[58] The law can foster "rectitude" in existing moral opinion by wisely applying the premises of that opinion to concrete problems, thereby helping the people to perceive what their standards of value really entail. And on occasion it can help to solidify public opinion when it is unsure or ambivalent. (Arguably, both of those functions were performed by our civil rights legislation and adjudication). In the absence of any such legal support or clarification, social standards of decency could degenerate into a collection of amorphous generalities, ambiguous in meaning and privatized.

On the other hand, it is important to recognize that the law has its limitations. Rousseau insists that "the censorship may be useful for the preservation of morality but can never be so for its restoration."[59] A morality that has lost its strength, that is no longer acceptable to the people, cannot be saved by legal enforcement. More generally, the state cannot successfully legislate an ethic that is without grounding in prevailing beliefs, no matter how worthy it might be from an abstract point of view.

This doesn't mean that the law is confined to the role of merely reflecting and transmitting the ethical practice of the present day; that it may never do anything to improve the moral status quo. Insofar as there is a conceptual problem here concerning the law's efficacy, Rousseau's illustration and resolution of it, by reference to the noxious practice of duelling, is illuminating.

> The employment of seconds in duels, which had been carried to wild extremes in the Kingdom of France, was done away with merely by these words in a Royal edict: "As for those who are cowardly enough to call upon seconds." This judgment, in anticipating that of the public, suddenly decided it. But when edicts from the same source tried to pronounce duelling itself an act of cowardice, as indeed it is, then since common opinion does not regard it as such, the public took no notice of a decision on a point on which its mind was already made up.[60]

The employment of seconds, which exacerbates the evil by extending it to second parties, could be corrected through edicts appealing to a sense of honor with a root in public opinion. But the evil itself cannot be abolished where the public fails to recognize duelling as dishonorable and isn't open to persuasion. Somewhat analogously, the pervasive commerce in and consumption of alcohol in the United States can be subject to special regulation (and "sin tax") but it cannot be abolished. And for similar reasons the blatant commercialization of sex can be restricted by the law insofar as common opinion finds the practice loathesome, but sexual promiscuity itself, or adultery, cannot be restricted if the public simply doesn't view it as an unacceptable vice (regarding it instead as an understandable human weakness or a lifestyle that people should be free to choose). The law can reinforce an existing ethos, helping to preserve it from disintegration, and it can even make improvements where opinion is indefinite, but what it cannot do is *create* an ethos. Hence, while the idea that a legal order both reflects and shapes the morality of a people is an idea with some complexities, it is not a hopeless paradox.

Any satisfactory case for legal enforcement of moral norms must include an account of the limitations of the enterprise. For analytic convenience we may regard most limitations as belonging to one or more of the following categories: constraints that are inherent in the enterprise because of the nature of law and society; those deriving from basic mandates of a liberal regime, and those imposed by current conditions and opinions in our society. The primary consideration in the first category is the one I've been discussing, which may be formulated thusly as a practical principle: the law should seek to enforce only such norms as are in harmony with an underlying social consensus. Since this principle could be inflated to a point where it would become an insuperable obstacle to any morals legislation at all, it should be clear that we aren't talking about a requirement of virtual unanimity on the particular norm in question.[61] The point is that the state may not undertake to impose upon the people standards belonging to an ethical outlook that is alien to them (because it is old and dead or because it is wholly new). Closely related to this criterion is the distinction between a legal proscription of gross indecencies and an effort to impose the highest standards one can envision. Civic law is not in the business of promoting sanctity or demanding a virtuous perfection of which only the most admirable persons are capable. There follows a third criterion: the legislator should be very hesitant to mandate ethical restrictions that cannot be observed by ordinary people without considerable hardship or suffering; at least ordinary human capacities and weaknesses have to be taken into account.

These relatively familiar guidelines are all counsels of moderation. In this context moderation means that the law must be informed by an awareness of the difference between a reasonably defensible moral purpose and a fanatical puritanism that aims to override or transform human nature. To provide some support for the monogamous family, and to counteract assaults upon valuable standards of human worth by a multibillion-dollar pornography industry—these are rationally defensible purposes. To eradicate vice from the face of the earth by means of a comprehensive censorship of temptation thereto—these are not. As we know, the greatest dangers of despotism arise from the ideological aspirations, epitomized by totalitarian regimes of the twentieth century, to transform radically the ethos of a people and create "a new man." And, totalitarianism aside, immoderately moralistic policies are often socially divisive, giving rise to hostilities and disunity, contrary to the unifying purpose of public morality. Wherever the legislation of a moral norm is most likely to produce more divisiveness than harmony or decency, there is a compelling case against the legislation.

These criteria for a moderate policy on behalf of public morality might be faulted as insufficiently precise. It's true enough that they are not precise rules; nor could they be. They are general principles requiring the employment of practical judgment in view of variable social circumstances. The judgment that a certain ethical standard is or isn't in harmony with the underlying social consensus is an exercise of practical wisdom about the community's tradition, its long-term public opinion, and the like. The decision that a certain moral demand would or wouldn't be too stringent for too many of our citizens is an exercise of both ethical and prudential judgment. The need for perceptiveness and insight of this sort is hardly confined to the field of morals legislation. To what extent an enactment would actually be obeyed and whether, under existing circumstances, it is likely to do more good than harm are pervasive factors in legislative deliberation. In principle, or under normal circumstances, it should not be too much to expect of our constituted representatives (to whom, after all, we are willing to give the great powers of war, peace, civil justice, and taxation) that they determine with care which vices to proscribe and which to leave unproscribed.

Of course in this as in other areas of the law the legislator (and the public) can go wrong. The second of the three moderating strictures referred to above should have precluded our Prohibition Amendment, which sought to eradicate the production and sale of alcoholic beverages everywhere in the United States. That was a classic example of the legal effort to promote not just decency but purity, an error unlikely to be repeated in our polity. As to sexual offenses, the first two of our strictures argue strongly for the decriminalization of adultery and promiscuity ("fornication"), even though these practices, if widespread, can threaten our way of life. As a matter of fact, laws against these practices are repealed or unenforced almost everywhere in our polity. In modern times it seems, to lawmakers and prosecuters as well as the population at large, both utopian and excessively harsh to act upon these lapses from virtue with all the force of the criminal law. Likewise, our limiting criteria seem to militate against the remaining (increasingly rare and rarely enforced) criminal statutes against homosexual conduct among consenting adults in private. Arguably, there are many people who could not conform to these restrictions without substantial suffering. And in view of the state of contemporary opinion about the matter—opinion significantly liberalized and yet intensely agitated—it appears that criminalizing this behavior contributes more to social divisiveness than to any ethical or civic purpose. But these limiting considerations are far less applicable to legal restrictions upon commerce in hardcore pornography, brutal entertainments, prostitution, sex parlors, "bathhouses," polygamy, narcotics, and a number of other so-called victimless offenses. Let's try these criteria out on sadistic pornography, prostitution, and cocaine. Does it make much sense to say that legal restriction of sadistic pornography, prostitution, and cocaine holds people to a puritanically high standard amounting to the demand for purity? And how much sense would it make to claim that ordinary people cannot abstain from these vices without substantial suffering? (Needless to say, one who has degenerated to the point of addiction cannot abstain from his drugs without considerable suffering, but that is true in some degree of any vice that has been allowed to become a full-fledged addiction.) Finally, these activities, unlike drinking and homosexuality (and, increasingly, gambling), are widely recognized in our society as vices.

The basic principles of constraint on legal enforcement that we've been considering are those arising from realities of human society that are more or less universal. There are other important constraints deriving from the distinctive principles and commitments of a liberal society. Apart from due process requirements, the most prominent limiting principles of this sort are freedom of speech and privacy. Any law against *advocacy* of immoral ideas or ways of life would surely and rightly be held unconstitutional. This basic liberal norm, which extends to serious imaginative literature and art, imposes substantial limits upon what the law may treat as pornography. And a presumption exists against intervention of the police in deeply cherished regions of privacy such as one's home. Hence, there is much to be said for Supreme Court rulings that do not allow the state to make the possession of pornography or use of contraception in the home punishable offenses.[62]

The final category of constraints on the law is harder to analyze abstractly but is not impossible to work with. These are constraints arising from contemporary social conditions and opinions that seem likely to persist. As I've noted, recent decades have brought a rather striking liberalization or relaxation in certain moral attitudes, particularly on sex-related matters. (The term *sexual revolution* captures some of it.) This new liberalization, which is especially prominent in the mass media, imposes obstacles to morals legislation that are not necessarily mandated by basic liberal principle. For example, some of the more blatant media exploitations of sex and violence are sanctioned far less by fundamental liberal principles than by a current combination of escalated libertarianism, relaxation of moral standards, and entrenched media interests therein. It is on account of these latter factors that legal measures are less effective than they used to be as instruments for dealing with obscenity, public vulgarity, or indecency, and more of that sort of thing has to be tolerated. But how much more is still a subject for practical judgment about underlying moral opinion, that is, about the contemporary balance between liberationist and traditionalist beliefs. After all, as indicated in the previous chapter, some elements of our traditional moral consensus remain intact. And it remains to be seen whether every tenet and attitude of the new liberalism is inevitably here to stay. Hence, there is still room for the law to act.

Before leaving this subject, let us take more explicit note of the various ways in which the law can act. The mode of legal action upon which we've been focusing here, and to which the limitations just discussed are most directly relevant, can usefully be labeled "enforcement." Enforcement includes criminal prohibition but it includes civil penalties and restrictions as well. A civil proceeding for shutting down a commercial sex establishment as a "public nuisance" is an example of the latter. And there are legal avenues beyond enforcement. The proliferation of pornography shops and theaters can be confined by rigorous zoning regulations. And in its role as proprietor of certain civic facilities, government could (in appropriate circumstances) deny access to programs deemed contrary to public decency. To illustrate: the municipality may decline to make its beautiful publically owned auditorium available for a conspicuously sadomasochistic performance; nor does the city have to make its library meeting room available to such groups as "The North American Man-Boy Love Association" (whose motto is "sex before eight or else it's too late").[63] The contrary, libertarian policy adamantly requiring equal access for all such things undermines public morality by strongly implying that the state is neutral about decency and indecency (or by implying communal endorsement of the indecencies). A policy that takes viciousness into account in the determination of access to some civically owned facilities can serve the purpose of affirming that the community is *not* morally neutral. And of course society can also make that point in its public schools; it can use the educational function to teach an ethic of self-control and encourage the virtues upon which the monogamous family relies. Moreover, the law may define "family" in such a way that sanction is provided for the monogamous heterosexual child-producing and nurturing union. Finally, there are occasions when the state can legislate positively on behalf of an ethic of restraint, as Congress did in the Adolescent Family Life Act of 1985. The Act disbursed public funds to private organizations (including some religiously affiliated organizations) for teenage sex education programs featuring restraint and a moral orientation to sexual experience.[64] None of this is meant to suggest that such measures are always unproblematic; the point is that the role of the law in support of public morality is a matter of some complexity, involving a relatively broad range of possibilities.

In our times it will often be prudent, if not downright necessary, for the legal support of morality to take the form of means other than strict "enforcement." Especially, in view of the current cultural milieu, it seems wise to rely less on the civil law in matters of public morality. So one might press the question—Why employ the criminal law at all in this area; why not abandon the criminal sanction entirely in favor of other apparently less coercive measures? The best answer, I believe, is that the practical availability and vitality of the other, less-coercive measures ultimately depends on the presence of more stringent enforcement policies somewhere in the legal system. The whole enterprise of public morality— the collective sustenance of moral norms—rests ultimately upon the willingness to censure emphatically the more extreme violations of those norms. And enforcement policies, particularly the criminal sanction, constitute the most unequivocally emphatic modes of communal censure that we have. A society that declines to condemn—to the point of penalizing— even the most violent or degrading kinds of pornography is hardly in a strong position to employ the milder kinds of regulation. A society unwilling to prohibit even "snuff films" (graphically simulated portrayals of the dismemberment and slaughter of women for sexual gratification) is sending the message that it regards individual freedom of expression (almost any expression whatever) as more important than respect for (any) standards of decency. And in view of that message, why should people submit to regulation that, after all, would require some sacrifice of passion or economic interest to standards of decency? As a way of demonstrating society's seriousness about certain norms (or egregious violations thereof), the criminal law has a modest but not wholly dispensable role to play in the moral life. Finally, in the total absence of such a role, it becomes increasingly hard to resist libertarian demands for more and more personal autonomy and less moral restraint.[65]

This conclusion is contrary to a currently prominent view that the criminal sanction is properly employed only against offenses constituting "gross and immediate harms," that the scarce resources at its disposal should be reserved for the security of life, limb, property and the like— securities that are indispensable conditions of living in any organized society.[66] The rationale for public morality can acknowledge the priority of those concerns on the agenda of the penal law; it is not an argument for devoting as much of the resources of the criminal justice system to pornography, prostitution, and gambling as to homicide, assault, and armed robbery. It is, however, a rationale for the law's concern with goods transcending the minimal, indispensable requisites of any social existence. It is a justification for what the law has always tried to do (nowadays with more obstacles and less confidence)—and what the majority of citizens evidently still wants it to do—devote some of its attention to the quality or worthiness of our social existence.

Equally important to keep in mind is the fact that the criminal law doesn't have to do most of the moral work. When effective, the criminal sanction acts upon the public ethos and sentiment as a kind of catalyst of elements already present; by condemning extreme incivilities, it can energize ethically oriented policies in civic affairs and support an ethic of self-restraint in areas of our lives that no law can reach. A moderate legislator will keep in mind that the crucial object of the enterprise is not that all vice is to be stamped out but that the existence of communal standards of decency is to be publically affirmed. What finally counts is people's confidence that we live in a moral community or at least that we ought to. And if nothing else, such (reinforced) confidence can provide the backbone for resistence to the further dismantling of moral norms and constraints.

IV. Counterarguments

The import of the position I have outlined in the three preceding sections will be more evident when we have examined two different ways of criticizing it. The first of these criticisms, deriving from a liberal perspective, is concerned with dangerous abuses thought to be endemic to public morality. The second derives from radical perspectives concerning the nature of society and humanity. A view of the case for public morality from these two adversarial postures can serve to illuminate its premises and implications.

In *On Liberty* John Stuart Mill writes: "But the strongest of all the arguments against the interference of the public with purely personal conduct is that, when it does interfere, the odds are that it interferes wrongly and in the wrong place."[67] Mill's idea here is that when the public acts to protect persons from direct palpable injury, it usually knows what it is doing, but when it intervenes to enforce notions of propriety (in matters of "personal conduct"), it is very likely to be governed by passions and prejudice. In the former case the people have only to judge of their own vital interests; in the latter they are free to judge by their mere likes and dislikes and will probably do so. Therefore, society must be denied any authority to legislate standards of decency, because to grant that authority at all is to place individual liberty at the mercy of nonrational tastes and antipathies.

Obviously, this line of argument rests upon a judgment about the defects or weaknesses of the public—the people in their collective capacity (and consequently the law); on matters of propriety or decency, the public is prone to subjectivity and error. Now assuming for the argument's sake that the premise is valid, one could logically conclude that there is a presumption against morals legislation and that the state should proceed with much caution on this subject. The lawmaker should have a burden of proof to meet and should be careful to employ limiting criteria of the sort that I (and others) have suggested, criteria designed to subject policy to reasonable considerations. This, however, is not the Millian conclusion; for Mill and contemporary inheritors of his outlook, moderation is no answer to the problem. As is well known, Mill insists upon a categorical principle that would forbid "absolutely" any compulsions, by law or public opinion, that are not designed to protect unconsenting persons from palpable harm.[68] The principle would altogether preclude legal proscription of indecency per se. But how could such an absolute prohibition follow from the premise that there is a human propensity to error in these matters; how could that premise entail anything more than a strong presumption against intervention? After all, if "the odds are" that the public will intervene wrongly it must be the case that sometimes they will do so rightly. Is it reasonable to conclude that because people are generally disposed to erroneous interference, no civilized state should *ever* be allowed to subject prostitution, polygamy, and pornography, as well as duelling and the use of hazardous drugs by consenting adults, to the constraints of the law? If that conclusion is believed to be compelling, it must be on the assumption (frequently discoverable in libertarian argumentation) that a rigid rule of the Millian sort is the only alternative to a regime of unlimited moralism. Logically, however, there is another alternative: civic education in the broadest sense—the enlightenment of the citizens or the lawmakers so that sensible discriminations can be made in application of sanctions to various kinds and degrees of vice. When this alternative is admitted into the discussion, the problem of dangerous abuses resolves itself largely into the question whether sensible discriminations can really be made and morals legislation confined by an educated moderation.

Apparently Mill takes a dim view of the educability of the public on this subject. He writes: "[T]o extend the bounds of what may be called moral police, until it encroaches on the most unquestionably legitimate liberty of the individual, is one of the most universal of all human propensities."[69] Now it is easier to see why Mill and his intellectual descendants will not settle for compromises. Mill seems to view that propensity to moral policing, that censorious impulse as others may refer to it, as a deeply ingrained human inclination unamenable to any real tempering and softening. You can never safely compromise with it (give it an inch and it will take a mile). This kind of perception underlies "slippery slope" arguments that so often appear on the liberal side of debates over censorship. The government must never be allowed to restrict even unmitigated pornography because—inevitably or at least very probably—the censorship will escalate and envelop serious literature and political ideas. (Once you grant them the right to impose restrictions upon *Hustler* magazine, *Lady Chatterley's Lover* is threatened and, after that, socialist and other unpopular ideas will be in danger.[70] The basic supposition is that human beings are infected with a powerful disposition to aggressive intolerance, which can only be combated by categorical principles denying it any opportunities for satisfaction.

But if the inclination is as intractable and uneducable as Mill's argument seems to suppose, one is hard put to understand how he could expect his principle of absolute noninterference to gain widespread acceptance. Yet *On Liberty* was written precisely to persuade the public or its leaders to envision the desirability of the principle and allow its firm establishment. If one can believe that *this* enterprise has a chance of success, how could one adamantly deny any prospects for a civic education seeking to instill respect for limitations that are less than absolute? Moreover, if there is a censorious disposition, answering somehow to urges rooted in human nature and intractable, is it altogether clear that the best policy would be to deny it any outlet whatever? Maybe the safest policy would be to compromise with some of its demands.

It is true that intolerance of ways markedly different from our own, and the desire to have such ways brought into conformity or excluded from the community, is a pervasive phenomenon in human experience. I've already noted some of the well-known problems and evils associated with this phenomenon. Yet what to do about it, through public policy and education, is not such a simple matter; appropriate policy is contingent upon how, essentially, we ought to conceive of this human propensity. Should we conceive of it simply as an unmitigated evil, compounded of thoroughly undesirable and indefensible traits—fear, prejudice, and lusts for domination? Those are the terms in which libertarian writers almost always talk about it, and of course they are right about certain forms of intolerance (racial and ethnic hatreds, for example). But some of the phenomena labeled intolerance are susceptible to a different interpretation. We can think of them as rooted, partly, in communalistic impulses and the defects of those impulses among most people most of the time. If, as I've argued, the spirit of community is built upon common beliefs and traditions, a shared way of life, then most people's resistance to the intrusion of alien and contradictory ways can be seen as natural and not altogether disreputable. Strong communal bonds and identity are based on "love of one's own," devotion to things distinctively "ours." And that feeling is not compatible with boundless toleration for every conceivable way of life or pattern of conduct.

Practices sharply at variance with our cherished commitments, and which we believe to be profoundly wrong, can be experienced as a challenge to the premises of our social union and a denigration of what we believe individually. Lest it be thought that these feelings are easily avoidable and dismissable, let us imagine practices that would be loathsome to almost everyone in the United States. Would you advocate toleration of *suttee* (the ritual burning of the widow on her husband's funeral pyre), or gladiator fights to the death for the excitement of audiences, supposing that the practice were voluntary? How about cannibalism (without homicide for the purpose)? Wouldn't virtually everyone, liberals and conservatives alike, feel that these "lifestyles" are abominations—and if we tolerate them, what kind of civilized society are we? Arguably, this sort of reaction is necessarily entailed by the beliefs we hold about human life and dignity. (To put it a bit differently, someone who would not have such a feeling could reasonably be suspected of lacking those beliefs or holding them tepidly.) Intolerance of this sort can be understood as a functional reaction protective of valued communal modes of life and ideas of humanity. And that protective feeling isn't normally confined to what goes on in one's immediate neighborhood; it extends to activities occurring in one's city and country (albeit often with some attenuation of its intensity in those cases). In other words, it extends to all communities to which we belong and with which we identify. You will probably experience moral distaste upon hearing of instances of *suttee* in India or homicidal violence as entertainment in some other place, but not a sustained outrage and sense of responsibility to do something about it; those countries are not *ours*. (On the same basis, we feel more strongly about a notorious crime or disaster occurring in the United States than we do about a similar event occurring in a foreign country, even when the former event is geographically more distant from us than the latter).

Unfortunately the special affective attachment to one's own people and institutions, and the community—serving impulses associated therewith, are often misdirected; they are not fully rational. Undeniably they contribute to parochial exclusivities, prejudices, and hostilities among cultural groups and nationalities. Yet these impulses are also the source of many affections, loyalties, "brotherhoods," from the familial to the civil, without which life would be poorer than it is. This is a deep-rooted inclination with complex dimensions. Its problems are not amenable to a simple and total resolution; policies seeking to eradicate or ride roughshod over it may properly be accused of immoderation. A reasonable orientation toward this human propensity is not a wholesale rejection but an understanding that endeavors to broaden by enlightenment its narrower parochialism, to contain by law its worst excesses, and to accommodate its better elements. In such a realistic orientation, involving (if I may be allowed the word) a measure of toleration for the wants and limitations of ordinary mankind, public morality has a role to play.

An oversimplified view of the "censorious" disposition, and belief that it can be denied but not educated, underlies the inability of libertarians to envision a middle ground between a regime of virtually unqualified liberty and one of rampant censorship. These suppositions, more or less Millian, prevent many libertarians from taking seriously the possibility of a mixed or balanced public opinion—one combining respect for basic liberties of thought and belief with a healthy antipathy for gross depravities of conduct. Yet, as I've tried to show, our contemporary public opinion *is* of the mixed kind in which some moralist and some permissive attitudes coexist, often tending to check and balance each other. My point here is not that our present situation is optimal or without serious difficulties, but that our experience in modern democracies contradicts Mill's view of human nature at this interesting point: the inclination to "moral police" is susceptible to a moderation that Millian philosophy fails to envision. At any rate, this question about the nature and educability of collective opinion on moral matters is an important factor in both the case for and the (liberal) case against public morality.

Other aspects of the case for public morality are highlighted when one views it from a more radical or leftist perspective. From the vantage point of classical Marxism, the project of this chapter would look like an utterly misguided effort to save a (necessarily) corrupt capitalist society by tinkering with its ideological and legal superstructure. Karl Marx is famous for having said that moral ideas, along with those of religion and metaphysics, are "ideological reflexes and echoes" of the "material life process."[71] That is, moral norms don't shape human affairs, they *reflect* the impersonal socioeconomic forces that are the real shapers. Moreover, advanced capitalism will inevitably destroy all the old moralities, replacing them with "naked self-interest" and "callous cash payment" as the only bond among human beings.[72] This degradation cannot be ameliorated within the system; it can only be abolished—by revolutionary transformation of the entire bourgeois liberal society. As for pornography, prostitution and the like, capitalism will naturally end up "commodifying" sexuality as it commodifies everything else.[73]

Proponents of public morality should acknowledge that the capitalist economy, especially in its mass consumption stage, has a community-weakening dynamic that is in part responsible for the decline of traditional norms. Obviously, such an economy (along with the advanced technology it generates) increasingly stimulates the desire for private profits and material gratifications, thereby cultivating a privatized citizenry. And recently, it has generated a large industry that finds considerable profit in catering to tastes for pornographic and violent entertainments. But one need not accept the Marxist economic determinism that wholly identifies liberal society with the capitalist dynamic and treats everything in the former as (ultimately) a result or reflection of the latter. The market economy is not the all-encompassing determinant of our social life; it is one among several major components, including political commitments, religious traditions, and ethical orientations. The rationale for public morality must reject doctrines that view material factors as the decisive ones and moral norms or opinions as always epiphenomenal; it is incompatible with any philosophies that view social life as the product of impersonal "forces" and therefore regularly speak of social affairs in the language of "inevitability."

Underlying the case for public morality is a philosophic outlook that accords substantial weight to ideas, including ethical ideas, in the shaping of our collective life. While it can allow for the importance of economic and technological factors in setting limits to collective self-determination, the philosophy is at variance with all materialistic fatalism. On the other hand, it is not given to the optimism characteristic of Millian liberalism concerning the rational capabilities of the autonomous individual. The view of human nature associated with public morality differs from that associated with Millian liberalism as to the quality of the choices that independent individuals can be expected to make; the former yields less confidence than the latter that persons liberated from communal norms can be relied upon to make virtuous or responsible choices. But, against the fatalists or technological determinists, it maintains that character matters a great deal, that what a people believes or can be persuaded to believe about good and bad is socially crucial. Hence, unlike both liberalism and Marxism, the philosophy of public morality attributes a significant role to the legal order as embodiment and cultivator of ethical opinion. To some of the more extravagant claims about personal autonomy, the philosophy can respond by pointing out that all societies necessarily shape human character for better or worse. It recognizes that most of us are imperfect enough to need the support of institutions, including the law, in our efforts to live a decent life. And it supposes that, within limits, we are able to provide such support for decent beliefs through the collective deliberative process that is law.

The leftist (including neo-Marxist) outlook generates an additional, and perhaps more interesting, critique. Radicals may claim that the phenomenon I've been calling public morality really functions as the ideological instrument of an exploitive economic system and even the (covert) agency of an exploitive class. The ethic of self-restraint is denigrated as an ideology arising from and supporting bourgeois interests; its main objects are the promotion of attitudes conducive to capitalist productivity, bourgeois law and order, and the power of property owners who are adept at restricting present gratification for the sake of long-term profit. Furthermore, this critique is often associated with the anticipation of a time when an ethic of self-restraint will no longer exist. It is expected that the morality of restraint or moderation will "wither away" when the oppressive social conditions that gave rise to the need for it have withered away and the new liberated man has arisen. This outlook appears some-times in the form of unarticulated assumptions or unargued assertions and sometimes in the form of more developed theory. Perhaps the most forceful and dramatic theoretical presentation of the view—especially in the area of sexuality—is to be found in Herbert Marcuse's *Eros and Civilization*.

Of course the ethic of self-restraint has economic effects; it can contrib-ute to productivity and is conducive to law and order that protects property interests. But the idea that it is simply an instrument at the service of (malevolent) capitalistic interests is far-fetched, especially in view of facts we've noted about the tension between public morality and the dynamics of modern capitalism. (And let's remember the Marxist exposé of the morality-destroying "cash nexus.") A more accurate account would recog-nize this complexity: while the morality of self-restraint does serve commer-cial society by supporting a work ethic, it also serves to limit commercialism by moderating our acquisitive impulses and passion for material goods. More importantly, the idea that a transformative liberation of the magni-tude that Marcuseans envision is possible sharply conflicts with the concep-tion of human beings and society that underlies the case for public morality. On the latter view, our need to bring certain unruly passions under rational control is hardly a mere product of transient, historical circumstances; it is a permanent feature of the human condition. The philosophy of public morality is an adversary of utopian philosophies that look forward to the radical transformation of our self-interested nature and the eventual disappearance of life's great conflicts. The self-interested passions and the conflicts will persist; they can be moderated by continuing effort—but not abolished. On this reality there is essential agreement (notwithstanding many other disagreements) in the great tradition of political thought extending from Aristotle to Locke and the American founding.

Moderation is a central virtue for beings who are as far from the angelic as they are from the simply brutish. And the support of moderation by a public morality is a necessity for individuals who are not by nature good enough to abolish the brutish, or the crudely selfish, but are by nature good enough to aspire beyond it and to create communities able to bring it under reasonable control. The case for public morality rests upon an understanding of our selves as composite rational animals, with the possibilities and the (more or less permanent) limitations thereof.

No doubt the rationale for public morality I've outlined here, lengthy though it is, will fail to persuade those who cannot accept one or another of its basic ideas. Of course it cannot persuade anyone who rejects wholesale its view of the human condition and the problems resulting therefrom (the condition and the problems from which the need for virtue arises). Hence, it cannot persuade ultraskeptics for whom good and bad, worthy and unworthy, are things utterly subjective or relative to parochial and ever-changing cultural conditions. One who is thusly convinced that there is no such thing as human well-being (beyond preservation and material security) will hardly be convinced by arguments that certain communalistic bonds and certain qualities of character are requisites of human well-being. These arguments will also be rejected by libertarians for whom it is an unassailable principle that personal freedom of choice is the overriding good, always taking precedence over communitarian or moral claims with which it might be in competition. Finally, among the likely objectors are liberal theorists who, while acknowledging that virtue is a matter of some importance, insist that a regime of free choice can be counted upon to produce, naturally, all the virtues ("liberal virtues") that our kind of society needs. Such views could not be *proven* wrong once and for all, but they can be subjected to critical dialogue, and an appropriate burden of argument can be imposed upon them. This effort continues in chapters to come.

NOTES

1. Edmund Burke, *Reflections on the Revolution in France, Two Classics of the French Revolution: Reflections on the Revolution in France and The Rights of Man* (New York: Doubleday, 1989), p. 73.

2. Richard Rorty, "The Priority of Democracy to Philosophy," in *The Virginia Statute for Religious Freedom*, Merrell Peterson and Robert Vaughn. (Madison: Univ. of Wisconsin Press, 1988), p. 265. The viewpoint cited is attributed by Rorty (approvingly) to John Rawls. The question for Rorty (and Rawls?) is how, on his terms, one could ever make a rational judgment that "how we live now" is defective. If the answer is that one cannot make such a judgment—because there is no recourse to standards transcending our contemporary culture—then the position would seem to be indistinguishable from sophisticated complacency.

3. Aristotle, *Nicomachean Ethics, Introduction to Aristotle*, book 1, pp. 309–10; see also book 2, p. 333.

4. Patrick Devlin, *The Enforcement of Morals* (New York: Oxford Univ. Press, 1965), p. 11.

5. H. L. A. Hart, *The Concept of Law* (New York: Oxford Univ. Press, 1961), p. 167. See also *Law, Liberty and Morality*, pp. 70–71.

6. See H. L. A. Hart, "Social Solidarity and the Enforcement of Morality," in *Essays in Jurisprudence and Philosophy* (New York: Oxford Univ. Press, 1983), particularly pp. 261–62.

7. Ibid., p. 249.

8. For further discussion of this topic see chapter 3.

9. Speaking of the far-reaching import of monogamy, the Supreme Court has said the following: "Upon it society may be said to be built, and out of its roots spring relations and social obligations and duties with which government is obliged to deal. In fact, according as monogamous or polygamous marriages are allowed, do we find the principles on which the government of the people, to a greater or lesser extent, rests. . . . Polygamy leads to the patriarchal principle, and which, when applied to large communities, fetters the people in stationary despotism, while that principle cannot long exist in connection with monogamy" (*Reynolds* v. *United States*, 98 U.S. 145 [1879]).

10. The conception of community under consideration here can be visualized in a variety of ways. Robert Bellah and his associates envision it as follows: "Communities, in the sense in which we are using the term, have a history—in an important sense they are constituted by their past—and for this reason we can speak of a real community as a 'community of memory,' one that does not forget its past" (*Habits of the Heart*, p. 153). They go on to say that "stories of collective history and exemplary individuals are an important part of the tradition that is so central to a community of memory." Hence, a "real community" is united by respect for a tradition that includes veneration for certain historic individuals whose characters are held up as exemplary. For a similar though not identical picture of what makes the bonds of community, see Sebastian De Grazia, *The Political Community: A Study of Anomy.*

11. De Grazia, *The Political Community*, p. 5. De Grazia built upon the work of the eminent French sociologist Emile Durkheim.

12. See Jean-Jacques Rousseau, *Politics and the Arts: Rousseau's Letter to M. D'Alembert on the Theater*, ed. Allan Bloom. (Glencoe, Ill.: The Free Press, 1960), ch. 11.

13. The virtual impossibility of a boundlessly tolerant multiculturalism is nicely illustrated by an event reported in the *New York Times* of January 10, 1993. Under the heading "France Jails a Gambian Woman Who Had Daughter Circumcised," the article notes that the French courts are beginning to penalize clitorectomy notwithstanding that it is part of "a cultural tradition" for thousands

of inhabitants. Apparently the French do not find everything tolerable, though they have welcomed immigrants of diverse ways of life. This is but one small illustration of a problem that is perennial in human affairs.

14. Sociologists Brigitte and Peter Berger make the point in the following way: "Americans have been ready to accept [cultural] differences *as long as*, and *only as long as*, the different groups could plausibly be seen as sharing some common values of the society. In that case, ordinary and initially prejudiced Americans are quite ready to conclude that these different people are 'really okay' " (*The War Over the Family: Capturing the Middle Ground*) pp. 183–84.

15. In this regard what comes quickest to mind are measures currently taken on academic campuses to impose "politically correct" viewpoints on behalf of "multiculturalism."

16. Thomas Paine, *The Rights of Man: Part Second, Reflections on the Revolution in France and the Rights of Man*, (New York: Anchor Books, 1973), p. 398.

17. Alexander Hamilton, James Madison, and John Jay, *The Federalist Papers*, p. 77.

18. Stephen Macedo, *Liberal Virtues: Citizenship, Virtue and Community in Liberal Constitutionalism* (Oxford: Oxford Univ. Press, 1991), p. 285.

19. Ibid., p. 258.

20. See my discussion of Devlin–Hart Debate and Note 5 above.

21. A week hardly goes by without news reports of citizens complaining about prostitution, pornography, and drugs in their neighborhoods—and calling upon public authority to help them do something about it. As Fred Siegel observes: "What unnerves most city dwellers . . . is not crime *per se*, but rather the sense of menace and disorder that pervades day-to-day life: the gang of toughs on the corner exacting their daily tribute in the coin of humiliation, the 'street tax' paid to drunk and drug-ridden panhandlers . . . the provocations of pushers and prostitutes plying their 'trade' . . . these are the visible signs of cities out of control, cities that don't protect either spaces or their citizens" ("The Loss of Public Space," *The Responsive Community* 4, issue 3 (1994); p. 43. Siegel also refers to uglifying practices such as urination in public places. It's true that these are not large moral evils or injuries, but they are the kind of incivilities that, little by little, destroy the quality of life and the sense of community.

22. I've considered evidence and analysis concerning the extent of moral consensus in America in chapter 1, Sec. II.

23. The problems to which my argument here is addressed are perhaps most dramatically articulated by a friendly critic of communitarianism in the form of the following "quandry":

> If what is required is a truly national community, the communitarian promise would seem to be a hopeless one, for clearly no modern industrial state can sustain this sort of community without stoking up the very hazardous fires of nationalism.

On the other hand, if what is sought is the autonomy of local communities as such, there is no assurance that this will not give further momentum to the relativization of tastes and morals that mandated liberal neutralism in the first place. So the appeal to community, far from resolving the quandries of liberalism, merely confirms them in another guise. (Ronald Beiner, *What's the Matter with Liberalism* [Berkely: Univ. of California Press, 1992], p. 31).

In the first part of his quandry, Beiner seems to have in mind a rather strong, Rousseauian fraternalism of the kind that the more radical communitarians affirm. My answer is that a realistically modified (hence, attenuated) patriotic communalism need not stoke up a dangerous nationalism. Beiner's second point is more difficult to grapple with. Even a modest policy of accommodating communitarian concerns would have to depend considerably (though not entirely) upon local communities, and that risks the further fragmentation of the country on the basis of localist—if not racial, ethnic, and religious—loyalties. That is definitely something to watch out for; it argues against an excessively localist communitarianism. But, fortunately, most of our towns, cities, and states are not thoroughly homogeneous ethnic or religious enclaves. And again, what I'm recommending is an accommodation of communitarian desiderata balanced and compromised by other, specifically liberal considerations. Beiner doesn't show that this recommendation is impossible. Finally, I agree with him that appeals to community alone cannot *resolve* the quandries of current liberalism.

24. Here is one perceptive observation focusing simply on the economic side of the problem. Surveying an extensive body of research, William A. Galston notes: "Some 80 percent of children growing up in two-parent families experienced no poverty whatever in the first ten years of their lives, whereas only 27 percent of the children in single-parent households were so fortunate . . . . It is no exaggeration to say that the best anti-poverty program for children is a stable, intact family" (*Liberal Purposes: Goods, Virtues, and Diversity in the Liberal State* [Cambridge: Cambridge Univ. Press, 1991], p. 284).

25. Sociologists Brigitte and Peter Berger put it in the following way: "The family permits an individual to develop love and security—and most important, the capacity to trust others. Such trust is the prerequisite for any larger social bonds. Only in the family are the individual's social tendencies aroused and developed and with these the capacity to take on responsibility for others. A person who has developed no family bonds will have a very hard time developing any larger loyalties in later life" (Brigitte and Peter L. Berger, *The War Over the Family*, p. 174). Of course, it would be contrary to the main theme of this chapter to maintain that the family is wholly sufficient for these purposes or that it needs no outside help in their execution. It is also appropriate to acknowledge that, as the title of the Bergers' book indicates, there is a current ideological controversy about the nature and value of the family. In lieu of an extended discussion of this "culture war," here are two points to consider. Critics of the monogamous

family and advocates of alternative arrangements are to be found in certain academic and professional circles far more than among the general public. And the critics are rebutted by steadily increasing evidence that children of "intact families" do better on virtually all the major indicators of well-being and pathology, including school attendance and achievement, teenage pregnancy, drugs, delinquency, crime.

26. For a more elaborate treatment of the subject, see Harry M. Clor, *Obscenity and Public Morality: Censorship in a Liberal Society* (Chicago: Univ. of Chicago Press, 1969), ch. 6.

27. Contemporary feminist writers take a rather different view of what is wrong with pornography and of the ethic appropriate for judgment of it. The feminist view is critically explored in chapter 5.

28. Perhaps the most interesting recent formulation of this viewpoint can be found in Murray S. Davis, *Smut: Erotic Reality/Obscene Ideology* (Chicago: Univ. of Chicago Press, 1983).

29. I have paraphrased the language affording constitutional protection to all works of "serious value" in *Miller* v. *California*.

30. *Paris Adult Theatre* v. *Slaton*, at 63.

31. The most forceful Freudian articulation of the problem in a social context is Sigmund Freud's *Civilization and Its Discontents* (New York: Norton, 1962). He presents a somewhat less pessimistic view in *New Introductory Lectures in Psychoanalysis*, ch. 7.

32. John Locke, *Some Thoughts Concerning Education, John Locke on Education*, ed. Peter Gay. (New York: Teacher's College, Columbia Univ., 1964), p. 32.

33. Richard McKeon, *Introduction to Aristotle*, p. 370.

34. Ibid., p. 373.

35. Actually, Aristotle provides *three* reasons for avoiding self-indulgence. He notes that "the self-indulgent man is so-called because he is pained more than he ought at not getting pleasant things" (McKeon, *Introduction to Aristotle*, p. 371). Perhaps this argument that the self-indulgent personality is miserable could deter hedonists who are unmoved by arguments about "dignity" or "freedom."

36. This Tocquevillian expression (see ch. 1, sec. III of this book) could have been uttered by Aristotle and Locke, as well as by Freud and in some contexts even by Rousseau.

37. *Nicomachean Ethics*, book 2.

38. Arguably, these are some of the reasons character and its analysis is such a prominent theme in great literature. It's a safe guess that most viewers of Tennessee Williams's *A Streetcar Named Desire* do not find the ultraselfish hedonist Stanley Kowalski an attractive human being. In the novels of Jane Austen, which are renowned for exploration of the subtleties of character, the basic questions are not exactly about "What is good character?" but are about the process of discovering it, the nuances of it, and the social consequences of it (or

its opposite). Especially prominent in novels like *Pride and Prejudice* is the virtue of reliability and its vicissitudes. Perhaps some readers will believe that the character theme is a prominent phenomenon in Western literature only. As an antidote to that idea I recommend the novels of Chinua Achebe, especially *Things Fall Apart* and *Arrow of God*, in which the characters of the leading figures—powerful Nigerian Tribesmen—are treated with profundity. And in both of these novels human vanity is a major theme—every bit as much as in Tom Wolfe's *Bonfire of the Vanities*.

39. McKeon, *Introduction to Aristotle*, p. 338.

40. Thomas Hobbes, *Leviathan* (Indianapolis: Bobbs-Merrill, 1958), p. 131.

41. *Some Thoughts Concerning Education*, p. 105.

42. On the deliberate denigration of the more "sublime" aspects of virtue by modern liberal philosophy, see Thomas L. Pangle, *The Spirit of Modern Republicanism*, especially pp. 67–73.

43. *Leviathan*, p. 125.

44. *Some Thoughts Concerning Education*, p. 105.

45. See H. L. A. Hart, *The Concept of Law*, ch. 9, sec. 2, "The Minimum Content of Natural Law."

46. *A System of Logic* (London: Longman's Green, 1949), p. 621.

47. The idea of such a spectrum is suggested, though in different language and for a rather different purpose, by Lon L. Fuller in *The Morality of Law* (New Haven, Conn.: Yale Univ. Press, 1964), ch. 1.

48. This is an appropriate place to take note of an interesting issue in the Devlin-Hart debate. With sexual morals in mind, Hart accuses Devlin of assuming that a society's morality is a "seamless web" that will unravel altogether if any part of it is abandoned. On the contrary, Hart suggests, norms concerning sexuality can be abandoned without any effect on norms concerning murder, cruelty, dishonesty, and the like. (See Hart, "Immorality and Treason," in *Morality and the Law*, ed. Richard A. Wasserstrom, pp. 52–53). Devlin replies: "Seamlessness presses the simile rather hard but, apart from that, for most people morality is a web of beliefs rather than a number of unconnected ones" (Devlin, *The Enforcement of Morals*, p. 115). My argument above is closer to Devlin's, than to Hart's, on this question. If Hart thinks that a social ethos is an aggregate of discrete norms, each standing on its own, it seems to me that there is no small burden of proof upon him. But my main point is not about the way moral standards are conceived of by most people, it's a point about character formation. If sexuality is as important a factor in human development as many thinkers, ancient and modern, have claimed it is, then the attitudes and habits one acquires concerning this passion and its objects will affect the whole character. To be sure, licentiousness in this area need not lead directly to relaxation of standards regarding murder and thievery, but it is unlikely to be without any impact upon one's general attitudes, interests, and capacity for moderation. Moral opinion

need not be a seamless web but character is, to a large extent, a whole. (Otherwise the term *character* could hardly have meaning). A highly fragmented personality is usually regarded as something pathological, isn't it?

49. James Q. Wilson and John J. Dilulio, Jr., "Crackdown," *The New Republic*, July 10, 1988, pp. 21–22.

50. Galston, *Liberal Purposes*, pp. 224–25.

51. Tocqueville refers generally to these "vices" throughout *Democracy in America*. For some direct references, see vol. 1, ch. 13, "Government of the Democracy in America."

52. James Q. Wilson, "The Rediscovery of Character: Private Virtue and Public Policy," *The Public Interest* 81 (1985): p. 3.

53. Ibid., pp. 5–14.

54. Hart, *Law, Liberty and Morality*, p. 75.

55. Herbert L. Packer, *The Limits of the Criminal Sanction* (Stanford, Calif.: Stanford Univ. Press, 1968), pp. 42–44. Pressing the point farther than Packer's (generally liberal) criminology does, Wilson and Herrnstein claim "punishment as moral education almost certainly reduces more crime than punishment as deterrence" (James Q. Wilson and Richard J. Herrnstein, *Crime and Human Nature* [New York: Simon and Schuster, 1985], p. 495).

56. Mary Ann Glendon, *Abortion and Divorce in Western Law* (Cambridge, Mass: Harvard Univ. Press, 1987), p. 139.

57. Ibid., p. 9.

58. Jean-Jacques Rousseau, *The Social Contract, The Social Contract and Discourses* (New York: E. P. Dutton, 1950), p. 128.

59. Ibid., p. 127.

60. Ibid., p. 128.

61. Herbert Packer offers this as a test for the required moral consensus: "[W]hen one is talking about immorality as a *necessary* condition for invocation of the criminal sanction, the inquiry should simply be whether there exists any significant body of dissent from the proposition that the conduct in question is immoral. Is there any social group that will be alienated or offended by making (or keeping) the conduct in question criminal?" (*Limits of the Criminal Sanction*, p. 264). If taken at all literally, this test is so stringent as to preclude all morals legislation and much else. It would strike down the whole policy of penalizing possession and commerce in drugs like cocaine and heroin. Under this principle the Sherman Anti-Trust Act of 1890 and similar prohibitions of monopolistic practices could not have been enacted, since a social group—a significant section of the business community—dissented from the proposition that "conspiracies in restraint of trade" are immoral. While apparently willing to acknowledge that the criminal law is a moral agent performing a socializing function, Packer argues for an extremely restricted view of the extent of that function. It's hard to reconcile the acknowledgment with these disabling restrictions.

62. *Stanley* v. *Georgia*, 394 US 557 (1969) extends First Amendment protection to possession of pornography in one's home notwithstanding the illegality of commerce in pornography. *Griswold* v. *Connecticut*, 381 US 479 (1965) protects, as a matter of constitutional "privacy," the right of married persons to use contraceptives. One may support the conclusions of those cases, as I do, without endorsing all the arguments therein. And one need not endorse libertarian efforts to inflate the personal rights involved to such an extent as to render virtually all public morality unconstitutional.

63. In case a reader thinks this example far-fetched, see "A Very Dubious Right: Pederasty in the Public Library," *The Responsive Community*, 2, (summer 1992), p. 9.

64. The Supreme Court upheld the AFLA against claims that it violated the separation of church and state. See *Bowen* v. *Kendrick*, 487 US 589 (1987).

65. Another illustration of the general proposition in this paragraph comes easily to mind. Consider the problem posed for school administrators by teachers whose "lifestyles" are apparently at variance with the moral function of public education; for example, a teacher who performs in pornographic films or magazines or one who participates in the group-sex activities of a notorious "swinger's club" (see ch. 1, sec. II). If you acknowledge the propriety of a policy against providing such persons with state-sanctioned access to the minds of the young, then you must consider the preconditions of its successful operation. Isn't it evident that the effectiveness of the policy, that is, the ability of the school system to maintain standards of "good moral character" as a condition of employment, depends finally upon a legal system that is *not* neutral about indecency? If the society doesn't care enough about indecency to penalize some of its worst manifestations, how will the educational system deal with the inevitable claim that both the behavior and the moral norms are private matters? To generalize the point, total abandonment of legal support for moral norms not only weakens them but encourages the promotion, by law or customs, of libertarian norms.

66. See Packer, *Limits of the Criminal Sanction*, pp. 296–98, 365.

67. *On Liberty*, p. 102.

68. Ibid., p. 13.

69. Ibid., p. 103.

70. I do not wish to suggest that slippery slope arguments are discreditable per se. Few writers on controversial topics manage to avoid them altogether. (This essay doesn't avoid them altogether. As I've suggested, it is arguable that the abandonment of certain moral standards can lead eventually to a general moral decline. In other words, slippery slope arguments are employable on behalf of morality as well). In the absence of reliable criteria distinguishing the acceptable forms from the unacceptable, one must evaluate them as they come. In each case, judgment will depend finally upon one's perception of the persuasiveness of the empirical evidence offered as to the likelihood of dangerous

escalation (or "sliding," to keep the metaphor intact). Some observers claim that the process of escalation is especially to be feared from restraints imposed upon *speech*, although Mill's argument implies that it is triggered by any and all "moralistic" restraints upon conduct. In my view the historical evidence is rather mixed. In the nineteenth century we had greater restrictions upon sexual literature and conduct than anything contemplated now, yet that was a century abounding in radical criticism of philosophic, ethical, political, and religious orthodoxy. For an interesting analytic study of the logic of the slippery slope mode of argument, see Frederick Schauer, "Slippery Slopes," *Harvard Law Review*, 99 (December, 1985).

71. *The Marx-Engels Reader*, ed. Robert C. Tucker. (New York: W. W. Norton, 1978), p. 154.

72. Ibid., p. 475.

73. See Harry Brod, "Pornography and the Alienation of Male Sexuality," *Social Theory and Practice*, 14, no. 3 (fall 1988): pp. 265–84.

3

Reflections on the Offensive, the Harmful, and the Good

Public morality, when defined and defended systematically, means that in principle the civic community has a legitimate interest in discouraging some ways of life and encouraging others. Hence, public morality is incompatible with a prominent contemporary theory mandating the rigorous neutrality of the liberal state toward alternative "lifestyles" or visions of the human good.[1] The implications of this requirement of neutrality, and certain concepts associated with it, call for more extensive examination than they could receive in the preceding general rationale for public morality. Especially in need of further examination are concepts of the harmful and the offensive—as these are employed in current (largely liberal) discourse on this subject.

The neutrality requirement can be said to rest upon claims of two different sorts, some positive and some negative in character. The positive claims, to be treated in the next chapter, are concerned with values of autonomy, or freedom of choice, and equality—for the sake of which the requirement is thought necessary. The negative claims are based upon radical skepticism concerning ideas of the good life; in one way or another they deny (or virtually deny) that there is any rational ground for judgment and consensus about what is humanly valuable. This latter outlook is what I am most concerned with here. But first it will be useful to note some of the practical ways in which a policy of state neutrality about the good is highly problematic, and, in its stronger versions, a quite unattractive prospect.

To begin with, it's no easy matter to determine what a policy of unqualified neutrality—or one taking that as its ideal standard—would actually amount to. As Ronald Dworkin defines the principle, "the liberal conception of equality prohibits a government from relying on the claim that certain forms of life are inherently more valuable than others."[2] How far does this prohibition go; how far-reaching is it? The answer depends in part upon what is meant by "form of life." Does prostitution constitute a way of life? What about drugs (a "drug culture")? And gambling? (It would seem to be such for the compulsive gambler). Insofar as these are to be considered lifestyles, then a thoroughgoing neutrality principle would apparently preclude not only criminal laws against them but, indeed, all state-sponsored efforts, including public policy, to discourage or discriminate against them. It's not at all clear what (if any) are the limits to the demands unleashed by this principle. Since the monogamous family and the alternatives to it are obviously forms of life, the Dworkinian principle, taken with utmost seriousness, would seem to preclude not only laws penalizing polygamy, but all entrenchments and endorsements of monogamous marriage in our law and social policy. Perhaps Dworkin and other moral neutralists would reply that this interpretation exaggerates their point; they are only talking about government coercion or direct legal constraints on liberty. Perhaps. But doesn't state endorsement of monogamous marriage, and refusal to grant alternative arrangements the status (and benefits) of "family," constitute some constraint on one's liberty to pursue and enjoy the alternative arrangements? Many polygamists, homosexuals, communalists, and the like will maintain that their liberty is significantly curtailed by the state's bias in favor of monogamy.

The neutrality doctrine, carried some distance toward its logical conclusion, might even provide grounds for complaints against the teaching of patriotism or an ethic of hard work and self-discipline in the public schools. After all, endorsement of patriotism or allegiance to one's country reflects a moral judgment by the public school, which is an agency of the state. Education on the basis of that judgment is conducted at the expense of alternative visions of the good life; for example, the idea that a worthy life is one of transcendent self-sufficiency beyond the narrow horizons of country and society (the Thoreauean view), or the idea that the authentic human being is the perpetual revolutionary (the view of Maoists and of Sartre in one of his theoretical moods). Wouldn't the Thoreaueans and revolutionaries have a complaint that the educational system is relying on the claim that their preferred form of life is less valuable than others? As for the teaching of a work ethic—and promotion of self-disciplined character—that policy runs counter to the kind of hedonism that finds all fulfillment in leisure, self-expression, and gratification now, not later. And surely present-oriented hedonism qualifies as a form of life embodying a conception of the good. Proponents of neutralism might wish to avoid these consequences by exempting public education from its operation—on the grounds that their principle doesn't extend to children or minors. But why not, especially in the public school situation where attendance requirements are backed by the coercive authority of the state? And what about the rights of parents; is it no constraint whatever on the liberty of hedonistic, self-expressive parents to have their children forcibly exposed to what they see as excessively statist, conformist, or bourgeois attitudes? Such are the issues likely to plague a regime really committed to thoroughgoing neutrality regarding alternative versions of good life.

The trouble with all this is not only that it prevents the civic community from promoting or supporting socially unifying norms but also that it tends to the dissolution of such moral unity as may already exist. Ideological minorities would be encouraged to press, as a matter of right, a far-reaching agenda of demands for the extraction of moral or "lifestyle" preferences from public policy—demands that the traditional majority is likely to find impossible (or intolerable) to grant. This is a formula for "culture wars." Perhaps some fine distinctions can be employed to rescue the neutrality concept from these extremities by placing acceptable limits on its reach. But then we would of course have a modified principle, inviting the question, "Why is it acceptable to draw the line where you've chosen to draw it?"

There is a possible resolution involving a set of distinctions prominent in liberal theory for some time. One could give up on the more sweeping demands for equal treatment of lifestyles and confine the idea of neutrality to the area of legal enforcement, that is, direct efforts by the state to penalize immorality. Then one could have recourse to the venerable (Millian) distinction between conduct palpably "harmful to others" and conduct merely deviating from accepted morality. The prevention of harm is a legitimate basis for the exercise of legal coercion; the support of norms reflecting ideas of the good or valuable is never a legitimate basis. This position can be supplemented with the proviso that people may be protected, by regulations against "public indecency," from involuntary exposure to blatantly offensive public conduct (a proviso that Mill himself endorsed, though virtually without justifying argument.) Hence, the law may proscribe as "offensive nuisances" such conduct as nudity, obtrusive display of pornographic advertising, and solicitation by prostitutes in public places. But for the contemporary liberals who subscribe to this view, it is essential that these enactments be regarded as "nuisance laws," thereby differentiating them from any legal enforcement or endorsement of morality. As protection for nonconsenting persons from unwanted assaults on their sensibilities, these laws are said to be no more concerned with the immorality of the conduct they proscribe than are ordinances against excessively loud noise in residential areas.[3] Thus, we find Professor H. L. A. Hart insisting upon "the need to distinguish between the immorality of a practice and its aspect as a public offensive act or nuisance."[4] It follows that streetwalking by prostitutes may be proscribed to protect ordinary people in the streets from emotional shock or distress, but prostitution itself may not be proscribed because it isn't "harmful" and its aspect as a moral vice (if any) is not the law's business. Should we settle for this way of resolving the problem?

This currently familiar outlook rests upon two distinctions; its proponents are distinguishing rather sharply between the harmful and the immoral and between the offensive and the immoral. If these things are as separable as the proponents suppose, then their policy may be said to serve a neutrality principle (in the area to which it applies), because it would effectively prohibit government from using coercive law to enforce norms about the relative value of ways of living. But what happens to the policy if these things are not entirely separable in important cases, if these distinctions can be maintained only in attenuated form? Insofar as the determination of what is "harmful" requires a moral judgment, and insofar as what is "offensive" is substantially a reflection of ethical commitment or ethos, doesn't the whole theory of a rigorous state neutrality become highly questionable? Some advocates of this principle might want to respond that, while it cannot always be maintained with utmost rigor in practice, it is the ideal standard to which liberal societies should aspire. In exploration of these themes, let us postpone the larger question about the "harmful" until we have considered the somewhat lesser questions about "offensive nuisances."

Does it make complete sense to say that the immorality of prostitution is none of the law's business but the offensiveness of its public exhibition *is* the law's business? It is hard to deny that moral disapproval of prostitution is the basic reason that people are offended by its public manifestations. And, as a matter of fact, the law cannot be wholly indifferent to the source of the feelings involved; neither the law nor liberal theory proposes to offer protection from everything that people in the streets might find unattractive. For example, assertive hawking in the streets to advertise the pizza parlor could well be a nuisance to many, but no one proposes to penalize and abolish it as "indecency." It appears that the distinction between the immorality of a practice and its aspect as a public nuisance cannot be drawn as sharply as Professor Hart's position requires it to be drawn.

For one thing, it is untrue that existing ordinances against public indecency have in fact nothing to do with the maintenance or endorsement of any moral norms. The sensibilities that the law protects from offense are surely derivative of moral beliefs, more exactly, some combination of ethical and aesthetic feelings about the decent and the disgusting. The persons who are disturbed by sexual conduct or representations thereof in public places are disturbed on account of their views of propriety that are deep-rooted in a traditional ethos (either because the conduct is deemed immoral per se, as in the case of prostitution, or because the public exhibition of it is thought grossly improper, as in the case of nudity or sexual intercourse in the city park). If standards of value were of no relevance here, why would law and social policy be particularly solicitous of the feelings of those persons as against the preferences of other, more liberated, individuals? After all, some people believe in public nudity and find the constraining conventional propensities deplorable. In response it will be observed that the former group is the majority and a large one. No doubt that is one justifying reason for proscription of public indecency, but it doesn't hold up well as the entire justification. In a liberal democracy majorities frequently have to encounter and put up with things they don't like. It would seem that public decency laws and policies are designed to protect the sensibilities of some persons not only on account of the number of those persons but also in recognition that the morality their feelings represent has a communal standing entitling its adherents to the law's solicitude. In this regard, consider the following language from the famous *Wolfenden Report* (famous for its affirmation that immorality as such, and hence the private practice of prostitution, is none of the law's business): "We feel that the right of the normal decent citizen to go about the streets without affront to his or her sense of decency should be the prime consideration and should take precedence over the interests of the prostitute and her customer."[5] Why the precedence? And on what premise is a certain category of persons designated as the normal, decent citizen? It seems most unlikely that the authors of the report were thinking of normality in a merely statistical sense.

My argument thus far is that an element of public morality is entrenched even in the relatively minimal and uncontroversial policy of protecting people from certain flagrant forms of "public offensiveness." This reality must be a cause of some embarrassment to neutralist liberalism. It would seem that one determined to maintain a neutralist position must choose between two alternative options. On the one hand, a relentless effort could be launched to reform social attitudes and legal assumptions so that the policy against "public indecency" will be wholly divested of its moral significance. On the other hand, society could be urged to abandon the policy altogether on the ground that it cannot be purified of moral or lifestyle bias.

The first alternative is no small undertaking. It would involve, in effect, abolition of the notion of public indecency and its replacement with an antiseptic notion of public nuisance that views exhibitions of sex-for-sale no differently than it views loud noises and distasteful odors; the only problem being that some people are involuntarily exposed to things they happen to dislike. Supposing that this (rather strange) purification of attitudes were possible,[6] would it be desirable? For example, do we want our civic community to regard billboards promoting a graphically violent "snuff film" as having no more ethical import than billboards promoting a furniture sale (condemnation and prohibition depending in both cases on how many people are displeased and how much)? To treat degrading practices as if the only socially relevant problem they pose is one of "offense" is to trivialize a moral evil by making it turn upon merely private likings and dislikings. A legal system adopting that practice is apparently announcing that it recognizes pleasure and pain but not degradation. No doubt people walking by a theater are entitled to some protection against emotional shocks they might receive from involuntary confrontation with blatant advertising of the sadomasochistic films within. But does the provision of such protection dispose of society's interest in the matter? In the light of traditional public morality, the fact that hundreds or thousands of people who voluntarily enter the theater are not shocked, indeed are entertained, by what they see constitutes a social problem not the absence of one.

Furthermore, in the unlikely event that public morality could be entirely dethroned and replaced by a nonethical public nuisance rationale, the odds are that the program would fail to achieve even its very limited purpose. Under that dispensation we would find it increasingly difficult to protect nonconsenting persons from offensive and shocking experiences. When the state allows an extensive and profitable pornography industry to flourish with impunity, it's no easy matter to confine the advertising and other social manifestations of the business. And, the economic factor aside, a legal order that refuses to censure pornography on account of its viciousness—which cannot even manage to make an overt moral judgment about its obtrusive public manifestations—is in a weak position to (rigorously) limit the pornographic to the interiors of discreet magazine shops, theaters, and reading parlors. Having given up its moral ground, confining its case within the tepid language of "nuisance," law and social policy will find themselves increasingly on the defensive against libertarian claims.

So, to avoid these difficulties, perhaps one should consider the alternative position—explicit abandonment of the social policy seeking to protect people's sensibilities from grossly offensive public conduct. Why not abolish the legal bias against lifestyles involving nudity and even sexual intercourse in public places? The proposition is not so far-fetched as to be without its proponents, including doctrinal proponents. The contemporary philosopher Jeremy Waldron faults John Stuart Mill's allowance for restrictions upon "indecent" public behavior; the admission of such restrictions, says Waldron, is at sharp variance with Mill's forceful case for "struggle and confrontation between opposing views of the good life."[7] Waldron continues:

> There is, surely, a debate to be had about the merits of public love-making; and making love in public would be, on Mill's own account, an important contribution to the initiation or the course of such a debate. If copulation in public were banned on the ground that it is "bad manners" or offends against public decency, it is difficult to see how people could ever get a real sense of the issues involved in this argument.[8]

In another context it might be tempting (if not highly illuminating) to linger over the assumptions and implications of such a view. What shall we make of the supposition that debate about sexual matters depends in some significant way upon the existence of public copulation? And is high quality reflective dialogue about issues the most likely result of the opportunity to observe copulating couples (or multiples, etc.) in the city park? One might also pursue an inquiry stimulated by the thought that bestiality too can represent "an opposing view of the good life." And what about whipping and beating of (naked) consenting masochists in the city park? The possibilities for the promotion of confrontation between opposing viewpoints seem endless. But let us not linger over these questions. I've cited Waldron's outlook in order to illustrate the implications of a thoroughgoing rejection of public decency norms and the concept of public morality itself. Waldron's outlook may be illustrative of what it would mean to carry liberal neutralism to its utmost conclusion (except for one value commitment—a remarkably absolutistic devotion to "debate"). Whatever else might be thought about it, a milieu so indifferent to the moral sensibilities of ordinary people would be hard for ordinary people to live in.

More could be said on this theme. I hope enough has been said to render plausible three observations. First, the maintenance of traditional public decencies—even those of the most elementary sort—is neither a simple matter nor something we can easily take for granted in our time. Second, laws or policies supporting such decencies cannot be, strictly speaking, morally neutral. Third, if a regime of unqualified neutrality toward alternative ways of life could be actualized, it would be a monstrosity.

Let us turn to the more far-reaching questions raised by the modern liberal position about the "harmful"—the "harm principle" as it is sometimes called. In *Law, Liberty and Morality,* Professor Hart writes: "A very great difference is apparent between inducing persons through fear of punishment to abstain from actions which are harmful to others, and inducing them to abstain from actions which deviate from accepted morality, but harm no one."[9] This kind of sharp disjunction between injurious conduct and (harmlessly) immoral conduct pervades the critical literature on legal enforcement of morality. Among practices belonging to the latter category, Hart includes prostitution, incest (among consenting adults), and bestiality. Since *Law, Liberty and Morality* does not provide a systematic analysis of what is and is not injurious to human beings, we are entitled to ask why such practices as those just mentioned may confidently be said to harm no one. (As we may ask for a defense of the implicit claim that the ethic that censures them is nothing more than a conventional opinion that happens to prevail among us). Perhaps Hart means to rely upon ordinary common sense perceptions; the activities in question, he observes, "involve nothing that would ordinarily be thought of as harm to other persons."[10]

Leaving aside for the moment the question of what is "ordinarily thought of" in this regard, the sharp distinction maintained by Hart and others is easiest to maintain on the basis of a narrow definition of "harm" that encompasses only physical and other palpable damages. Conducted with due care, prostitution, bestiality, and incest (among consenting adults) need not cause physical or material injury; that is also true of pornography. As we've seen, however, Hart is willing to allow legal constraints to protect people from offensive nuisances shocking to their sensibilities. Apparently Hart's concept of the "harmful" is broad enough to encompass certain emotional shocks, but that is its outer limit.

Why stop with emotional shocks? One reason for doing so could be to furnish public policy with a concept that it is uncontroversial and, to the greatest extent possible, neutral among competing ideas of the good or the valuable. Of course, even the narrowest conception that identifies the harmful strictly with palpable or material injury isn't thoroughly neutral; it presupposes that life, safety, health, and property are valuable goods. I won't make much of this rather obvious factor, which may be considered trivial—though it becomes less trivial insofar as what is presupposed is that life, safety, physical health, and property are the most valuable things. What is more interesting is that, by its inclusion of "offense" among the things to be regarded as injuries, Hart's perspective may be said to teeter on the edge of recognizing that there is such a thing as nonmaterial or nontangible harm. And this opens the door to some controversial questions.

What Hart's doctrine apparently will not recognize is nontangible effects that are subtle, long range, and ethically injurious. For example, what about the possibility, referred to by Justice Harlan in an obscenity case, that "over a long period of time the indiscriminate dissemination of materials, the essential character of which is to degrade sex, will have an eroding effect on [important] moral standards"?[11] In other words, what the liberal perspective under consideration decisively precludes, or seeks resolutely to ignore, is the idea of *moral harm*—that human beings can suffer injury from degradation of mind and character as well as from painful assaults upon the feelings or deprivation of life, liberty, and property. The idea of moral harm is an imprecise one, standing in need of clarifying analysis. The pernicious effects upon character with which it is concerned will often occur gradually; they are not perceptible in the way that a material damage or blatant emotional shock is perceptible. Yet even in its relatively imprecise form, the idea has a claim to consideration; certainly it is worthy of attention insofar as a proper understanding of the harmful is allowed to turn upon what is ordinarily thought of as such by ordinary people. One might ask average persons in the street or in the jury box, if they view prostitution and incest as harmless to adult persons who choose to engage in them—or if they think habitual indulgence in sadistic pornography has any deleterious effects, whether or not it leads directly to antisocial acts. These practices are unlikely to get, from ordinary folks, a clean bill of health as things that "harm no one." We might even ask this question: "Suppose that when your children come of age someone entices them into prostitution, pimping, or bestiality, and suppose also that they could pursue these lifestyles in security from venereal disease; do you think they would suffer any damage and that the enticer has done them any wrong?" Few would answer: "As long as there's no danger of disease or violence, they're going to be perfectly well off"; the responses are far more likely to reflect (however inelegantly or inarticulately) the notion of a moral corruption that is injurious to the person who undergoes it.

The idea of moral harm is taken seriously in traditional philosophy and classical literature; indeed that is what much of classical ethics is about. In contemporary liberal theory, however, moral harm is generally ignored; when acknowledged at all it is usually dismissed as something too remote and speculative to warrant substantial attention, or as something inimical to the principles of a liberal society.

One of the few exceptions to the previous observation is the contemporary liberal theorist Joel Feinberg, who takes the idea of moral harm seriously enough to make an argument against it. The argument is worth examining. Feinberg does not deny that good and bad character is a reality of some sort; what he denies is that the possessor of a bad character is at all injured by it, unless he happens to desire a better one. "Morally corrupting a person, that is, causing him to be a worse person than he would otherwise be, can *harm* him . . . only if he has an antecedent interest in being good."[12] By "interest" here Feinberg means, essentially, a desire or subjectively valued goal. He notes that everyone has an elementary interest in the indispensable material means to the achievement of goals (physical health, a sufficiency of wealth, etc.). But beyond these elementary needs, people's interests are definitively exhibited by their subjective wants or aspirations; therefore, it is with respect to these wants and desires that people's well-being can truly be assessed. The upshot is that people are well off insofar as their objectives—whatever they may happen to be—are achieved.

Now if all that matters is how one wishes to define a term, we may grant that Feinberg (like everyone else) is entitled to give the term *interest* the conceptual content he chooses. If, however, what is at stake is our understanding of human well-being, the problem here is no small one. From Feinberg's analysis it would follow that a person totally incapable of love, friendship, cooperation with others, higher learning, appreciation of beauty, or any aspiration whatever beyond physical gratification, is as well off as one who has these capacities—as long as he doesn't feel any want of them and can take care of his material urgencies without them. Indeed, it follows that someone whose desire is to spend his whole life watching television soap operas, or simply scratching where it itches, would be *harmed* (would suffer an invasion of his interests) if he were required to desist long enough to watch a Shakespearean play or help someone in distress. No doubt Feinberg would include this person in his category of "contented moral defective." Why defective? In context, the negative judgment can only refer to the fact that such a person does no good for others, that is, doesn't serve their interests. It could not refer to anything intrinsically unsatisfactory about such a life. So why not be a contented moral defective? If goodness is in no way good for me unless it is something I happen to desire, why would it be reasonable for me to *develop* this aspiration and endure the sacrifices of immediate gratification that its realization demands?

Moreover, why should parents assume the laborious task of bringing up a child to be something more than a successful hedonist? Says Feinberg: "The moral corruption or neglect of an unformed child . . . is no direct harm to him, provided he has the resources to pursue his own interests anyway, but it can be a very real harm to his parents if *they* have a powerful stake in the child's moral development."[13] Moral corruption or neglect couldn't injure a child because he or she could have no antecedent "interest" in being good. If children acquire that interest, it is because the parents have imposed it upon them by instilling the notions of good in which *they* have an interest. And this, we are told, is what moral education is about.

On this view of what moral education means, "it's for your own good" could only be a falsehood or a kind of myth, the truthful translation of which would be "because that's how we want it." It's an interesting question how children are likely to be raised when all educators have come to see that moral development and debasement are irrelevant to the well-being of the educatee. Will moral training be abandoned (except for injunctions against blatant assaults on the elementary material interests of others)? Or will it be replaced by some sort of preparation for the thoroughly autonomous choice of one's standards of good and bad? (Feinberg's preference perhaps.) On the other hand, those in charge of children might feel considerably freer than they do now to impose whatever tenets and instill whatever character traits they happen to like. Why not?

To be sure, this critique does not prove the case that moral harm exists; nor does it settle certain basic questions. Rather, it draws out the extreme, and for most people rather unattractive, implications of the contrary view. Some liberals will want to make that view more attractive by modifying or broadening it somewhat. This could be done by expanding the conception of enduring human interests so as to include the capacities for self-esteem and authentic choice of one's lifestyle.[14] Hence, a person would be *harmed* by activities resulting in substantial loss of self-esteem or ability to make significant decisions as to the purposes or goals of one's life.

But on that basis wouldn't it have to be acknowledged that involvement in prostitution is something truly harmful—insofar as it results in loss of respect for oneself? And it would follow (wouldn't it?) that parents who allow their children to perform in pornographic productions—indeed anyone who persuades others to do so—have harmed them if self-respect is thereby impaired. On the other hand, if that is what truly matters, engaging in intercourse with animals for a leering audience would have to be declared harmless whenever it can be done with self-esteem intact. But what about the putative human interest in the ability to *choose* one's goals and forms of life? Insofar as real choosing depends upon a (considerable?) capacity for reasoned deliberation and self-control, wouldn't we be obliged to regard as injurious corruptions those influences upon a person's character that undermine rational self-control? Then the regular involvement with pornography, as well as drugs and a "drug culture," could be indicted as sources of real harm to the extent that they unleash irrational passions tending to overwhelm the deliberative faculty. Undeniably, we often consider narcotic drugs to be a problem not only because of the physical damage they cause but also because of the degradation of mind and character, that is, the moral damage. And if self-respect and self-control are to be considered as human interests, impairments of which are injurious, what about other vital interests and impairments? Why not entertain the idea that influences that make us weak and cowardly, or undermine the capacities for affection and trust among us, are also morally harmful?

From these reflections the following inferences may be drawn. First: the narrow conception of the harmful prominent in liberal theory is anticommonsensical (or, as they say in academic philosophy, counterintu-itive). Second: if that conception is broadened to accommodate the objec-tions, it's hard to avoid a slippery slope toward those large questions of traditional moral philosophy that the narrow conception was meant to preclude. Third: notions of what is harmful to human beings are ultimately linked to ideas of what is good for us; what we think of as harmful is ultimately dependent upon what we recognize as well-being. And what is recognized as well-being depends finally upon ideas or intuitions about the kind of beings we are, that is, human nature.

The linkages I've just noted, and the views of moral corruption embod-ied therein, can be illustrated by reference to the classical thought in which they received their first systematic recognition. The idea of a "cor-ruption" that is injurious to the person undergoing it has its philosophic origins in the Platonic thought that there is such a thing as the good health—and consequently the ill health or disease—of the human soul. In other words, the concept of the healthy and unhealthy applies not only to our bodies but also to our minds and our lives—to the whole person. We find this perception articulated and explored at a number of points in the Platonic dialogues; it is graphically presented in *The Republic*, book 9. As an illustration of what is properly meant by good and bad, Socrates formulates an "image of the soul" that is said to be composed of these parts; a many-headed beast, a lion, and a human being. The beast, with some savage heads and some tame ones, represents the irrational or primal sensual appetites; the lion represents "spiritedness," the seat of anger, pride, lust for power; the human being is the rational element. The soul can flourish only when the most human element within it "take[s] charge of the many-headed beast—like a farmer, nourishing and cultivating the tame heads, while hindering the growth of the savage ones—making the lion's nature an ally and, caring for all in common, making them friends with each other and himself, and so rear them."[15] Let us observe in passing that the irrational inclinations are not simply to be suppressed; some of them are to be cultivated and others restricted. But this discrimination is possible only when the reasoning part, the part that has or can acquire knowledge, is in the authoritative position.

This is, to be sure, a metaphorical construction, an image of the sort that the great philosopher-poet periodically employed to provide complex or elusive realities with concrete embodiment. While the image by itself doesn't prove the things it seeks to illustrate, it does perform two functions of real import. One of these is to locate the grounds of ethical judgment in certain crucial facts of human nature. With this picture of the soul in view, Socrates can assert that the distinction between "the noble" and "the base" is appropriately made on the ground that the noble things are those that "cause the bestial part of our nature to be subjected to the human part," while the base things are those that "enslave the tame to the savage."[16] The picture also shows Socrates' interlocutors, in a manner both graphic and plausible, why *it isn't in their interest* to indulge the bestial part of themselves at the expense of the distinctively human part; why it's against their interest to become "base." What the image is meant to portray is that baseness entails dehumanization, whereas one's well-being is inextricably linked to one's humanness. Moreover, baseness is shown to render impossible that harmony of the soul, that fulfilling "friendship" among its constituents, which can only occur when the thinking part of us governs, educates, and reconciles the many and conflicting nonrational elements.

On this teaching, in which baseness and moral corruption are equivalent, persons are corrupted insofar as their higher human capacity for deliberative self-direction is weakened and subordinated to the lower and less-human inclinations. Succinctly: the soul or human nature consists of elements that are both diverse and unequal in status; the healthy condition is an appropriately hierarchical balance among these elements and consequently a coherent life. To destroy that balance—in oneself or others—is to cause real injury by undermining the capacity to actualize the distinctively human mode of being. And that, ultimately, is the most far-reaching (though not the most obvious) "harm."[17]

It is important to recognize the nondogmatic character of this teaching. This general vision of the healthy and the corrupted does not dictate precisely what one has to do to achieve the former and avoid the latter; it doesn't issue in a body of moral rules or categorical imperatives. Instead of rules and commandments, we are presented with a model of what it means for a human being to be in good condition and the reverse—a model that can inform judgment or provide reasonable perspectives concerning the particular circumstances of our lives. And, of course, this perspective is in considerable contrast with the minimalist model of our "interests" currently presented by Feinberg and others.

The validity of this vision is not unchallengeable; nothing in a Platonic dialogue (and, I believe, in moral philosophy) is so demonstrably valid as to be unquestionable. One can challenge this viewpoint by denying that our natural endowment includes bestial inclinations in conflict with more benign dispositions *or* by acknowledging that the bestial exists in us but insisting that it is entitled to equal status with the rational element. In other words, it is always possible to claim either that the harmony of the soul is a spontaneous occurrence (not a difficult project that faces large obstacles)—or that it is arbitrary to regard wholeness as an important desideratum and disorder in the psyche as an evil.[18] But such claims are easier to assert than to defend.

It will be said that this line of argument about the good and the bad neglects the sophisticated skepticism or relativism with which we are confronted in twentieth-century philosophy. Let us consider at some length three prominent viewpoints of that sort.

First there is the argument that basic conceptions of the good are irreducibly and irreparably diverse; ultimately they are incompatible and the conflicts between them unresolvable. In a famous essay, Isaiah Berlin says: "The world that we encounter in ordinary experience is one in which we are faced with choices between ends equally ultimate, and claims equally absolute, the realization of some of which must inevitably involve the sacrifice of others."[19] What makes a liberal pluralistic regime "truer" and "more human" than others is that "it does, at least, recognize the fact that human goals are many, not all of them commensurable, and in perpetual rivalry with one another," and among which therefore a person must choose.[20]

To this viewpoint two critical responses are possible, one short and the other more elaborate. The short response: even if we accept in its entirety the thesis that there is no rational resolution of conflicts among ultimate ideas of the good, it doesn't follow that we are unable to judge some ways of living to be bad and harmful. Some things can be reasonably condemned without reference to or agreement about final ends. As John Gray puts it: "One may assert that the conceptions of the good expressed in the lives of Mother Teresa and Oscar Wilde are incommensurable, and yet confidently assert that the life of a crack addict is a poor one."[21] How can such distinctions be made? It does seem easier to discern, and agree upon, the bad and the injurious than the good and the fulfilling. We can perceive the disabilities that render the crack addict unable to live either in compassionate service to others *or* in devotion to the arts and social criticism (and, for that matter, in devotion to education, friends, community, and much else). Similar disabilities—not just physical or material but of mind and character—are noticeable in lives centering upon prostitution, pornography, gambling, sadistic sexuality, brutal entertainments, and the like. But are these things evident without any reference whatever to conceptions of what is worthy or valuable for human beings? It makes sense to say, as William Galston does, that we can agree on the badness of certain things "without having a fully articulated, unitary account of the good."[22] But can we really do so without any reliance at all—even tacit—upon notions of the good? It is because of this doubt that I cannot regard the short answer to Isaiah Berlin's proposal as sufficient.

A more complete response requires more direct confrontation with Berlin's central claim that our final ends or fundamental conceptions of the good are in perpetual and unresolvable rivalry. We should begin by recognizing the valid insight here. Berlin wishes to discredit the simplistic and dangerously utopian view that all good things, or all legitimate human aspirations, can be harmoniously encompassed and fulfilled by a properly designed social regime. His point is that "not all good things are compatible"; it is endemic to the human condition that to opt for the realization of some valued things is to neglect or sacrifice others. The insight that you cannot have it all—especially in a political society—is both valid and important to remember. This thesis realistically cautions against grand expectations for the final solution of the great human problems and social conflicts. All regimes (including, let us note, the liberal pluralistic one) are inevitably defective in that some significant aspects of the human good are neglected or subordinated.[23]

But this does not mean or need not mean that there is simply no human good, that all conceptions thereof are utterly subjective, or that any conception is as worthy as any other. Berlin himself doesn't seem to want to go that far; though not entirely clear about it, he appears to settle for the idea that there is a plurality of (ultimate) goods that cannot be ranked or reconciled by any transcendent principle. Unfortunately, Berlin provides virtually no examples of these unrankable and unreconcilable alternatives.[24] Here are two possible examples: Commitment to the monastic worship of God and search for personal salvation *versus* commitment to achievement of social justice and economic well-being through an active political life; commitment to a life of heroic virtues and triumphs (Alexander the Great, Caesar, Napoleon) *versus* devotion to the abolition or relief of suffering and conflict (Tolstoy, Albert Schweitzer, Florence Nightingale). The diverse conceptions of the good expressed in these two sets of alternative lives appear to be "ultimate" and hence unamenable to rational inquiry and judgment of better and worse. This is true of the first set—insofar as it reflects an antimony between the other-worldly religious life and the activist secular one; such commitments do seem incommensurable. The second set of alternatives, however, is not exactly of that sort; one could still press an inquiry as to the contribution of each of these modes of life to the flourishing of a rational and social animal. (Why heroism and victory? Why is suffering such a bad thing?) They could both be discussed in relation to a broader or more fundamental human good that they implicitly claim to serve and on the basis of which their partial claims could be evaluated.

While the latter of the two antinomies just considered is amenable to reasoned theoretical evaluation, neither of them seems amenable to resolution by actual compromise. The opposing positions are so sharply adverse that it's hard to see how one side could make any substantial accommodation to the other. (What concession could Napoleon make to Tolstoy's view or Tolstoy to Napoleon's?) But many of the supposedly unresolvable tensions of moral life are not exactly like that. Devotion to the realization and expression of one's individuality (through the arts or otherwise) and devotion to a social good transcending one's individuality are wholly incompatible only if these competing versions of the good are absolutized. And they need not be absolutized; both of them can be, and usually are, modified in one way or another so as to make possible an accommodation of individuality and community. Of course, such compromises may be condemned by a Henry David Thoreau for promoting an attenuated individuality and by a radical communitarian for promoting an attenuated human solidarity. But there is no need to view our moral experience as if such unalloyed, puristic commitments were conclusively characteristic of it. Even devoted individualists regularly moderate the demands of authentic selfhood in favor of friends, family, country, and obligations thereof—that is, in recognition that there are other goods. Another frequently encountered antimony of moral life is the tension between loyalty to one's friends and respect for standards of justice that demand impartiality in certain great antagonisms of life. To this pervasive, difficult, and sometimes tragic, ethical conflict there is surely no easy doctrinal answer. But that doesn't mean that you can only make an absolutistic choice of one or the other side of the dilemma. The principle "always stand by your own people regardless of any consideration of justice or public interest" would place intolerable obstacles in the way of any larger human bonding or obligation.[25] The diametrically opposed principle, "never in any circumstances give loyalty to friends or loved ones a priority over impersonal standards of right," would be virtually as destructive of bonds among such imperfect beings as we are. With the aid of some practical wisdom, it is not (usually) hard to avoid these dogmatisms; one could reasonably conclude that justice overrides friendship in certain grave cases (where the friend is engaging in criminal, traitorous, or grossly dishonest activity, for example)—and that friendship can take precedence in certain lesser cases (e.g., I wouldn't denounce or abandon a loyal friend who has made an unfair accusation against a political enemy). It might well be that in the borderline area between these situations there is no clear answer, and one simply chooses "subjectively." But it's one thing to acknowledge that in this world there are such situations of ethical stalemate—and another to claim that they *characterize* the moral life. Likewise, it's one thing to say that the moral life is difficult because what is good for us is a complex matter involving diverse desiderata—and quite another to say that the human good is only what I wish or decide to regard as such.

The kind of "soft relativism" represented, at its best, by Isaiah Berlin stops (somewhere) short of the latter and most radically relativistic position. For a clear and relentless affirmation of the radical position, we can look to one of its most famous proponents, Jean-Paul Sartre. In brief, Sartre's existentialism says that, since there is no God and no human nature whatever to establish "values" or norms, each of us must create "alone, unjustified and without excuse" the standards of moral action and judgment. Things—actions, commitments, ways of life—have value only when and because I choose them. To illustrate that this is the inescapable human condition, Sartre tells his now-famous story of the young man who came to him for ethical advice during the Nazi occupation of France. "The boy was faced with the choice of leaving for England and joining the Free French Forces—that is, leaving his mother behind—or remaining with his mother and helping her to carry on. He was fully aware that the woman lived only for him and that his going-off—and perhaps his death—would plunge her into despair."[26] The dilemma, as Sartre presents it, is a stark confrontation between two kinds of action and two kinds of ethics: on the one hand, a concrete action of immediate benefit to one individual and associated with an ethic of personal devotion; on the other hand, an action in the service of a distant national collectivity and involving "a broader ethic, but one whose efficacy was more dubious."[27] (Maybe it would turn out that he would have no effect on the war effort.) Sartre tells us that no preexisting morality could possibly provide any guidance to this young man. For example, the Kantean principle, which commands that one never treat a person simply as a means but always as an end, is apparently violated by either course of action; if the boy goes with the Free French, he treats his mother as a means to the collective good, and if he stays with his mother, he risks treating his political comrades as a means. Sartre's advice: "You're free; choose, that is, invent." That is, you must invent the right and the good by choosing either an ethic of personal devotion or an ethic of public commitment and standing by it.

As I've suggested, moralists ought to acknowledge that life will sometimes present us with "tragic" choices between what appear to be equally compelling ethical imperatives or devotions. The situation Sartre depicts might be one of these. But as to its broader implications for moral philosophy, we ought to take account of the following considerations.

1. It is of import that both of the options here are relatively decent and possibly even noble courses of action. Hardly any thoughtful moralist would say that it is contemptible to stand by one's needy mother in these circumstances (and put up with the likely misunderstanding and hostility of the patriots who are risking their lives). Nor are there many who would denigrate the young man if he reluctantly abandons his mother to fight for the grand cause of freedom from the Nazis. These are both respectable courses of action because they involve some personal sacrifice for a worthy object—in the one case devotion to a loving and dependent person and in the other case devotion to country and fellow citizens at a critical time. In the extreme circumstances of this situation, it might well be that the competing claims of family and country, or intimate and communal relations, cannot be ranked by appeal to some overriding moral standard. Then, it is appropriate to say (though this wouldn't be the only way to put it) that one can only "choose" a priority or act upon some previous commitment to the predominance of one claim or the other.

2. Yet this conclusion hardly tells the whole story about moral judgment. What would we think of someone who rejects both family and country in favor of material self-interest or personal pleasure? Suppose that Sartre's young man had decided to stay put because he couldn't tear himself away from a lucrative business or a mistress or the gambling tables or the drug culture. Would Sartre—more importantly would we—be willing to say that each of these options is perfectly ethical and in no way inferior to the young man's original options—because, after all, individual choice is the only source of value?[28] There is little doubt that the choice of self-centered material interest or sensual gratification in this kind of situation would be deemed nonrespectable by almost everyone almost everywhere

in the world (even though, as a matter of fact, such choices are not infrequent). Why? We could discuss it in terms of human responsibility or dignity or sociability. But in whatever terms the moral judgment would be couched, it would rest upon a perception that higher goods or worthier ends have been abandoned in favor of interests considerably lower or less worthy. And this perception of ethical priority and its violation would usually be accompanied by criticism of the character—the self-indulgence and cowardice—of someone who thusly sacrifices the higher to the lower.

3. The moral dilemma that Sartre means to illustrate can arise and acquire its tragic status because family and community are both vital human goods. Without the former, prospects for the attainment of any loving attachments with other human beings and personal development as an individual are at best dim. But without the latter we would be confined within the rather narrow moral and intellectual horizons of kinship relations and denied the larger perspectives, friendships, and modes of human cooperation that civic life makes possible. The problem is that these indispensable desiderata are at least sometimes in conflict, a conflict pervasive enough to be recognized and dramatized by Sophocles, Plato, Rousseau, Freud, and others. Yet, the conflict is not always, or even often, at such a dramatic fever pitch as we find in *Antigone*, book 5 of Plato's *Republic*, and Sartre's example; fortunately we are not often faced with a stark and unavoidable either/or. In the concluding part of *Macbeth* the tyrant's overthrow is accomplished through the alliance of men who are profoundly moved by attachment to both family and country. And it is one of the perennial tasks of social and political life to arrange accommodations involving such practical rankings as will preserve valuable elements of both.

The pervasive problems of moral life can be said to derive from two root causes. First, elementary passions and gratifications resist, with frequent success, demands made upon them on behalf of more elevated desiderata. Our experience of this problem persists despite denial or neglect of it in sophisticated contemporary philosophy, and I have made it the core of the argument for public morality in the preceding chapter. Secondly, as suggested in this chapter, the human goods are many—or, more precisely, there is a human good but it is complex and many-sided. Pervasively, and despite large differences among conventions and "cultures," we human beings desire certain things that are perceived as basic goods. These include the preservation of life in relative comfort (what Hobbes called "commodious self-preservation"), bonds among people transcending self-centered utilitarian calculation (or what I can get out of you), the fruition of such bonds in friendship or love, the development and exercise of our natural faculties as thinking beings, and a measure of respect (from self or others) that depends in part upon the experience of agency—that one has some control over the direction of one's life. These good things are various, and the conditions of their realization—principles, institutions, commitments—can come into conflict; hence the moral dilemmas. In some ways, this actual human situation is harder to live with than that envisioned by Sartreans, where the good is something created by one's unconstrained volition.

It is important to recognize the variations and the dilemmas, but it's at least as important to recognize what belongs to our common humanity. Though a conclusive answer is hard to come by, we must consider why such desiderata as I've listed above are appropriately deemed good for human beings as such. The first desideratum—self-preservation on terms not unduly painful—will be generally acknowledged; one has to go far toward utmost cultural relativism or postmodernism to find its universality denied. Why is it desirable to have bonds of community, friendship, and love? If one is unwilling to settle for these as goods in themselves, there is the further argument that the human mind (or soul or self) is thereby enlarged; consider how narrow people can be—and are—when isolated in their solitary selves. Why be enlarged? One can answer that only thus are we in a position to exercise the faculties or develop the potentialities that identify us as human. Do we not regard certain capacities—sociability and speech or ideation—as qualities that it is normal to possess and abnormal, as well as most unfortunate, to be without? Few of us would be prepared to argue that a child who is unable to speak, or an adult who can hardly think or imagine anything that isn't immediately present, is in adequate human shape. We lament such conditions as disabilities or defects; we try to prevent, correct, or compensate for them. As for self-respect, and the capacity for self-government often associated with it, these qualities seem to be vital requisites for any substantial achievement—the development of natural potentialities, service to community, friendship. If someone continues to press the question why these are (usually) good things, there is no clear and more final answer than that such are the crucial ingredients and contributors to our ability to live in a distinctively human way and achieve the fulfillments thereof. What is good for us, in the last analysis, is what promotes the sustenance and flourishing of our kind of being—which is a conscious, thinking, imagining, and loving being.

Anthropological or cultural relativists are anxious to affirm the great variety of ways of being human, while debunking the idea of normality. But it is not clear that even the most radical among them have meant to assert that only the variety is real and the "human" is nothing but a verbal construct. At least, the ultrarelativist view, according to which everything human (or "human") is the result of (diverse) cultures and nothing is attributable to our nature, is rarely maintained with thoroughgoing consistency. One suspects that it cannot be. Anthropological relativists are most bent upon rebutting claims about things normative, or universally valuable for mankind, because they fear that such claims render professional open-mindedness and social toleration impossible. As Clifford Geertz, a leading champion of this perspective puts it, "What relativists, so called, want us to worry about is provincialism—the danger that our perceptions will be dulled, our intellects constricted, and our sympathies narrowed by the overlearned and overvalued acceptances of our own society."[29] Well enough as far as it goes. But Geertz doesn't exactly explain, nor does he even explore the question, why dulled perception, constricted intellects, and narrow sympathies are bad things. Is it because, and only because, they are so regarded by the provincial norms of the culture that has nurtured modern Western anthropologists? If pushed (farther, apparently, than he wants to be), Geertz might find it necessary to admit that having very constricted intellect and sympathies is not an admirable or flourishing condition for members of our species.

It is one thing to insist that there are different ways of manifesting the human qualities of consciousness, thought, imagination, friendship, and love; surely that is true. But it's quite another thing to deny outright that these are qualities definitive of our humanity and that it is usually better to have more of them than less. Most relativistic anthropologists do not seem prepared, unambiguously and with Sartrean determination, to go that far. It's a hard thing to deny altogether the reality of a common humanity and its needs. And there is a heavy burden of proof on someone who, while acknowledging that reality to an extent, wishes nonetheless to insist that nothing is good (or bad) for human beings as such. Efforts to adopt, or presuppose, such positions are virtually bound to be infected with ambiguity.[30]

To be sure, there is always room for disagreement—both across and within cultures, as well as among theorists—as to exactly what belongs on a list of basic human goods.[31] Universal consensus, however, is not a necessary condition for the validity of judgments about human well-being and its ingredients. (Indeed, the claim that universal consent of mankind is a necessary condition reflects a particular view of the good or the right.) The several desiderata I've emphasized are those most difficult to take lightly in principle and most likely to be recognized in actual experience, cultural differences notwithstanding. After all, who wants to be considered ignorant and thoughtless; in what society do they regularly admire the perpetual drunk or the person who is unable to persevere in any serious purpose, cooperate in a communal project, or care about anyone or anything except the accumulation of pleasurable sensations?[32]

Assuming that these theoretical considerations have some validity, how do they bear upon public policy in a liberal society on matters of ethical import? I believe they should apply, in an indirect though significant way, by affecting assumptions that we bring to our thinking about social problems. In other words, it makes a practical difference whether the following ideas or their opposites are prominent among the premises with which we approach our civic problems. Good and bad (appropriately understood) are realities, not simply subjective opinions always relative and parochial. Generally put, there are distinctively human potentialities— those of a reflective being who can live, love, and build communities reflectively; good is whatever promotes these capabilities and bad is whatever weakens or undermines them. On this basis it makes sense to recognize moral harm as an actuality to be taken seriously; morally harmful conditions are those involving the substantial disabling of mind and character.

Liberal societies have in fact taken account of these realities to some degree. Underlying our heavy emphasis on education, and devotion of resources thereto, one may discern a supposition that cultivation of the human faculties is a good—over and above its instrumental contribution to career and wealth. And among the reasons for policies supporting the monogamous family, one can discern an assumption that enduring affection and careful discipline nurture minds and hearts in desirable directions (or that lack of such affection and discipline is injurious to minds and hearts). Some policies for "beautification" of public places seem to rest on a recognition that an aesthetically attractive environment is good for us (for people as such, not just for whites or blacks, men or women, liberals or conservatives, Westerners or non-Westerners), and that the ugliness of slums or "urban blight" is bad for one's moral health as well as physical health. And some provisions of the criminal law—including restraints upon pornography, prostitution, drugs, gambling, brutal entertainments—can be seen as activated in part by concern about influences destructive of character.

These purposes are not always easy to recognize for what they are; often the ethical desideratum is concealed in a utilitarian rationale or obscured by the materialistic language in which it is presented. Modern liberal philosophy fails in large part to provide the language or concepts with which to think about moral health and harm; modern liberalism tends to discourage the discussion and the perception of social affairs in these terms. It seems that our theory obscures an aspect of social reality with which our practice is still (however tacitly or ambiguously) engaged. We cannot afford to have this aspect of reality perpetually obfuscated; our practice needs to become more thoughtful.

None of this is meant to suggest that everything that may be deemed morally harmful is a fit object for legal repression. Some moral injuries or dangers thereof are appropriately addressed by penalizing them; others that can't or shouldn't be subject to punishment may be discouraged by public policy (and the opposite, beneficial conditions encouraged) in a variety of ways. And for some evils the only answer is education or efforts thereto. I have provided these distinctions with some illustrations in the previous chapter. What is most important, however, is the clear awareness that there are significant nonmaterial harms (as well as goods) and that, contrary to prominent contemporary outlooks, degradation of character can be as real and injurious as loss of material opportunities or civil rights or political power. Confusion about this reality can be attributed to a number of sources; prominent among them is the persistent doctrinal oversimplification of "the harmful." It is such an oversimplification to maintain, or regularly to imply, without argument, that if something putatively bad for us isn't a palpable material injury, then it must be only an offensive nuisance. Equally obstructive of clear thinking is the associated doctrinal illusion that a liberal society can and ought to be strictly neutral among alternative visions of the human good.

The orientation I'm presenting and favoring in this book is surely not without difficulties. Moral harms are usually harder to ascertain and to address than physical or material ones; dealing with them (especially as a matter of public policy) requires considerable exercise of practical wisdom or prudential judgment about degrees of injury and threat of injury. It would be less troublesome if we could preclude the contingent judgments by recourse to a body of absolute or categorical principles of right and wrong to tell us just when the state should and when it shouldn't intervene in the moral life. While I don't believe that we can do without clear ethical principles, neither can I believe that human affairs, with their variability and uncertainties, allow for the resolution of this perennial problem by strict deduction from necessary principles of a categorical moral law.[33] In this unruly (yet not wholly chaotic) world, absolutistic moral rules are as often inappropriate as absolutistic libertarian rules. When what is good for us concretely depends upon questions like "How substantial is the moral harm?" and "What preventions or remedies are likely to be effective?" there is no escape from the need for prudential insight about the social circumstances. That fact is half the story. The other half is the need for ideas of the good that are grounded in an understanding of what we are—the qualities and challenges that make us human beings.

NOTES

1. See Bruce Ackerman, *Social Justice in the Liberal State* (Yale University Press, 1980); Ronald Dworkin, *Taking Rights Seriously* and "Liberalism," in *A Matter of Principle* (Cambridge, Mass.: Harvard Univ. Press, 1985); and Charles Larmore, *Patterns of Moral Complexity* (Cambridge: Cambridge Univ. Press, 1987).

2. Dworkin, *Taking Rights Seriously*, p. 274.

3. Currently, the position under consideration is most aggressively articulated by the liberal theorist, Joel Feinberg. See, especially, Feinberg, "Harmless Immoralities and Offensive Nuisances," in *Rights, Justice and the Bounds of Liberty.*

4. Hart, *Law, Liberty and Morality*, p. 43.

5. *The Wolfenden Report: Report of the Committee on Homosexual Offenses and Prostitution* (New York: Stein & Day, 1962), p. 140.

6. The following questions represent some of the practical problems likely to confront a "public nuisance" policy from which the moral norms and supports have been thoroughly extracted. How many offended people are enough to trigger the restriction? How offended (angry?) do they have to be? In cases like streetwalking and pornographic advertising, how can one be sure that the offensiveness of a practice has been truly separated from its perceived immorality? Finally, if "offense" of a majority were to be taken as sufficient justification for restriction (without any moral element), wouldn't such a policy threaten personal liberty more—not less—than the current one?

7. Jeremy Waldron, *Liberal Rights* (Cambridge: Cambridge Univ. Press, 1993), p. 129.

8. Ibid., p. 130.

9. *Law, Liberty and Morality,* p. 57.

10. Ibid., p. 25.

11. *Roth* v. *U. S.,* 354 US 476 (1957), Justice Harlan concurring.

12. Feinberg, *Rights, Justice and the Bounds of Liberty,* p. 50. Italics in the original.

13. Ibid. Italics in original.

14. In *A Theory of Justice,* (Cambridge, Mass.: Harvard Univ. Press, 1971) John Rawls includes self-respect among the "primary goods," and having or choosing a "plan of life" as an essential feature of "moral personality." See sects. 67 and 77. In subsequent writings Rawls calls these "higher order interests" of persons, apparently to accord them a more prominent status among basic human goods. See Rawls's "Kantian Constructivism in Moral Theory," *Journal of Philosophy,* September, 1980.

15. *The Republic of Plato,* ed. Allan Bloom (New York: Basic Books, 1968), p. 272.

16. Ibid.

17. I am far from suggesting that this formulation represents Plato's last word on the subject. Platonic dialogues are notoriously complex, and the complexity is inflamed by the fact that various dialogues view these themes from various perspectives. My claim for the theme formulated above is that it is a very prominent one.

18. For an argument that seems to prefer diversity in the soul to harmony or wholeness, see Stephen Macedo, *Liberal Virtues,* pp. 234–40.

19. Isaiah Berlin, *Four Essays on Liberty* (London: Oxford Univ. Press, 1969), p. 168.

20. Ibid., p. 171.

21. John Gray, "Neutrality," *The Responsive Community,* spring, 1793.

22. Galston, *Liberal Purposes,* p. 182.

23. This, I believe, is the teaching of Plato's *Republic,* contrary to Berlin's notion that it teaches "a final Harmony in which all riddles are resolved, all contradictions reconciled" (*Four Essays on Liberty,* p. 168). Allan Bloom observes: "Socrates constructs his utopia to point up the dangers of what we would call utopianism" ("Interpretative Essay," in *The Republic of Plato,* ed. Allan Bloom). At least Socrates makes clear enough all the valued things that we would have to sacrifice to get a perfectly just regime governed by philosophy, that is, by truth alone. A similar insight is at the core of Rousseau's political philosophy. The human independence and individuality extolled in the *Second Discourse* must be considerably subordinated to achieve the fraternal unity and harmony of the good society in *The Social Contract.* You cannot get it all together in any single social arrangement or mode of life.

24. The closest he comes to a clear example is his presentation of the conflict between the "negative" liberty of individual rights and the "positive" liberty

associated with community or fraternity. (Locke vs. Rousseau?) But Berlin cannot help manifesting his preference for the former and arguing its superiority.

25. For an exploration of the ravages of parochial "familialism" or clannishness, see Edward Banfield's classic *Moral Basis of a Backward Society* (New York: Free Press, 1967).

26. Jean-Paul Sartre, *Existentialism* (New York: Philosophical Library, 1947), p. 29.

27. Ibid., p. 30.

28. No doubt Sartre would think very little of someone who abandons both mother and Free French for any of these material gratifications. The interesting question is how in the world of Sartre's existentialism one can legitimately condemn such choices. Sartre would wish to condemn them as *mauvais fois*—bad faith or self-deception, refusal to face the demands of one's situation and the human condition. But why should we accept *this* moral norm? Why not deceive ourselves and run away from (unpleasant) responsibility? From another angle, what if the young man actively and in full self-awareness collaborates with the Nazis to get special privileges for his mother?

29. Clifford Geertz, "Anti Anti-Relativism," *American Anthropologist* 86 (1984): p. 265.

30. One very interesting example of such ambiguity is Ruth Benedict's seminal *Patterns of Culture* (Boston: Houghton-Mifflin, 1989). Having explored several extremely diverse North American cultures (including one apparently sadistic one), the author declares that all cultures are "equally valid." Yet she also manages to criticize competitive societies such as that of the United States. Another outstanding illustration of the point can be found in the writings of Max Weber. In language similar to that of Isaiah Berlin, Weber says "the ultimate possible attitudes toward life are irreconcilable, and hence their struggle can never be brought to a final [rational] conclusion. Thus it is necessary to make a decisive choice," from *Max Weber: Essays in Sociology*, ed. H. H. Gerth and C. Wright Mills (New York: Oxford, 1958), p. 152. Yet, Weber manages to condemn the lust for power without responsibility as "a product of a shoddy and superficially blasé attitude toward the meaning of human conduct" (Ibid., p. 117) and to praise the man who assumes responsibility as a "genuine man" (*Ibid.,* p. 127).

31. Two interesting enumerations of basic human goods are provided by John Finnis and William Galston. See Finnis, *Natural Law and Natural Rights* (Oxford: Clarendon Press, 1980) and Galston, *Liberal Purposes*, especially chapter 8. For a psychological perspective, see A. H. Maslow, *Motivation and Personality* (New York: Harper Bros., 1954). Despite large differences in the philosophic orientations of their authors, these three "lists" of the human needs and fulfillments present striking similarities.

32. In the Platonic dialogue *Gorgias* Socrates torpedoes the nihilistic Callicles, who has insisted that there is nothing good but personal pleasure and nothing

in the world to be ashamed of. Socrates asks, "Tell me first of all, can a man who itches and wants to scratch and whose opportunities for scratching are unbounded be said to lead a happy life continually scratching?" Callicles responds, "How fantastic you are, Socrates, and how thoroughly vulgar" (Plato, *Gorgias* [New York: Penguin Books, 1960], pp. 94–95). Even Callicles has to admit that there must be more to life than what Socrates describes. The point, simply put, is as follows: anyone who is willing to think at all can't really think that, as far as the value of ways of life is concerned, anything goes as long as one happens to like it.

33. This is an appropriate place in the argument to recognize a theory of public morality alternative to the one I am presenting. Taking his bearings largely from an interpretation of Kant, Hadley Arkes maintains that neither moral judgment nor legal constraint can properly rest on "contingent truths"; they can only be grounded in categorical right and wrong, that is, principles true "as a matter of necessity" (Arkes, *The Philosopher in the City: The Moral Dimension of Urban Politics* [Princeton, N.J.: (Princeton Univ. Press, 1981], p. 392). Arkes argues that legal restraints cannot rightly be justified merely upon empirical calculation of cumulative material injury, and (if I understand him correctly) that consequentialist reasoning as such is not a legitimate justification. Hence: "If it is hard to establish the ground of principle on which gambling can be considered a wrong, it is inadvisable to argue that what is not unambiguously wrong in the particular case becomes wrong somehow in the aggregate. And still less justified would it be to complete the current by arguing that, if gambling is undesirable in its aggregate effects, the law may restrain its particular incidents" (Ibid., p. 399).

As opposed to my viewpoint, this one apparently makes a sharper distinction between ethical and consequentialist reasoning. On my view, since gambling is an activity with a potential for moral harm, there would be some latitude for practical ethical and legal judgment to determine the seriousness of the threat, as well as the prospects for a remedy that would be reasonably effective and free of undesirable side effects. Moreover, it seems to me that even Arkes's purposes are not well served by the stringent requirement that unless each instance of an activity, by itself, is a categorical wrong, the use of the law against its aggregate effects is unjustified. Arkes himself finds it necessary to consider the *effects* of pornographic and other degrading entertainments; he finds that "people who can cultivate a certain sadistic pleasure in watching the suffering of others" probably leave the theater having been made "substantially worse" and making "the polity . . . a worse place for having them present" (Ibid., p. 421). These are consequentialist considerations of a sort, perhaps the sort that I've been labeling moral harms.

The other side of Arkes's position, as I read it, is that if each instance of an activity *is* unambiguously wrong the law ought to (must?) proscribe the activity.

He doesn't quite say so, but it would apparently follow from the wrongness of adultery (betraying a loved one in violation of a solemn promise) as such, that the law is *obliged* to criminalize it. On my view we needn't regard one day at the races, one pornographic transaction, or even one lapse from marital fidelity as necessarily and categorically evil. Yet, we can see that the inclinations associated with these behaviors, when frequently or habitually indulged, are probable corrupters of human minds, characters, and relations. And, under the prudential limits I've suggested, such aggregate threats to a decent society are cognizable by the law.

4

Choice, Equality, Dignity: Contemporary Liberal Perspectives

A central theme of this book is that liberal society needs a certain kind of ethic that it does not spontaneously produce. This can be characterized briefly as an ethic of moderation, publicly supported and serving to counteract or modify some problematic tendencies that liberal society does spontaneously produce. In order to articulate and present that moral and political outlook in its own terms, I have, until now, avoided systematic confrontation with the current outlooks that are most inimical to it. Most prominent among these are two variations of contemporary liberalism: the libertarian view that stands for the primacy of individual freedom of choice, and a strongly egalitarian view that rests, ultimately, upon a conception of what human dignity means.

These two perceptions are not wholly separable; at their foundations one can discern rather similar, if not the same, views of human personality. They do, however, give rise to somewhat different ways of rejecting and debunking public morality. And the egalitarian doctrine (more than the libertarian one) actually presents itself as a public morality by laying claim to the status or the functions of an authoritative ethic for our society. Hence, we shall have to consider its adequacy as a replacement for the traditional virtues to give it a fair critique. It will also be useful to consider how these currently dominant liberal doctrines compare (especially vis-à-vis public morality) with the classical liberalism that presided over the origins of our polity. What can be said about the new liberalism from the perspective of Lockean political theory? Once we have addressed these questions, we should be in a position to evaluate the argument, advanced by some interesting contemporary thinkers, that liberalism does indeed provide an ethic of virtue that a worthy community needs, the claim that what is required and provided is the "liberal virtues." What, after all, are the essentials of a liberal society and what kind of human being does it generate?

I. Autonomy

Autonomy—a condition of personal independence, freedom of choice, or self-determination—is the subject of a great deal of celebration and glorification in our society nowadays.[1] It is also the subject of a considerable amount of attention in academic argumentation. As Joel Feinberg states the case, "the fully voluntary choice or consent of a mature and rational human being concerning matters that affect only his own interests is such a precious thing that no one else (and certainly not the state) has a right to interfere with it simply for that person's 'own good.' "[2] Let us leave aside the much-debated question as to what those matters are that "affect only" a person's own interests, and whether the line of demarcation between the personal and the social good to which Feinberg alludes can actually be drawn with confidence. The questions most in need of exploration here concern the "preciousness" of individual choice—the value of the act of choosing and its status among the elements of human well-being. While the following analysis concentrates upon theoretical issues, the subject has, of course, large practical import. Consider the following typical assertion by an enthusiastic proponent of the liberation of pornography: "The more important issue turns on the fact that a great many people *like* and *enjoy* pornography, and *want* it as part of their lives. . . . This fact means that censorship is an interference with the freedom and self-determination of a great many people, and it is on this ground that the conservative harm argument must ultimately be rejected."[3] Claims of this sort (which abound on many subjects) apparently assume that the self-determination of an individual is a thing of such value as conclusively to override competing considerations of value—or, to say virtually the same thing in other words, that the opportunity to choose is normally more important than *what* is chosen.

On what rational grounds can it be affirmed that free or autonomous choice per se (apart from the object or content of the choice) is a precious thing? Four distinct rationales suggest themselves. First, freedom of choice is an essential, defining condition of human respectability or dignity. Second, the individual is the best judge of his or her own interests. Third, the act of choosing is the crucial agency whereby the human faculties are developed and excellence is achieved. Fourth, the opportunity to make decisions for oneself, and in fact making them, is indispensable to the process of discovering or actualizing one's own distinctive potentialities. Each of these rationales can be formulated as an indictment of public morality. Yet they are different rationales; although the goods to which they refer—dignity, interest, excellence, and individuality—can and do overlap in some ways, they are different goods. What they have most in common is their focus upon the well-being of *the individual*. Each of them is a source of argument against public morality on behalf of the individual, though secondarily, or by extension, some of these arguments can be addressed to the social good. Finally, there is an additional libertarian rationale deserving attention according to which personal liberty is valued primarily as an indispensable condition of social development and "progress."

The first rationale is one heard frequently in modern times. To summarize a prominent version of it: the very idea of human dignity or respect for persons presupposes free agency and responsibility. Persons (unlike nonhuman things) are the kinds of beings who can assume responsibility for their lives, and the fulfillment of this essential capacity depends upon opportunities to choose among alternative ends or values, that is, ways of life. One's respectability, therefore, is directly proportional to his or her self-determination. This line of reasoning has something to be said for it; in some contexts there is much to be said for it. Among the qualities on account of which we think of humans as having a status that other beings (dogs and cats, for example) don't have, certainly the ability to be active agents in the direction of their lives is high on the list. My cats are lovable, but I cannot *respect* them, or regard them as having dignity, insofar as what they do and what they become is the entire result of instinct or cause and effect.

But, especially as applied to our topic, this line of reasoning poses a number of problems. Is freedom of choice to be regarded as a *sufficient* condition of dignity and self-respect? If so, my dignity would remain fully intact even if what I have chosen is the lifestyle of the pimp or, for that matter, a perpetual television-consuming "couch potato." A way of life modeled on the images in sadomasochistic novels and films will suffer no loss of respectability as long as it is the result of a decision. Moreover, does self-determination entail a degree of rational self-command? Feinberg's terminology—"the fully voluntary choice of a mature and rational human being"—suggests an acknowledgment that it does. But then knotty questions arise as to the degree of maturity and rationality requisite before

one's choices are entitled to be regarded as "precious." (Maybe the preferences of irrational persons aren't really choices in the full sense.) And if
that is so, couldn't persons lose their dignity as a consequence of having
opted for courses of action that disable the capacity and inclination for
reasonable self-command (i.e., opting to become immersed in a "drug
culture")? Perhaps it will be conceded that autonomous choice is not to
be viewed as a sufficient condition of dignity, but then one wants to hear
about the other conditions before embracing the practical conclusions to
which this rationale points.[4]

The second rationale—that individuals are the best judges of their
own interests—is usually aimed at "paternalistic" laws and policies. (As
suggested in Chapters 1 and 3, the case for public morality is not necessarily
paternalistic; at least, when properly understood it isn't a pure case of
paternalism.) This claim can be advanced in various ways, some more
qualified and therefore more persuasive than others. The claim is hardly
credible unless one stipulates that it applies "normally" to adults in good
mental and emotional condition. Given this stipulation, proponents can
make a valid point that, normally, an individual *cares* about his or her
own interests much more than the legislator can care about them. But
as to the *understanding* of one's interests, matters would seem to be more
complex.

In the latter regard distinctions might have to be made among kinds
of interests, for example, my short-range and long-range interests or my
special concerns as a unique individual and the more universal concerns—
the potentialities that I have as a social being and member of the human
species. Is every legally adult person supposed to have a better grasp than
legislators or policy makers (or communal institutions and traditions)
could have concerning one's long-term interests and requisites for the
development of one's human potentialities? The proposition is not far-
fetched that individuals involved in lifestyles conducive to drug addiction,
compulsive gambling, prostitution, and such are poor judges of what is
good for them (or are incapable of acting on their better judgment)—and
that, in these respects, the lawmaker probably knows better. From a
broader perspective, isn't it true that most of us tend to be defective in
awareness or pursuit of what is requisite for development of our *higher
human faculties*? Left to ourselves—without some prodding by social norms
or expectations—we often prefer the easy path, declining the exertions
and sacrifices necessary for actualization of higher intellectual, aesthetic,
and moral capabilities. And, left to ourselves, many of us would be quite

a bit more self-centered, and hence narrower people, than an enlightened view of our interests (acquired with effort over time) will dictate. So, apparently, the renowned proposition that individuals are the best judges of their own interests needs a sizable proviso concerning the adequacy of their education in the broad sense of the term. And this invites a further inquiry: does adequate education include any moral training, and is moral training at all dependent on authoritative social norms that favor some definitions of "interest" and disfavor others?

The third rationale, which has impressive credentials, maintains that the act of choosing is to be greatly valued as the indispensable stimulator and cultivator or our higher faculties. To make a real decision on matters of importance to one's life is, as Mill says in *On Liberty*, to exercise and strengthen "the human faculties of perception, judgment, discriminative feeling, mental activity, even moral preference."[5] Where people are disabled or deterred from the activity of choosing—by a paternalistic regime or by "the despotism of custom"—these potentialities will remain undeveloped and the person will be little more than a characterless mediocrity. This is not primarily an argument about freedom of choice as something belonging to one's human dignity or instrumental to the satisfaction of one's interests. It is about the act of choosing as a promoter of excellence or virtue, and the absence of choice as a major reason why there are stunted minds and weak personalities.

While Mill is probably the most famous proponent of this outlook in our time, it was affirmed with equal forcefulness by his great predecessor John Milton. In his *Areopagitica* Milton says: "I cannot praise a fugitive and cloistered virtue, unexercised and unbreathed, that never sallies out and sees her adversary . . . that which purifies us is trial, and trial is by what is contrary."[6] And he added: "When God gave [man] reason, he gave him freedom to choose, for reason is but choosing."[7] What is striking about the Miltonian argument is its justification of freedom of choice with a view to *moral virtue* (not just personal autonomy). A true morality is one freely chosen in full awareness of the alternatives; a cloistered virtue is at best a poor imitation. While the language in which John Stuart Mill makes his case is somewhat different (among other things, he doesn't invoke the Deity), the central concern is very similar. The fundamental desideratum in Mill's case for liberty is the development of human character; the crux of the position is that the opportunity and the act of choosing produces better human beings. We might say that this rationale for liberty takes the high road.

This "high road" position militates most forcefully against a thorough-going paternalism that would condemn us to mediocrity by depriving us of the chance to make meaningful judgments or commitments about the good and the bad, better and worse.[8] Yet we may doubt that the considerations it advances are conclusive in favor of personal choice in all situations and against any paternalistic intervention or any intervention on behalf of moral norms. To be fully persuasive, the case would have to be modified by qualifications similar to those I've suggested concerning the arguments about dignity and interest. The proposition will not be denied, when stated in the abstract, that the elements involved in the cultivation of a person's higher faculties are many and complex. The exercise of choice is often a vital contributor, but isn't it *one of several* vital contributors? Apart from sophisticated moral psychology, doesn't reflective common sense inform us that not all decisions per se have this beneficial effect? Quite a bit depends upon the ideas or attitudes, the inclinations or aspirations, by which a decision is inspired and directed—in other words, upon the character of the decision-maker. Liberal theorizing often concentrates so much upon the act of choosing that one is in danger of forgetting the importance of who is choosing what and to what end. (One might say that it abstracts too much from the human context of choice.) Consider a person who has deliberately opted for a life completely devoted to maximizing material comforts and sensual gratifications (or what, in his *Utilitarianism*, Mill called "the lower pleasures");[9] is it a plausible contention that the "faculties of perception, judgment, discriminative feeling, mental activity and moral preference" are likely to be developed by *that* choice? The point here is the simple one that there are better and worse choices, and that some can be destructive of the very desiderata for the sake of which the opportunity to choose is extolled.

Persons regularly inclined to make destructive choices might be well advised to submit to the authority of decent communal norms; arguably they would be better off with less autonomy. A Miltonian liberal could reply that in submitting to communal norms, people would be losing the opportunity for attainment of real virtue and therefore settling for the counterfeit. Admittedly, authentic moral worthiness, or worthiness at its heights, entails autonomy; you aren't entirely good unless you are freely choosing the good for its own sake. But one must keep in mind those persons who cannot attain the good in this way, persons whose decency is, in significant degree, dependent upon moral habituation or the internalization of social norms and customs. (More than a few of us?) What about those who, if set free from customary constraints, would choose not the virtuous but the vicious course? Would John Milton say that at least choosing such a course is better than a cloistered virtue? Consider the following two hypothetical men: the orderly bourgeois family man whose decency is largely the result of moral indoctrination or deference to tradition—and the liberated nihilist who chooses in full self-consciousness the lifestyle of the Marquis de Sade. It's hard to envision Milton giving such priority to the consideration of authentic choice as to prefer the latter. That would be the preference of Jean-Paul Sartre but certainly not John Milton.[10] No doubt my hypothetical bourgeois person is not an inspiring figure; the nihilist might be more intellectually interesting (from a distance, anyway), but which of them would you rather have for your neighbor or fellow citizen?

In case this illustration might seem far-fetched, we can tone it down a bit. Most of our citizens have not become supporters of the principle "all men are created equal" by choosing it after a full Miltonian or Millian confrontation with the alternative doctrines. Insofar as we embrace and act upon this and other fundamental norms of our polity, that is largely on account of "the way we were brought up," that is, because of processes that resemble social indoctrination more than personal choice. Now, someone resolutely determined to decide for himself or herself on all important ethical matters should begin by seeking liberation from habitual valuations and loyalties that are the results of such indoctrination. This person should then fully confront the alternative valuations or principles to make rational decisions about ethical behavior. ("That which purifies is trial, and trial is by what is contrary.") Indeed, shouldn't we encourage everyone to examine the alternatives on the premise that thereby we would get an entire citizen body rising above cloistered civic virtue to real—fully chosen and knowledgeable—civic virtue? If the idea sounds a bit humorous, it is probably because of its sanguine simplicity. One reasonably suspects that, while some of these voluntaristic adventurers may rise above a cloistered virtue, many others would sink below it. Usually, it is easier to lose faith than to replace faith with demonstrable truth. A likely result is that, for many, the habitual patriotic ground of allegiance to these principles would be weakened or replaced by sophisticated skepticism, ordinary apathy, or disaffection.

I have introduced the consideration of citizenship in this context in order to make the classical point that, however valuable the act of choosing might be for the human development of some individuals, a civil society cannot live by that alone. The standards and commitments of a civil society are sustained largely by custom or tradition—by authoritative social norms and respect for such norms.[11] Insofar as that is so, there would seem to be a substantial tension between the preciousness of personal choice and society's need for customary bonds and allegiances. And the tension appears not to be wholly resolvable. Perhaps it can be reduced by certain compromises, but Millian libertarianism is not inclined to compromise; it is inclined to regard the demands of custom as a "despotism."

As we've seen, Mill's animus against custom or tradition is attributable to his view of the relation between choice and excellence. "He who does anything because it is the custom makes no choice. He gains no practice either in discerning or desiring *what is best*"[12] (emphasis mine). But the animus is equally attributable to another, rather different consideration. Mill says: "If a person possesses any tolerable amount of common sense and experience, his own mode of laying out his own existence is best, not because it is the best in itself but because it is his own mode."[13] Here we arrive at the fourth rationale for the primacy of personal choice. The act of choosing may be regarded as a precious thing because of its association with a person's "individuality," a desideratum that Mill calls "one of the leading essentials of well-being."[14]

What exactly is this desideratum and why is it such a good thing? Whatever else individuality might mean, it means at least that one has a way of thinking, feeling, and acting that is uniquely or distinctively one's own. The root idea, apparently, is that "being myself" is a condition of great value—independently of those qualities, traditionally called virtues or excellences, which are deemed valuable for all human beings alike. From this perspective what is most important about freedom of choice is its relation to the discovery or determination of "who *I* am."

This outlook, deeply entrenched in modern liberalism since Mill, raises some very interesting questions about human well-being. Does one have a "unique self"? Is the actualization of the unique self—or, to put it more modestly, one's own distinctive proclivities—a greater good than actualization of those potentialities that belong to the human species as such? How much of my well-being is invested in pursuing *my own* way and how much is invested in the development of universal virtues such as intelligence, courage, self-control, sociability, love? Questions of this sort are of social interest, bearing practically upon public policy in a number of areas, including education, governmental support for the arts, and public decency. In other words, these questions have a bearing on policies relevant to "culture."

It will be argued that these goods—individuality and virtue, to put it simply—are not mutually exclusive, that indeed they are wholly complimentary, hence there is no real problem. Of course, they are not mutually exclusive, but neither are they always complimentary; there *is* a problem. Ordinary experience provides plenty of occasions in which considerations of individuality are in competition with other imperatives of a good life and the superiority of the former is not self-evident. Suppose a person finds that his distinctive proclivity is to be a highly inventive practitioner of sadomasochism, or an extraordinarily risk-taking gambler, or a remarkably creative pornographer. Should these activities be resolutely pursued because they express "who I am"—or should they be restrained and reformed in deference to qualities that are deemed requisite for the dignity or fulfillment of the human being *per se*? (And from which of these orientations should public opinion ordinarily take its bearings?)

The concept of individuality should be subjected to more philosophic scrutiny than it usually gets. For example, is individuality supposed to be valuable in itself or because of its consequences; is it an intrinsic or an instrumental good? In this regard it is useful to focus on Mill, the first major philosopher to devote an entire chapter (chapter 3 of *On Liberty*) to exposition of the concept. While Mill's exposition is not without ambiguities requiring interpretation, I believe that one can reasonably conclude at least the following. For Mill, "individuality" designates a desirable form of human personality, characterized by energy and originality. To choose your own plan of life on the basis of your own inclinations, as distinguished from merely adopting the conventional norms, is to develop an active, energetic character, rather than a passive, apathetic one. You will also possess originality in that you will think and experience the world in new and out-of-the-ordinary ways. Don't we need energetic characters and original minds; aren't these qualities superior to passive and sluggish conformity? Ultimately, I think Mill's case for these qualities comes down to the following two claims: they are necessary conditions of "genius"[15] and human improvement, and, even where no genius or improvement results, the person possessing them has more vitality and "fullness of life."[16] In short, individuality is one of the leading essentials of well-being because it sometimes produces excellence and always involves vitality. In this way, Mill and Millians may argue that individuality is both an indispensable instrumental good—instrumental to excellence—and a good in itself, insofar as personal vitality is desirable for its own sake.

The first half of the argument might be illustrated by reference to such outstanding individuals as Leonardo da Vinci and Socrates (the latter a figure upon whom Mill lavishes praise). But we have to note that Socrates (and as far as I know Leonardo) did not pursue individuality for its own sake or as a leading essential of his well-being. Socrates sought not to maximize his unique characteristics per se but to achieve virtue and wisdom. Nor did he (in the *Apology*) criticize his fellow Athenians for failing to make personal choices but for caring more about bodily satisfactions and comforts than about excellence and truth. To be sure, Socrates was a strikingly unique individual; by all the testimony we have, there was no one like him. But, evidently, that is the result rather than the prime objective of his relentless engagement with philosophy. Similarly, it is most likely that those Athenian citizens who were deeply influenced by Socrates acquired thereby more freedom of choice, more agency in the direction of their lives. But that is hardly because their mentor celebrated, in the manner of modern libertarians, the primacy of choice and selfhood in the good life.

As to the second half of the argument—the desideratum of personal vitality—it's hard to avoid the observation that certain "vitalities" are better than others. By itself, this desideratum could be exemplified by a Don Juan or a Marquis de Sade as well as a Socrates or a Leonardo. The Marquis was certainly an energetic and original individual who dared to adopt his own plan of life at variance with dull custom. I'm not suggesting for a moment that John Stuart Mill would approve of the Marquis de Sade or regard him as an example of worthy originality and vitality; he could not.[17] But de Sade does appear to fit a number of the criteria by which individuality is defined in Millian doctrine. If a libertarian devotee of that concept wishes to say "Oh, that's not what I mean at all!" we are entitled to ask why. Perhaps he or she would want to acknowledge that there is such a thing as a bad or undesirable kind of individuality. But if this complication must be admitted, shouldn't one stop extolling the libertarian society for its maximization of individuality as such—and start thinking about the kind of regime that would promote its desirable and discourage its undesirable forms? This orientation would require a model of good character in which individuality is only one of the qualities recognized as worthy or in which it is modified by certain other qualities. And the modifying elements cannot simply be taken for granted.

Wishful thinking aside, it is very unlikely that either a good character or an authentic personality can be expected from a regime of simple moral laissez faire. A serious individuality (as distinguished from a superficial or merely apparent one) requires sustained effort at self-understanding and depends upon considerable integrity of purpose. As Nietzsche taught, nothing (not even a meaningful "self") comes without self-disciplined devotion to some end or cause. And discipline and devotion are not spontaneous products of the relaxation of external restraints; when these qualities are acquired in any substantial degree, much is usually owed to the fact that demands have been made upon the individual by some community or another.[18] And such demands are often rooted in traditions or social habituation. It follows that libertarians who persistently denigrate social habituation and custom on behalf of free choice are exhibiting an inadequate, insufficiently complex view of individuality itself. There is much more to it than "letting go."

As should be evident, I'm not arguing for the opposite extreme, that individuality counts for nothing and universality for everything. Who could deny that the individuation of personalities is a vital element in our appreciation of what it means to be human and in the enjoyment of life? It is, apparently, a major ingredient of friendship and love; romantic love is inspired in large part by the perceived uniqueness of the loved one. ("There's no one like you.") And even in the moral life, the question "What do I really want?" is often relevant to the determination of what is the right or good thing to do. Moreover, though I've been making a case for custom or habituation in human affairs, we do not ordinarily admire someone who is *entirely possessed* by his or her habitual dispositions. Such a person would be incapable of self-criticism and self-improvement. Serious self-examination and choice are apparently grounded in a capacity for detachment from one's present inclinations, aims, and opinions (a phenomenon to be explored when we discuss "liberal personality" in the concluding part of the chapter).

On the other hand, common sense recognizes a role for custom and habituation. Who would want to live with utterly unpredictable people, or to be oneself utterly unpredictable? For theoretical purposes we need an account of personality that accommodates the various desiderata that ordinary experience recognizes as necessary for a good life. We need a theory of personality that explains how choice and individuality, habituation and virtue can exist together coherently in the life of a rational being. A fully satisfactory account of that sort is hard to come by.[19] At any rate, it is not provided by theories that give such priority to choice and individuality as is given by the libertarian rationales we've been considering. These are, in this regard as in others, one-sided doctrines.

There is, however, a somewhat different rationale that ought to be noted before we turn to the egalitarian theme. In this outlook freedom of choice is valued not so much because of any relation it might have to personal dignity, virtue, or individuality, but on account of its relations to social progress. In its simplest terms the argument is that freedom of choice promotes variety ("the different experiments of living," as Mill called it), and variety is a prime mover in social improvement. Uniformity causes "stagnation," whereas diversity stimulates the mind and promotes experimentation with new and better ways of doing things—in both the material and the cultural spheres of life. And, as proponents of this outlook often assume, the opportunity of individuals to experiment with new ideas and ways promotes moral along with intellectual and technological progress. In other words, there is a process of spontaneous social growth that needs no direction or constraint from civil law and public policy. The basic injunction to government is "prevent coercion, provide for the security of life and property, and then leave it alone!"

This well-known viewpoint gives rise to a number of well-known questions. Why should personal liberty and diversity (unsupervised) necessarily lead to progress? The answer of course depends upon what one means by *progress*. It does make sense to say that relentless experimentation with various techniques in the production of material goods or in architecture or in medicine leads to demonstrable improvements in these fields. But one can hardly speak as confidently of progress in culture and ethics. And the viewpoint under consideration is notoriously vague as to the standards by which real progress in these areas is to be distinguished from mere change. Nor, as a matter of empirical observation, is it clear that our culture is improved by advances in video technology or our morality by such cultural diversities as "heavy metal" rock music.

The justification of personal liberty as instrumental to the social welfare and betterment finds its strongest support in modern economic theory. It owes more to Adam Smith than to John Stuart Mill, and its greatest contemporary exponent is Friedrich Hayek. Applying Smith's insight into the workings of a free market economy, Hayek observes:

It is through the mutually adjusted efforts of many people that more knowledge is utilized than any one individual possesses or than it is possible to synthesize intellectually; and it is through such utilization of dispersed knowledge that achievements are made possible greater than any single mind can foresee. It is because freedom means the renunciation of direct control of individual efforts that a free society can make use of so much more knowledge than the mind of the wisest ruler could comprehend.[20]

In the free market where each individual is able to employ his own special piece of relevant knowledge for his own ends, there are two desirable results: a system of spontaneous cooperation in the production and exchange of goods *and* a vast increase in the amount of goods available in society as a whole. That the system is one of spontaneous cooperation and that the total amount of goods available is increased are results of the same cause—each individual is strongly motivated by self-interest to engage in such productive activities and transactions with others as will enlarge his possessions. This in brief is Smith's central thesis; Hayek's distinction is in his application of it well beyond the economic sphere to the development of society, culture, and civilization. On this model our civilization is the product of "spontaneous forces of growth" made up of the multifarious small experiments of multitudinous individuals seeking to improve their situations. Hence, not only tools but also ideas, values, and customs are continuously tested, modified, and replaced in a process whereby "the ineffective will be discarded and the effective retained."[21] Government could never muster the knowledge requisite to control or direct this complex process, and the effort to do so could only obstruct the process by imposing, as a kind of straitjacket, whatever knowledge or values we happen to have right now. Therefore, it cannot be a legitimate function of government to support any existing standards of value, except those requisite for maintaining the spheres of personal liberty from which new values arise.[22]

With regard to technical inventions and economic procedures, there's validity to the proposition that in a free market "the ineffective will be discarded and the effective retained." (At least for a sufficiently long run; in the short run there are unhappy consequences of which we are all aware.) But how much sense does this optimistic evolutionism make when applied to cultural norms and moral standards? Self-interested motivation and perceptions might be adequate to guarantee that a market economy will produce more of the material things that people want, but is it an equally reliable guarantee that a culture will produce worthy standards of value? Hayek would no doubt reply that we are not in a position to determine, in any conclusive way, what values are worthy, because principles of good and bad are also evolving; progress will bring not only new things but also new ends and perceptions of good. This comes perilously close to admission that ethical "progress" means nothing more than change and variety. But one can take seriously the idea of moral or cultural progress only insofar as there is a relatively clear, defensible criterion by which to affirm that the new state of affairs is better than the old one. Furthermore, it seems to me, we can have confidence in the moral or cultural experiments of individuals only insofar as we can have confidence in the character of those doing the experimenting. In other words, the benign outcomes expected by Hayek are dependent upon certain ethical prerequisites.

Hayek is not wholly unaware of this problem. Unlike Millian liberals, Hayek explicitly endorses a degree of traditionalism or conformity to customary norms. He notes as an important fact that human beings can understand and get along with each other spontaneously because most people most of the time conform unconsciously to conventional rules. "Paradoxical as it may appear," he says, "it is probably true that a successful free society will always in a large measure be a tradition-bound society."[23] In the absence of unifying traditions and habits, society would be obliged to promote observance of necessary rules by coercion. Indeed, "freedom has never worked without deeply ingrained moral beliefs."[24]

From my perspective it is certainly to Hayek's credit that he observes and explicitly acknowledges this reality. And it might not be such a paradoxical idea that a free society needs an established morality that unifies and constrains its members. What is paradoxical, however, is the relation between such a traditional morality and the progressivist dynamic of Hayekian free society. It's hard to envision the maintenance of a long-standing ("deeply ingrained") communal ethos amidst the continuous innovations of self-interested individuals that this kind of society must encourage. To put it most simply, an experimental attitude toward social norms is incompatible with a reverential one, and the ceaseless change generated by the former—in cultural as well as material life—is bound to undermine the latter. One should not be at all surprised to see that this is in fact what tends to happen in advanced capitalist societies, that is, those which have "progressed."

On Hayek's behalf someone might respond that there is really no ambiguity here; what Hayek envisions is incremental, nonprecipitous change under the mild constraint of somewhat flexible conventional rules that "can be broken by individuals who feel that they have strong enough reasons to brave the censure of their fellows."[25] But this kind of defense will not do. Hayekian society must welcome innovation in the expectation of improvement; therefore it will need more than a few of such innovative and independent-minded individuals, and it will need a milieu generally supportive of them. Why then is Hayek entitled to expect that the necessary traditionalism—the requisite deference to the past—will survive the individualistic progressivism that his theory unleashes? The expectation that traditional norms, and allegiances to them, will continue to exist sufficiently to perform their indispensable function does seem to be little more than a confident assumption. Hayek's doctrine does not allow for actions of the state addressed to the maintenance of conventional standards of value; compliance has to be wholly "voluntary" or spontaneous. This position virtually ignores the fact that, historically, the common morality— that is, the tradition upon which Hayekian theory relies—was supported (and thought to be in need of support) by law and authority in various ways.

The tensions in this outlook seem to reflect an effort (prominent in modern liberalism) to have it both ways. Yet one can have little doubt which way Hayek would have to go if it would become undeniably evident to him that tradition is not holding up. Although he does occasionally suggest that coercion might have to be used in the absence of sufficient deference to conventional rules, his philosophy as a whole mandates a strict reliance upon "the spontaneous forces of growth." At bottom this is a utilitarian philosophy resting on a certitude or resolute faith—that the autonomous choices of individuals employing their own resources for their own ends must eventually prove to be good for the greatest number.[26]

The assumption I've just summarized is also the underlying faith of John Stuart Mill (in the moral and cultural sphere at least). It is not too much to say that Hayek and Mill, each in his own way, takes social morality for granted. In the final analysis, both of these two seminal philosophers of the libertarian outlook presuppose that the extensive moral experimentation and choice they advocate will occur within an adequate ethical framework or context. And they presuppose that the ethical framework (whether it be provided by tradition or by the spontaneous processes of advancing civilization or by human nature) need not be established or maintained by deliberate acts of the polity. These assumptions—

sometimes acknowledged, more often not—pervade autonomistic doctrines on the great questions of public morality.

II. Equality

Most of the libertarian arguments against public morality turn out to be utilitarian or consequentialist arguments in the broadest sense of these terms. In one way or another they claim that people are better off—happier, more virtuous, more vital, or better equipped with the means to live well—as the result of a regime that maximizes freedom of personal choice. The egalitarian doctrines, on the other hand, tend to be nonutilitarian; they are mostly concerned not with the consequences but with (putatively) categorical principles or rights.

To summarize the relevant argument in advance: the maintenance of a public morality amounts to wrongful state discrimination in favor of some people's lifestyles and against others. For example, laws and policies restricting prostitution and pornography affirm that some ways of life are worse than others, thereby disfavoring or denigrating groups of citizens with regard to a subject (personal lifestyles or values) that is none of the state's business. Such discrimination violates the fundamental principle that citizens are equal in stature or that they have the right to be treated equally.

This outlook would seem to get some support from the principles of the Declaration of Independence. After all, the Declaration does indicate that the business of government is the security of individual rights, including the equal right of all to "the pursuit of happiness." And, one may conclude, that means the private pursuit of whatever a person regards as happiness or a requisite thereof; the state may not authoritatively determine for its members a correct conception of happiness. While this, as far as it goes, is a very plausible interpretation of what the Declaration means, three questions arise. Is it credible that the philosophy of the Declaration is utterly relativistic about what constitutes happiness, such that all personal preferences are deemed equally conducive to it and all ways of life equally worthy? This question almost answers itself; Thomas Jefferson and his colleagues never asserted and wouldn't have countenanced such an extreme (modernistic or "postmodernistic") position. Nonetheless, did they think that the state must be morally neutral, because the public interest of a republican regime is unaffected by any differences of "lifestyle"—and therefore it is no legitimate concern of civil society how its (equal) members may choose to live? Presumably no one believing that could say, as Jefferson did: "It is the manners and spirit of a people which preserves a republic in vigor. A degeneration in these is a canker which soon eats to the heart of its laws and constitution."[27] And, insofar as this is thought to be true, doesn't one have to entertain the idea that there is some outer limit to the inalienable right to pursue one's own subjectively defined version of happiness? Could the generation that established the Republic really have envisioned an unqualified right of all conceivable lifestyles to be treated by government as equally valuable? That is, to say the least, very doubtful.[28]

But our contemporary egalitarian doctrine has little to do, in any direct way, with the philosophy of the Declaration and the Founders. Its distinctive features are of rather recent vintage. Let us explore the doctrine as expressed by its most emphatic proponent, Ronald Dworkin.

In his first major work, *Taking Rights Seriously,* Dworkin states the position thusly:

> The central concept of my argument will be the concept not of liberty but of equality. I presume that we all accept the following postulates of political morality. Government must treat those it governs with concern, that is, as human beings who are capable of forming and acting on intelligent conceptions of how their lives should be lived. Government must not only treat people with concern and respect but with equal concern and respect. . . . It must not constrain liberty on the ground that one citizen's conception of the good life [or one group's conception] is nobler or superior to another's.[29]

Dworkin maintains that this principle of "equal concern and respect" defines liberalism and is the fundamental principle of our liberal society. I postpone for the time being critical attention to these two suppositions: that "we all" can be persuaded to accept these postulates, and that equality, rather than liberty, is our primary norm (Dworkin thinks that the important liberties are derivatives from it). What is initially crucial for an understanding of the Dworkinian perspective is the categorical character or function of this egalitarian principle; it is not treated as one principle among several but as a sovereign norm overriding (in almost all cases) any competing social considerations, policies, or standards of value. That is because principles are said to outweigh (or, in Dworkinian language, "trump") considerations of public utility or policy. To put it a bit differently, one has a personal *right* to equality of concern and respect, and rights must take precedence over "utilitarian" calculations of social welfare.

Why? That is an involved question. Sometimes we are told simply that such is the "logic" of the concept of rights. Sometimes (and more interestingly) we are told that basic rights and liberties reflect "an idea of human dignity," that to violate such a right is to treat someone as less than human. To illustrate: for Dworkin, the freedom of speech encompasses a right to express oneself publicly in any language, however vituperative or obscene, that one finds satisfying—because it is "an assault on human personality" to tell someone that he cannot express fully the "outrage" that he feels.[30] When the law tries to impose standards of civility in public discourse, it is arrogantly denying the equal respect due to the dissenters by forcing upon them the majority's orthodox attitude about propriety. The upshot of all this is that the state is violating the inviolable right to equal respect and is assaulting human personality whenever it acts against a practice because that practice is regarded as indecent, degrading, or uncivil.

Before we get to the foundations of this doctrine, there are some issues closer to the surface about the consequences of its way of using concepts like *respect* and *dignity*. The specific objective of the Dworkinian free speech argument that I've just summarized (as is obvious in his text) was to immunize from legal restraint the sort of public expression often heard from radical dissenters in the 1960s. It is well known that those utterances involved the vilification of one's adversaries by obscene invective ("mother . . . ing fascist pig!" and the like), and threats, addressed to society at large, of violence, arson, and various desecrations.[31] Now there might be good old-fashioned reasons such speech ordinarily has to be protected by the First Amendment, but we are concerned with the Dworkinian reason. Isn't there an anomaly somewhere in a theory that derives the right to expressions of that sort from the respect owed to human personality? Of course Dworkin is preoccupied with the respect supposedly owed to the speaker, but the obvious result is the licensing of much utterance that is disrespectful (at least to its objects) and degrading by deliberate intention.

Why exactly is it an assault on human personality to restrain someone from publicly expressing his attitudes in as hostile or vulgar a manner as he wishes? Dworkin says that "a man cannot express himself freely when he cannot match his rhetoric to his outrage."[32] That is true enough—if one equates *free* with *spontaneous*, but it would take more argument than Dworkin provides to show that the dignity of human personality depends upon unlimited freedom to vent one's passions, whatever they might be and without any semblance of rational dialogue or effort to persuade.

The majority (supporters of those "orthodox methods of expression" to which Dworkin refers) may believe that dignity, including that of the speaker, is enhanced when self-expression is limited by certain rules of civility. It is not obvious why their view is wrong. Dworkin says that the traditional view precludes equal respect for the dissenters. It does of course preclude the supposition that all modes of expression are of equal value, a supposition also rejected by laws against pornography and nudity in public places (and by all rules of politeness). In any event, the Dworkinian conception of the grounds of free speech yields the curious result that dignity and equality mandate a virtually unlimited right to express one's hatred and contempt of others.

It is important to remember what kind of argument Dworkin is *not* making. He isn't claiming that the sort of expression justified by his theory is harmless or that society is better off when it allows all such utterances than when it tries to suppress them. That claim would be a "utilitarian" argument about the general welfare; Dworkin's is emphatically an argument about individual *rights* independent of social welfare considerations. "If someone has a right to something then it would be wrong to deny it to him even though it would be in the general interest to do so"[33] (and, apparently, even though the general interest would clearly be injured by allowing it). So what if the Dworkinian free speech principle would facilitate a significantly greater amount of hatred and contempt than would a more moderate free speech policy allowing for some rules of civility? Dworkin makes no real effort to show that such an outcome need not be feared. Hence, the doctrine (when strictly applied or taken seriously) entails the predominance of an absolutist claim to equal respect, even if the predictable consequence is a society worse off by all the usual criteria, including happiness, rationality, civility, and even mutual respect.

At the root of much that is unsatisfactory about Dworkin's theory is a sharp dualism: claims about rights are always treated as matters of high principle, while competing claims are regularly treated as nonprincipled considerations of social policy or utility. One is left with this strongly dichotomous picture of social life: there are certain personal rights that are compelling ethical mandates, and then there are various expediential advantages and disadvantages that, while of more or less importance, are not (really or compellingly) ethical mandates. Where conflicts arise, the conclusion seems irresistible that a society wishing to be principled must not only decide them in favor of the former but also be prepared to put up with substantial sacrifice of the latter (utilitarian losses) in doing so.

In this way a proliferation of comprehensive rights (of a certain kind) is guaranteed, while the moral issues actually confronting society are distorted or evaded. It's simply untrue that personal rights are the only principled considerations, or that social values that may be opposed to claims of right are always inferior to them in ethical import. There are quite significant moral considerations—desiderata of civility, decency, or virtue among them—that are not about personal rights *and* are not able to be dismissed as mere matters of utilitarian gain and loss. In the language of contemporary academic philosophy, Dworkin's dichotomy embraces the distinction between the right and the good. Dworkin may wish to argue, along with his philosophic mentor John Rawls, that the right must have priority over the good.[34] But he is not entitled to argue as if the good has no real ethical status or never presents a compelling moral claim.

Contrary to the Dworkinian view, the rationale for public morality embraces the idea that there is more than one compelling civic principle— and that, therefore, claims about good life (or decent life) are often eligible to be weighed against claims of right. To be sure, this comparison hardly disposes of the principle of equal concern and respect; I do not maintain that there is no such principle in our liberal thought and civic life. The critical issue is whether it means all that contemporary egalitarianism says it means and condemns public morality as much as they assume it does.

Our traditional ethic of decency, and the legal policies associated therewith, has indeed presupposed that some ways of life are more (or less) worthy than others. For example, the traditional ethic prefers the values, attitudes, or experiences of monogamous love to those of polygamy, prostitution, and pornography. It also prefers the responsible citizen to the drug addict for reasons that include a judgment about moral character. (Proponents of public morality will do well to recognize this reality and not to try to argue around it.) Does the traditional ethic thereby violate the American principle of equality? Whatever the equal rights of citizens might entail, it is far from evident that they encompass an entitlement to have one's value preferences respected by the state as much as anyone else's value preferences. From the postulate that the individual citizen is entitled to *respect*, does the conclusion necessarily follow, as a matter of logic, that the community is obliged to esteem equally whatever type of life individuals might wish to live? To say that this conclusion does follow is to equate or conflate respect for the person as a human being (or fellow citizen) with respect for his or her particular desires, interests, personality, and character. Isn't it sometimes the case that respect for a person's humanity is quite compatible with emphatic disapproval of a lifestyle that the person has adopted or contemplates adopting? ("We respect you too much to stand by while you devote yourself to alcohol and idleness; get a job!")

As for the equal *concern* that a liberal community owes all its members, there are situations where a paternalistic policy is compatible with—or even a requisite of—true concern. As John Finnis observes: "Paternalists may well consider that, for example, to leave a person to succumb to drug addiction on the plea that it is his 'business' is to deny him the active concern one would show for one's friend in like situations."[35] Of course, one can imagine a version of equal concern and respect that would categorically prevent the community from intervening to protect that person because it would oblige the community to regard a drug-centered "lifestyle" as the moral equivalent of any other. But to embrace that version one has to inflate the concepts of respect, concern, and equality well beyond their ordinary meanings in our civic life and thought.

Although his principle would seem to entail the equal status of a drug-centered lifestyle, Dworkin has not (to my knowledge) attempted to deal with that subject. The argument he is anxious to make is about pornography. In a more recent work, *A Matter of Principle*, Dworkin reformulates (somewhat) his basic concept as follows.

> People have the right not to suffer disadvantages in the distribution of social goods and opportunities, including disadvantages in the liberties permitted to them by the criminal law, just on the ground that their officials or fellow citizens think that their opinions about the right way for them to lead their own lives are ignoble or wrong. I shall call this (putative) right the right to moral independence.[36]

This right is, in Dworkin's view, still a principle of equality; it is an equal right to be treated as a morally independent being. What difference, if any, the substitution of "moral independence" for "respect and concern" is supposed to make is not quite clear; I believe it makes very little difference. As Dworkin applies this general notion to the pornography issue, the right is violated whenever a system of regulation "includes the hypothesis that the attitudes about sex displayed or nurtured in pornography are demeaning or bestial or otherwise unsuitable to human beings of the best sort, even though this hypothesis might be true."[37] The crux of this argument appears to be that when the state regulates pornography on the premise that the attitudes involved in it are bestial or base, it is denying the independence of the person who holds those attitudes by denigrating his capacity to decide for himself what is good for him. In the language of our author's earlier formulation, the lawmaker or the majority is showing the individual profound disrespect by legislating constraints contrary to his moral opinion about how he should live.

Notice that the right not to have one's opinions on such matters overridden by the state is supposed to prevail even if the state's position is true; that is, even if pornography really does nurture bestiality and degrade people. Of course, there is nothing in Dworkin's writings to suggest that he actually takes that possibility seriously; the point is that the right must "trump" even the truth. And that is a claim of sufficient magnitude to warrant more than the casual stipulation it gets.

Now let us look more closely at the (supposed) right to moral independence in the case of pornography. The case can be stated thusly: It is my inviolable right to act on my opinion that pornographic attitudes and experiences are valuable for me. Now, we can envision someone who has thought about the matter and arrived at a clear and definite opinion of the sort just mentioned. But, we might ask, do people who indulge a taste for pornographic films and magazines really act on such a basis? It seems as evident as anything on this subject could be that persons entering a "peep show" are acting upon an appetite or passion rather more than a settled idea or a decision arrived at by reflection about how to live. Perhaps this distinction doesn't matter at all to Dworkin, and the word *opinion* in the statement of his principle could just as well be replaced by the words *desire* or *inclination* or *urge*. But then wouldn't the principle lose much of its ethical force? (A solemn categorical right to the independence of one's urges, including the urge of a group of revellers to enjoy "stag films"?) Arguably, it wouldn't stand up well in light of Dworkin's own rationale—that government must treat persons with respect *because* they are beings "capable of forming and acting on intelligent conceptions of how their lives should be lived."[38] Why, on this basis, should the community be obliged to treat the claims of irrational taste or impulse with the same deference that is due to "intelligent conceptions"?

To continue: suppose that the root of someone's interest in pornography is an inclination (call it an urge or an opinion, whichever) to find sexual gratification in portrayals of sadistic violence, including scenes of erotically presented torture and mutilation. Dworkin's doctrine, as he presents it, would compel the conclusion that the law's interference with the (pornographic) pursuit of that inclination, on the supposition that it is wrong, is a moral outrage. After all, the law, and the citizens who sustain it, are presuming that the attitudes involved in a practice that this person enjoys are ignoble or demeaning. While "moral outrage" is not Dworkin's exact language, that is clearly the tone of his argument about the regulation of pornography. He maintains that to embody in law the opinions of those who oppose pornography is to violate moral independence in essentially the same way as it is violated by legal embodiment of a Nazi opinion that "Jews [should have] less of their preferences fulfilled just because of who they are."[39]

The analogy with Nazis is, to say no more, astonishing. Suffice it to say that the ordinary proponent of antipornography statutes is not demanding that disfavored people be disenfranchised and worse; nor is he or she maintaining that lovers of pornography should be made to suffer because of who they are—because they possess irreducibly inferior characteristics. What is maintained is that people should be discouraged from finding their gratification in scenes of eroticized dehumanization—by the legal deterrence of those who would entice them to it for commercial profit. It is true that any thoroughgoing justification for the restriction of pornography will ultimately hold that some qualities of character or types of personality are undesirable. But the objective is protection of people, or rescue where possible, from certain degrading or corrupting influences that are prominent in modern society. This isn't fascistic hatred; it is, as many citizens see it, an effort to facilitate real moral independence and real respect.

Dworkin doesn't discuss violent pornography, "snuff films," and the like. He undertakes no refutation of the view that the attitudes about sex and human beings exemplified in such productions are actually degrading. He does not advance the usual liberal claim that the pornographic (or the mass media as such) has no significant effects on mind and character. Believing (with some justification) that such "utilitarian" defenses of pornography cannot adequately defend it, he relies upon a "rights-based" defense, with the rights grounded in an indefeasible principle of equal respect for everyone's moral autonomy.

What is the foundation or justification for such a norm? If one asks why "equal concern and respect" or equality of "moral independence" is so fundamental, if one asks for the authoritative source of the principle, there are two kinds of answers discoverable in Dworkin's writings. The principle is said to be a mandate of our underlying communal morality, a basic tenet of our liberal political convictions. But it is also suggested that the imperative can be justified on a more universal basis; that it can even be defended (in some complex manner) as a "natural right" owed to human beings as such.

With regard to the first claim, I hope it is evident by now that Dworkin's "equal concern and respect" is not *our* American principle in any ordinary sense of these words. Of course, it is relatively easy for citizens of a liberal democracy to agree with the abstract proposition that some basic modicum of concern and respect is due to every person; it also comes naturally for us to think of people as being, in some vital respects, independent individuals rather than subordinate parts of a collectivity. But just how and where the abstract proposition is to be concretely applied is a rather problematic business. Dworkin's theory capitalizes on this situation. What it offers is an acceptable generality with considerable potential for flexible extension to cases beyond the terms of the abstract agreement. And it advances this elastic generality as a controlling, preemptive moral demand.

In other words, while Dworkin can "presume that we all accept [his] postulates of political morality"[40] at a very high level of doctrinal abstraction, it is most unlikely that we all accept what, more concretely, the postulates come to mean in Dworkin's hands. Certainly, most Americans do not believe that our national principle of equity mandates respect for attitudes toward human sexuality embodied in pornography. Nor would many Americans find acceptable (or even coherent) an obligation to respect a sadomasochistic lifestyle as much as a loving and mutually respectful one. To put it simply, there is abundant evidence that the far-reaching Dworkinian conception of equality is not rooted in any solid consensus of American moral belief. If the actual scope and consequences of the doctrine would be explained to them, multitudes of our citizens would disagree with it in whole or in part.[41]

But perhaps what Dworkin wishes to argue is that this is the ethic upon which our institutions actually rest, even though citizens don't recognize it or hypocritically refuse to accept its necessary consequences. The ethic, however, is incompatible with allegiance to the monogamous family as a vital institution of our society. And it is not the ethic that presided over the American Revolution and the founding of the Republic. And, in its derivation of liberty from a more fundamental egalitarian imperative and in the priority it gives to equality over all public desiderata, especially those of private property, it is not the ethic of the American Constitution. The Constitutional conception of equality is violated by state discrimination against black people or Jews or (more recently) women on account of their race, ethnicity, religion, or gender; but no court has ever held authoritatively that refusal of the state to esteem equally everyone's opinion about how to live is repugnant to the Constitution. Finally, maybe Dworkin's real claim is that his comprehensive egalitarian principle is at the core of liberal philosophy, that it is the ethic that best explains what liberalism is about.[42] But that claim is not true of classical liberal philosophy; Dworkin's doctrine of equality is not that of Locke, Jefferson, or Mill. It does, however, represent a viewpoint prominent in contemporary liberalism; Dworkin is an important interpreter of a current trend in liberal or neoliberal thinking. But then what his claim finally comes down to is the unargued premise that basic American and liberal morality should be identified with a relatively recent ideological trend.

Since there is no good reason for accepting that premise, we are left with the other, more universalistic ground for acceptance of "equal concern and respect" as a fundamental norm. Dworkin rejects the idea that there are natural rights in the old-fashioned, Lockean sense, yet he holds that certain rights "are *natural* in the sense that they are not the product of any legislation, or convention, or hypothetical contract."[43] On this (somewhat elusive) ground, Dworkin has maintained that his equality principle describes a natural right, indeed *the* natural right. His ultimate philosophic support for this conclusion is in the teaching of John Rawls that equality of respect "is owed to human beings as moral persons."[44] At this level Dworkinian theory tends to merge with that of Rawls.

The aspect of Rawlsian doctrine most relevant to our purpose here is his conception of "moral personality" and its relation to the egalitarian principle. In *A Theory of Justice* Rawls presented the conception in the following way:

> Moral persons are distinguished by two features: first they are capable of having (and are assumed to have) a conception of their good (as expressed by a rational plan of life); and second they are capable of having (and are assumed to acquire) a sense of justice, a normally effective desire to apply and to act upon the principles of justice at least to a certain minimum degree.[45]

The apparent function of this concept is to identify the distinguishing features of human beings on account of which we are entitled to be respected or to make claims of right (as other creatures, horses, for example, are not). Rawls recognizes here that moral philosophy needs a rational answer to the question of what is special about our species. Rawls's answer is that these two qualities are what makes us the type of being—persons—to whom considerations of justice are applicable. For contemporary egalitarian liberalism, much depends on the meaning of this answer.

Rawls's claim is that, since virtually all human beings can be said to possess these two qualities in the requisite minimum degree, "equality is supported by the general facts of nature."[46] To sustain this claim, Rawls must stipulate that the criteria defining moral personality are "not at all stringent"; they are met by the most rudimentary capabilities and dispositions. At one point Rawls asks his reader to "imagine someone whose only pleasure is to count blades of grass in various geometrically shaped areas," and then goes on to indicate that this person qualifies as a possessor of a conception of his own good and rational plan of life (if he actually plans for the satisfaction of his desire).[47] The first condition of moral personality is apparently fulfilled by any pattern of activity deliberately desired as an end. Further, "the minimal requirements defining moral personality refer to a capacity and not to the realization of it."[48] Regarding both conditions, a bare "capacity" is enough. (Although Rawls says, rather ambiguously, that moral persons are "assumed to acquire" a "normally effective" sense of justice.)

As a foundation for the equality of "respect which is owed to all persons," this formulation has some problems. One may wonder how such a minimalist definition of moral personality can mandate a substantial respect for everyone (or anyone). Yet, if the tests were made more demanding (or watered-down less) numbers of people would fail them, much to the frustration of Rawls's egalitarian intentions. Rawls's definitions aside for the moment, it is a matter of ordinary experience that the capabilities and inclinations associated with a rational plan of life and a sense of justice can be possessed by different persons in vastly different ways and degrees. (As to the former, consider the life of Immanuel Kant and that of a drug cultist who remains just rational enough to plan his periodic bouts of oblivion. As to the sense of justice, consider Abraham Lincoln and Jefferson Davis or, from another angle, Pol Pot.) The disparities among us in these regards are striking and pervasive in all times and places. So, while equality might be supported by some of the general facts of nature, inequality is supported by others. Rawls is not unaware of these realities (indeed, in other parts of his theory they are prominent), but he doesn't squarely confront the question why the equalities should be treated as the naturally decisive phenomenon. Why should we be obliged to accord equal respect to all persons on account of qualities that they possess very unequally? Why not say that a certain elementary respect is owed to the potentialities of humanity found in anyone—and more to those in whom the potentialities are realized?

Rawls recognizes that "presumably individuals have varying capacities for the sense of justice," but he adds that, "this fact is not a reason for depriving those with a lesser capacity of the full protection of justice."[49] Of course, everyone is entitled to justice; the question is whether they are entitled to Rawlsian justice and, most pertinently, to the same degree of respect. The question is clouded by the fact that Rawls doesn't define "respect" or explicitly consider how far the imperative of equal respect is supposed to extend. Does it encompass an entitlement of all individuals to the same amount of social esteem, to be accorded the same regard or honor by society, regardless of achievement, character, or other forms of merit? Rawls never makes this claim in precise terms but he says things close enough to it. (And Dworkin seems to agree with this interpretation.) It's hard to avoid the conclusion that the concept of moral personality is an effort to derive much from little—a rather stringent mandate that persons be respected from a very nonstringent formulation of the essential qualities that make all of us respectable.

Perhaps what current egalitarianism really means to say is that differences among human beings are matters of degree while the distinction between human and nonhuman beings is qualitative and hence fundamental. What we have naturally in common is more important than our differences and inequalities (a formulation likely to be acceptable to Locke and Aristotle). But what should result from this foundation? Logically, it should certainly follow that no human being may be treated as (we think) animals may be treated. And it is reasonably inferred that, because of the regard due to the elementary characteristics of human nature, even malefactors are entitled to a lawful procedure, and even utterly selfabsorbed hedonists should not be subjected to gratuitous injury or degradation. What *doesn't* follow (beyond this elementary level of entitlement) is that society is forbidden to recognize varying degrees of excellence or deliberately bestow esteem on some ways of life and not others.

But Rawlsian theory has another, rather different reason for rejecting a meritocratic social policy. Rawls is much impressed with the importance of the psychological need for self-respect, and he views one's self-respect as heavily dependent upon the esteem of others. For this reason (in

addition to the claims of moral personality), his just society is designed
to assure "equality in the social bases of esteem." This is provided in part
by the equal civic rights of citizens and in part by limitations upon social
or economic inequalities that could reduce the self-esteem of the least
fortunate (or capable) members of society. Further, "as citizens we are to
reject the standard of perfection as a political principle, and for the
purposes of justice avoid any assessment of the relative value of one
another's way of life. . . . This democracy in judging each other's aims
is the foundation of self-respect in a well ordered society."[50] Assessment
of ways of life by some standard of "perfection" (that is, excellence or
worth or virtue) will cause those who fall short of such standards to think
less of themselves. Evidently, "democracy in judging each other's aims"
means that, to the greatest extent possible, the aspirations of all citizens
should be treated as equally valuable.

Rawls, I believe, is certainly warranted in attaching considerable psychological importance to self-respect as an element of our well-being. He is
also correct about the pervasive fact of life (for most of us) that what we
think of ourselves is much dependent upon how others regard us, our
conduct, and our aspirations. The difficulty lies in the moral and political
conclusions Rawls draws from these facts. Should we join Rawls in the
conclusion that a well-ordered society is one that seeks to assure self-
respect to everyone by granting an undifferentiating (or nonjudgmental)
esteem to the activities, aims, and characters of all citizens alike? (I'm
assuming that one's character is shaped by one's activities and aims.) That
society would not be easy to maintain, since it would contradict another
pervasive fact of life—the idea that the ends for which it is possible to strive,
and the personalities it is possible to acquire thereby, differ significantly in
value. Isn't this widespread belief also a factor of psychological importance?
And, according to the moral outlook associated with it, genuine self-
respect cannot be guaranteed to anyone, least of all by means of unearned
esteem. Self-respect (as distinguished from an easygoing self-satisfaction)
comes from trying to meet the demands of a good life and earning the
esteem of those who do likewise. Rawlsian esteem demands little of us.
Assuming that Rawls's well-ordered society could actually be maintained,
isn't it far more likely to obstruct than to promote excellence or higher
aspirations? Some Rawlsian formulations suggest the response that, as the
comprehensive principle of equal respect would be applied to the public
side of life only, the private sphere would provide an adequate arena for
hierarchical judgments of value. But that vision of a bifurcated society is

problematic in two ways. It establishes an uncomfortably (and unrealistically?) large disparity between our public and our private lives, what we value as citizens and as individuals. Moreover, the public sphere (or the polity) undoubtedly affects and shapes attitudes in the private sphere, especially where the former is as large and important as it is in Rawlsian theory.

Thus far I have noted two justifications of Rawlsian derivation for a comprehensive imperative of equal respect. The first justification affirms fundamental rights or entitlements on the basis of a concept of moral personality that looks very much like an idea of human dignity (or the functional equivalent thereof). The second justification concerns one's need for self-esteem and consequent dependence upon public support for external confirmation of one's worth. This resembles a conception of human frailty and weakness more than human dignity.

There is a third line of argument prominently advanced in *A Theory of Justice* on behalf of its egalitarian thesis. Rawls is at pains to refute the classical idea that it is just for people to be recognized and rewarded in proportion to merit and achievement. On the contrary, Rawls maintains, since a person does not "deserve" the natural qualities or abilities that enable him to achieve more than someone else, he cannot be said to deserve any greater advantages that may result therefrom. The point has some validity as far as it goes. But Rawls continues: "The assertion that a man deserves the superior character that enables him to cultivate his abilities is equally problematic; for his character depends in large part upon fortunate family and social circumstances for which he can claim no credit. The notion of desert seems not to apply to these cases."[51] The obverse point is that those with "inferior" or weaker character do not deserve lesser advantages; they are not responsible for their lack of motivation and effort to develop such natural endowment as they have. But if we are without any responsibility for our characters in this regard, then we must be without responsibility for them in any other regard. No one would deserve esteem for pursuing worthy ends and no one would deserve blame for pursuing base or narrowly selfish ends, because the persons we are, and consequently the lives we lead, are determined by our circumstances rather than our volition. But how much dignity or respectability can be attributed to beings thusly described? And what does it mean to say that such beings without agency are moral personalities capable of having a rational plan of life?[52]

This sort of radical environmentalism is even more incompatible with the definition and status of moral personality as elaborated by Rawls in writings subsequent to *A Theory of Justice.* In the somewhat revised version, moral persons are said to be

> characterized by two moral powers and by two corresponding highest-order interests in realizing and exercising these powers. The first power is the capacity for an effective sense of justice, that is, the capacity to understand, to apply and to act from (and not merely in accordance with) the principles of justice. The second moral power is the capacity to form, revise and rationally to pursue a conception of the good.[53]

Insofar as he means "form, revise and rationally pursue" in the ordinary sense of the words, Rawls is now acknowledging that we do in some meaningful way choose our conception of the good (as distinguished from just *having* one). It would follow that we are in some degree responsible for the kinds of persons we become and the lives we lead. If this interpretation is correct, then Rawls has in effect abandoned the thoroughgoing environmentalist stance that was so prominent in *A Theory of Justice.*[54] Whether Rawls can really afford to do without that stance, that is, how much his egalitarian doctrine as a whole depends upon it, is an interesting question that I will not undertake to explore here.

Rawls's reformulated version also seems calculated to enhance the status of moral personality through its assertion that persons have a "highest-order interest" in realizing and exercising the two powers. In other words, the two powers are not only qualities that we possess but qualities that we have a fundamental interest in *developing*. It is not clear that this new element is entirely compatible with a principle of equal respect for all lifestyles or conceptions of the good. Perhaps Rawls's grass-counting citizen could claim to have a "realized" or sufficiently developed conception of the good. But maybe our highest-order interests would be best served by a social regime that favors some more fully developed conceptions or some plans of life that exercise the basic human capacities a bit more.

There is also a question about the sense of justice. Rawls is now saying that a person has a vital interest in realizing the capacity to "act from" (which must mean on the basis of a commitment to) "the principles of justice." If this were a claim that human beings have such an interest by nature, it is not at all evident why that would be so, unless one is entitled to assume a rather idealistic vision of human nature. Maybe all that is meant by the propostion is that in the optimal (Rawlsian) society persons would have an interest in acting from the principles of justice. Such a conclusion, however, is not without its difficulties; it presupposes that we *can* all be trained or socialized to (as Rawls puts it in his latest book) "understand, apply and to act from the reasonable principles of justice that specify the terms of fair social cooperation,"[55] and to exercise this sense of justice "for its own sake."[56] When has it ever been the case that large numbers of people act substantially on such relatively elevated moral understanding and motivation? Once again, we encounter an apparent effort to derive much from little. Most thoughtful people could agree with Rawls's modest initial premise that humans normally possess a "capacity" for a sense of justice "at least to a certain minimum degree." But it's quite another thing to accept the current Rawlsian conclusion that human nature makes possible whole societies of people who are devoted to the principle of fair social cooperation for its own sake.

That conclusion is contrary to the view of the American Founders that most of us most of the time are going to be motivated by self-interest, even when we are observing norms of justice. Evidently, Rawls expects rather more of ordinary people than did Tocqueville, who urged, as the best that can be expected from our society as a whole, an ethic of "self-interest rightly understood."[57] Rawlsian theory seems to reflect one of two assumptions about our natural dispositions: that they are predominantly benign or that they are almost wholly malleable and hence susceptible to being molded by benign social norms. (Or sometimes the one and sometimes the other?) But Rawls does not undertake a systematic analysis of our natural dispositions (such, for example, as one finds in Hobbes, Rousseau, or Aristotle).

Recently, Rawls has begun to reformulate his doctrine in such a way as to render unnecessary and irrelevant any such analysis of human nature; he has begun to back away from all "metaphysical" understandings of his theory. He now observes that his theory is "intended as a political conception of justice for a democratic society, it tries to draw solely upon basic intuitive ideas that are embedded in the political institutions of a constitutional democratic regime . . . it starts from within a certain political tradition."[58] This is perplexing in more ways than one. What made the original theory interesting was its apparent effort to *justify* democratic ideas and institutions (of a certain kind); it presented itself as political philosophy in the business of determining not merely what we happen to believe in modern Western democracies, but what, for good reasons, we *ought* to believe. Insofar as it is now to be considered a culture-bound doctrine, an interpretation of "our" liberal attitudes, doesn't it lose much of its import? But there is a perplexity more directly relevant to the theme of this chapter. What now is the status of "moral personality"; is this too only an extract from the intuitive ideas, that is to say, the deep-rooted opinions of our democratic society? Rawls seems to say so; "Now the conception of persons as having the two moral powers, and therefore as free and equal, is also a basic intuitive idea assumed to be implicit in the public culture of a democratic society."[59] Is that all it is? If so, then the conception of moral personality does not, after all, represent any claim that human beings actually have the capacity for a rational plan of life and sense of justice, or for that matter any interest therein! It is not about reality, but about a (putatively) prevailing belief system.

Overall, Rawls's reformulated doctrine entails a paradoxical result: "moral personality" is elevated to the status of a paramount human good ("highest-order interest")—and then (so it seems) reduced to the status of a mere assumption of one particular political culture. Insofar as the basic argument now reduces to a claim about the content of our moral consensus, or what principles actually underlie our political tradition, it is, I think, dubious in the same way that Dworkin's doctrine on the same subject is dubious.[60] What is more crucial here, however, is whether Rawlsians can avoid in this manner a reliance on conceptions of human nature and well-being as such. I think not. They must be able to show, at least, that the modern opinion about moral personality from which the theory takes its bearings is not false. Suppose it were the case that what the theory has to say about the sense of justice is at variance with powerful natural dispositions, in other words, that such basic inclinations as humans might have to act "from" a concern for fairness are very weak in comparison with contrary impulses. (Or that Pol Pot's conception of justice is as much in accord with human nature as Rawls's.) And suppose it were the case that the capacity to actualize a rational plan of life needs to be nurtured by a social milieu that actively discourages irrational lifestyles, that is, that does *not* scrupulously "avoid any assessment" of ways of life? Rawlsians owe us much more of a demonstration than they provide that human nature accommodates their ideal of a highly egalitarian and nonjudgmental society. And beyond this consideration, can one really be satisfied with an argument about the right and the good that has as its foundation nothing but the assertion that a certain "we" (modern Americans? Democrats? Liberals?) happen to have certain beliefs or commitments on the subject? That is a tenuous foundation, especially where a concept like moral personality, with its implied idea of human dignity, is at issue.

It is characteristic of the kind of liberal philosophizing represented by Rawls and Dworkin that binding moral principles are advanced in relative abstraction from fundamental considerations of human nature—our perennial inclinations and conflicts, our weaknesses as well as our strengths. More often than not these factors are dealt with simply by stipulation (increasingly so in Rawls) or by the adoption, with scarcely any argument, of an optimistic view. Sometimes they are ignored as irrelevant to moral argument and obligation. Equally distinctive of contemporary egalitarian liberalism is the tendency to rely upon an ideal of human dignity that is severed from ordinary concerns about human character. Almost never in the arguments of Dworkin, and not often in those of Rawls, do the differences between types of character make any significant difference. Or, more precisely, the only difference between better and worse character that is allowed to matter is that between those who do and those who do not conform to the principle of equal respect. This notion of dignity tends to denigrate the ethical importance of the substantive ends or goods for which persons might choose to live. It emphasizes instead an inherent claim to respect that no one has to earn and no one (except perhaps persons violating Rawls's egalitarian norms) can lose. Taken together, these two distinctive features yield a "dignity principle" (as we may call it) that undermines good character by liberating from social restraint attitudes, conduct, and lifestyles inimical to the maintenance of good character and its communal supports.

Recent egalitarian liberalism affirms the primacy of the right over the good, and rights over virtue, on the basis of the rather abstract concepts of personality, dignity, and respect. It is not my intention to maintain that such ideas have no role to play in our moral and political life. What I am trying to show is that, as applied to our civic affairs by their contemporary advocates, they are more ambiguous and less attractive than at first one might think.

III. Classical Liberalism

At the foundation of contemporary liberal political theory one finds either a concept of freedom of choice or of equal dignity (or some effort to combine the two). Despite differences between these orientations, they have in common one politically massive result—personal rights are proliferated and the idea of a publicly supported ethic of decency or moderation is delegitimized. Yet the centrality of rights is hardly an invention of recent theory; it has powerful origins in classical liberalism, most prominently the teaching of John Locke. Accordingly, one might want to say that the old liberalism is scarcely more hospitable to public morality than the new. A brief comparison of the two can serve to show why this isn't quite so, and, in the process, facilitate exploration of the ethical basis of liberalism.

As is generally known, the fundamental Lockean natural right is not exactly a right to choose one's lifestyle or to be respected equally, but a right to self-preservation with which liberty and property are associated. The natural rights to life, liberty, and property are grounded in certain basic natural needs and conditions: the predominance (in almost all of us) of the desire to survive, and the fact that liberty and material possessions are necessary conditions of survival in this world.[61] The need for corresponding civil rights is derived from an additional, and rather harsh, fact of life. Summarizing this consideration in his harshest terms, Locke says that "the pravity of mankind [is] such that they had rather injuriously prey upon the fruits of other men's labours, than take pains to provide for themselves."[62] Hence, we have established civil authority and civil liberties for protection from the consequences of our self-centered, self-aggrandizing natural passions. In his *Thoughts Concerning Education,* Locke says: "I told you before that children love liberty. . . . I now tell you that they love something more, and that is dominion: and this is the first original of most vicious habits that are ordinary and natural. This love of power and dominion shows itself very early."[63] For purposes of education, the conclusion Locke draws is the necessity for substantial, as well as judicious, parental authority to instill habits of self-control.

The Lockean doctrine of individual rights is accompanied by a sober, "realistic" view of human nature, an understanding of our ordinary weaknesses, and the consequent need for restraint or guidance. This cannot be said of the new liberalism, especially in its egalitarian form. Proponents of that outlook, who demand the expansion of personal rights as a categorical imperative of justice, give very little indication that they have grappled with certain unattractively contrary aspects of the human scene. Dworkin, for example, regularly advances new and enlarged rights—claims against the state with almost no attention to facts of life that have a crucial bearing upon how those rights are likely to be employed. The pervasiveness at all times of self-interested strivings and intense conflict among passionately held conceptions of justice are realities addressed by Lockean much more than by Rawlsian thought.[64]

Of course, this fact by itself does not show that Lockean liberalism is more friendly to a public ethic of decency than is contemporary liberalism. What it does indicate is that Locke recognizes the fundamental human problem—the existence of powerful nonbenign natural passions requiring restraint and refinement—to which public morality has been a response. One is not surprised, therefore, to find Locke insisting upon certain "moral rules which are necessary to the preservation of civil society," and which government has an interest in maintaining.[65] The point, made in Locke's *Letter Concerning Toleration,* is designed to illustrate the limits of toleration. But what rules are these? A careful reader of Locke's *Letter* can most plausibly infer that the morality with which he is predominantly concerned is that addressed to the keeping of promises (contracts) and the maintenance of civil peace (desiderata much threatened by religious fanatics who would use political coercion for the establishment of some religious orthodoxy). This leaves open a question whether, in the Lockean perspective, there are any other kinds of moral rules necessary for civil society and that might therefore be eligible for governmental support.

In *Thoughts Concerning Education* Locke does indeed recognize a broader ethic of civility that must be inculcated in the young to promote moral habits conducive to decent social relations and civic responsibility. These admonitions, however, are addressed to the family of the educatee not to the civil lawmaker or magistrate. In particular, they are addressed to an upper stratum of the population, the class of "gentlemen," a presumably enlightened and public spirited class interested in producing ethically respectable offspring.[66] Needless to say "the gentry," as a group with power, has disappeared in modern liberal society, and the family as such has lost a significant share of its influence on the formation of moral character (to other influences such as peer groups and mass media). In view of these factors would Locke countenance any adjustments in his teachings? Could Lockean philosophy acknowledge any role for government and law as moral educators under conditions where the family and other private agencies (like the Church) cannot be relied upon to inculcate sufficiently the standards of civility that society needs? A conclusive answer is hard to come by. What we do know is that Locke acknowledges society's interest in a civilizing morality but assumes that nonpolitical agencies will provide it.

It cannot be said that Lockean liberalism positively favors a public morality. What can be said is that it does not disfavor public morality to the extent that contemporary liberalism does. While both sets of doctrines stress individual liberty, they take rather different views of its grounds and dimensions. The human liberty that is central in Lockean thought is the freedom from any "absolute, arbitrary power," no matter where it may come from—a liberty indispensable to the security of one's life and property. In civil society, that liberty is associated with the rule of law.

> Freedom of men under government is to have a standing rule to live by, common to everyone of that society, and made by the legislative power erected in it; a liberty to follow my own will in all things where the rule prescribes not; and not to be subject to the inconsistent, uncertain, unknown, arbitrary will of another man.[67]

We find here no emphasis upon personal autonomy as such; no glorification of cultural diversity and freedom of choice about lifestyles. This is a soberly political conception; it is to law and the institutions of law that this idea of civil liberty is most closely linked. What matters the most is that a person should not be at the mercy of the unpredictable, arbitrary will of another, as we are in a "state of nature" where there is no impartial law and constituted authority. And so, while it mandates a legal order that will in effect protect one's freedom of choice from a number of restrictions, classical liberalism does not focus, as libertarian theory does, upon the preciousness of individual autonomy per se. It provides little encouragement for those who would single out, and continuously celebrate, the act of choosing as a good in itself or as the foundation of all good and dignity.

Nor does Lockean theory provide much support for a Dworkinian principle of "equal concern and respect" as the fundamental norm of a liberal society. The Lockean conception of equality in a state of nature entails the ideas that no human being is naturally in a position of superiority or subordination to another; authority among us is no natural fact but only a man-made convention. What follows is that political authority exists by the consent of the equals who created (contracted for) it. There is nothing here about the equal dignity of all personal lifestyles. (Indeed, this portion of Lockean teaching points to a principle of majority rule and the contractual obligation of the citizen to abide by the decisions of the majority.)

The point I'm making here is a negative one: classical liberalism does not present such formidable obstacles to public morality as are presented by current autonomistic and egalitarian doctrines. The negative factor, however, is of importance; it provides one key to the explanation of a phenomenon that otherwise might seem quite perplexing—our long history of actions by the liberal state in the sphere of morality, and their accommodation by the judiciary of the liberal state.[68] In all probability, we would not have this history if the current doctrines of freedom and equality had presided over our polity from the beginning.

Yet, the other side of the story must be acknowledged; Lockean liberalism does present some significant obstacles to the maintenance of a public morality. The most direct way to make this point is to cite the definition of a legitimate civil society offered in the *Letter Concerning Toleration.* Locke says:

> The commonwealth seems to me to be a society of men constituted only for the procuring, preserving and advancing their own civil interests . . .
> Civil interests I call life, liberty, health, and indolency of body, and the possession of outward things, such as money, land, houses, furniture and the like.[69]

Locke's ostensible objective in the *Letter* is to distinguish in the sharpest terms the functions of civil government from those of religion. The interests of a civil community are so defined as to preclude absolutely the claim that a legitimate government can have anything to do with the salvation of souls. In language somewhat different from Locke's (though faithful to his intention), we can say that our civil interests are "material" not "spiritual" interests.

This idea constitutes the origin and the foundation of all political liberalism. I mean not only that the separation of church and state is fundamental for liberalism, but that the material ends for which society is thought to exist are fundamental; we do not become members of society for salvation in another life *or* for the improvement of our characters in this one. That is common ground. Contemporary liberals will seek to use government in ways not envisioned in Lockean thought; they will legislate with a view to expanded economic well-being and substantive equality, but in doing so they do not challenge the basic idea that organized society is largely about preservation of life, with economic security, opportunity, and prosperity. These are in essence the Lockean civil interests. Rawls and Dworkin rarely speak in any direct way of the purposes of civil society, and when they do allude to the subject, it is without pointedly materialistic language concerning "money, land, houses, furniture and the like"; they prefer to speak a more elevated language of inviolable principle. Yet much of the equality they advocate is equality in the acquisition or possession of these things. And no more than Locke (indeed less than Locke if my interpretation is valid) will they countenance governmental intervention in support of moral decency or character as such. Modern liberals inherit from Locke a view of the polity in which virtue is definitely subordinated to liberty and property. And they inherit an outlook that cherishes an enlarged private sphere of life—the private pursuit of happiness—as against the public or communal sphere. When contemporary liberalism transcends Locke it takes along with it these premises and commitments.

IV. Liberal Virtues?

Moral character, or the maintenance of an ethic of civility, in the human community has never been a central concern of liberal political thought. Though liberalism needs persons of character and an ethic of decency, other considerations are at its core. Furthermore, where those moral needs are recognized in liberal theory (as they are in Locke and Mill more than in Dworkin and Rawls), the theory almost invariably takes for granted that ample means will be available to satisfy them. Typically, it is assumed far more than it is argued that a sufficient morality will be nurtured. The conclusion seems inescapable that liberalism, in all of its varieties, relies upon virtues or traditions that it does not generate, does little to support, and even tends to undermine.

Yet isn't this an unduly harsh conclusion? Doesn't liberalism itself produce a morality and virtues of its own that are slighted by this analysis? Arguably, an ethic of individual rights is also an ethic of reciprocal obligations. Thomas Paine stated the elementary point as follows: "A Declaration of Rights is, by reciprocity, a declaration of duties also. Whatever is my right as a man is also the right of another; and it becomes my duty to guarantee as well as to possess."[70] Furthermore, insofar as the rule of law is crucial in all or most of its versions, liberalism must generate an ethic of respect for law, that is for general rules impartially applied. And insofar as a liberal society makes its civic decisions by public, deliberative processes, doesn't it tend to foster deliberative habits of mind and a respect for reason?

These worthy qualities are good candidates for consideration as liberal virtues. It's far from my intention to deny that liberal society has any virtues; it surely has some. The critical question, however, is twofold: whether they are adequate for the maintenance of a desirable human community and whether even they aren't undermined by contrary tendencies of liberal thought and practice. Apropos of Tom Paine's point, some reciprocal rights and duties are worthier than others; ethically, what are we to think of a (putative) right to produce and enjoy bestial pornography or hate-filled rock music, which entails the corresponding solemn duty to guarantee that those who like it get to do it? The existence of such a duty would hardly redeem, or render ethical, the exercise of such a right. With regard to the respect for law and for reason that liberalism can be said to promote, it is a questionable proposition that liberalism, by itself and from its own resources, can sustain the type of moral character upon which these worthy qualities depend. To put it simply: the liberal ethic that encourages these qualities often seems weaker than the libertarian permissiveness that undermines them by weakening the social supports for self-restraint and civility.

But let us not dispose of the question so simply. There are some contemporary liberal thinkers who, unsatisfied with the kind of preoccupation with individual rights found in ordinary liberal theory, wish to emphasize virtues and character. Says Stephen Macedo: "Part of the case for liberalism (though perhaps not the most important part) is that it promotes types of character that may be esteemed virtuous and kinds of community that are attractive as communities."[71] Most directly relevant to the theme of this chapter and this book is Macedo's claim that liberalism promotes *moderation*. He observes: "The principled moderation I am defending is a liberal virtue justified by the respect owed to our shared reasonableness and the difficulty of occupying a common moral standpoint, of exercising our common capacity for reasonableness in the same way."[72] The following is, I hope, a tolerably fair brief summary of what Macedo means. A basic liberal principle (if not *the* basic liberal principle— one isn't quite sure) is that respect is owed to all human beings because they are by nature rational creatures. A basic liberal perception of reality, however, is that we exercise our rationality very differently and therefore frequently disagree about moral standards. Agreed-upon moral truth is hard to come by; diversity of viewpoints is a persistent fact of life. From the combination of these two insights, the optimal liberal will draw the conclusion that one should moderate one's claims and demands in the political arena, in accommodation of those who differ with us and who are, after all, rational beings too. This is a step beyond tolerance; it is an expression of respect for the reasonableness of others, as well as the inevitability of ethical diversity.

This is, I believe, an attractive formulation (perhaps the most attractive formulation) of the egalitarian liberal position. The acknowledgment that respectably reasonable people can and often do disagree is an important ingredient of practical wisdom and openness to learning, openness to reflection upon perspectives that one does not (now) hold. And in the political arena this disposition is a vital contributor to that willingness to compromise that is so essential for the viability of pluralistic democratic regimes. To appreciate the importance of this aspect of liberal society, one has only to consider, as a stark alternative, the kind of society that is ruled by zealots; for example, the regime of the Mullahs in Iran or Leninists in Cuba.

This argument, if I've got it right, leans rather heavily on rationality as the essential human quality and the ground of our respectability. It seems to me that the argument works well only insofar as one makes more of, or gives more ethical weight to, the fact of our common possession and use of reason than liberal theory usually does. At any rate, I'm not sure that a very far-reaching demand for equal respect can be established on this basis (or how much Macedo even wishes to stress *equality* of respect in these passages). Plato and Aristotle also understood that "man is the rational animal," the only animal who really needs and seeks knowledge, without ever suggesting that we have this characteristic equally or in equally respectable ways and degrees. And they would never suggest that the respect owed to our shared capacity for reasonableness mandates the accommodation of every "lifestyle" claim that persons or groups could make. Nor do I understand Macedo to be carrying the point necessarily to that (Dworkinian?) extremity. His prime example is that "on policy issues like abortion, which seems to come down to a fairly close call between two well-reasoned sets of arguments, moderation would lead us not only to respect our opponents but to compromise with them, to find some middle ground."[73] Indeed it would, and one can only wish that the moderating principle (liberal or otherwise) were more operative in our politics over abortion. But what about the many cases where there is no such thing as a fairly close call between two well-reasoned sets of arguments? What if one side presents little more than an unreasoned demand to do as we like because we like it? It's hard to say whether Macedo's liberal principle would mandate accommodation of the hard-core pornographer and the drug-taker *or* would allow for their restriction because the taste for these things is subrational. To generalize the point, if Macedo's perspective does recognize significant outer limits to the principle of equal respect, then it is (to its credit) deviating from mainstream contemporary liberal theorizing. If it does not, then it is endorsing a principle that legitimates (and encourages) the claims of the irrational and the immoderate.

It is surely a point worth making that liberal theory may support and liberal society can promote a certain kind of moderation. The problem, as indicated, is whether that fact isn't outweighed by the permissive libertarianism and egalitarianism that is endemic and increasingly prominent in liberal theory and practice. The influences in that direction are several. A heavily rights-oriented liberalism may encourage righteous intransigence rather than moderation and compromise. (On the abortion issue both sides of a badly polarized situation have been marching under the banner of categorical rights.) A strongly autonomistic liberalism is, in practice, more likely to inspire self-centered "individualism" than any real interest in reasonableness or compromise (all the more so when associated with a passion for material goods and enjoyments.)[74] And, insofar as a thoroughgoing doctrine of "equal respect" tends to undermine distinctions of better and worse, reasonable and unreasonable, even respectable and unrespectable, as to valuations and standards of good, it becomes difficult to sustain an ethic of moderation. Liberal politics is in need of people who can engage in thoughtful dialogue and compromise out of respect for human rationality and frailty, but liberal politics, by itself, doesn't produce the kind of human character required to sustain that process in good health. The requisite qualities of self-control and civility are not easily nurtured in a social milieu where what always counts the most is the equal liberty to live as one pleases and the pursuit of material happiness.

Liberal society indeed depends upon the virtue called moderation. But the need is one thing and the (sufficient) development or inculcation is quite another. Defenders of the idea of "liberal virtues" tend to blur this distinction, and that, I think, is the underlying difficulty with their position. Very often an argument that liberal society requires self-controlled citizens is offered as if it were an argument that it actually produces them.[75] The precise theoretical question is whether the ethic that liberalism needs is intrinsic to its theory and practice or is, so to speak, brought in from elsewhere (for example, preliberal philosophy or religion). The

argument I've been making amounts to the answer "Some of the former
but much of the latter." Insofar as what is needed is a countervailing
ethic, one that tempers—or places limits upon—certain egalitarian and
libertarian tendencies, this function is not adequately provided by liberalism itself. In neither the philosophy nor the institutions and ethos of
liberalism is there a sustained focus upon the subject of good character.
Locke and Hayek apparently recognize a need for some countervailing
ethos, but they hardly make any substantial provision for it. Rawlsian
doctrine, for the most part, neglects (or denigrates) the subject. More
often than not the traditional liberal theory takes for granted, while the
more radical liberal theory assaults, the moral preconditions of good
character or moderation. And if the institutions of our democratic society
are doing a little better in this regard than contemporary theory does,
that is largely because certain nonliberal aspects of tradition still survive
to support what remains of the liberal virtues.[76]

V. Liberal Personality

I have reserved for the last what is perhaps the most difficult dimension
of the subject. As is often noted, liberal society—with its pluralism, its
experimental, if not skeptical, attitude toward established norms, and
its openness to change—tends to generate a pluralistic, experimental,
changeable type of human personality. Is this largely a good thing or a
problematic thing? Arguably, it is a very problematic thing; pluralistic and
changeable personalities are divided and ephemeral personalities, achieving
neither inner harmony nor lasting devotion to any end or cause. But,
arguably, the liberal personality is a good thing; it is open to a variety of
ideas, hence it is thoughtful and capable of self-improvement.

The liberal case on this topic is stated most pointedly by Macedo.

> The inner experience of value conflict encourages a degree of tentativeness
> in our commitment to any set of values, and this provides room for
> reflection, self-criticism, toleration, moderation and an openness to reevalu-
> ation and change. . . . The internalization of diversity and conflict allows
> the reflective self to maintain some distance from any single end or the
> values of any particular community with which we happen to identify.[77]

Two large questions arise here: one about internal conflict and the other
about moral tentativeness or "distance" from one's values and ends. These

are psychological questions in the broadest sense, questions about what we used to call the good (and bad) condition of the soul.

As indicated in the previous chapter, the harmony or wholeness of the psyche has long been regarded as a vital condition of its well-being. In Plato's *Republic* "faction in the soul" is treated as a serious evil, and to create out of the "many" in the soul a unity is regarded as the central task of a human life.[78] This perspective is hardly confined to classical philosophy; unresolved conflict in the psyche is viewed as a source of human suffering and failure in Freudian and neo-Freudian psychology and in numerous other outlooks on personality. To be sure, neither Plato nor Freud taught that internal conflict can be totally eradicated; they taught that most of us will have to put up with a fair amount of it. But they regarded its reduction, and an approximation to coherence in aspiration, belief, or purpose, as a large part of what success in living means. Indeed, isn't that view amply supported by ordinary experience? We do not wish to be divided against ourselves. One wishes to have an "identity." A real victim of the "internalization of diversity and conflict"— one in whom truly diverse elements are roughly equal in strength—would most likely fail to achieve any coherent aspirations and would, strictly speaking, lack identity or integrity. No doubt this is not what Macedo and other "internal pluralists" have in mind. Perhaps their point is only that *some* degree of diversity in the soul is a prerequisite for any self-critical and creative thinking. That is a valid and interesting point, but the pluralists should acknowledge that there is a problem to be wrestled with here or a price to be paid (maybe substantial) for the good they envision.

A similar point can be made about the moral tentativeness that is celebrated as a virtue of the liberal personality. Arguably, in order to remain free to reflect upon and revise one's values, commitments, and qualities of character, one has to regard them as provisional in some degree. That is, as a thinking being I cannot afford to be wholly consumed or identified with whatever purposes or attachments I have now, however deeply felt they may be. I must maintain a "distance" even from characteristics that provide my sense of identity. Otherwise, how could I reflect critically upon them?

There are some perplexities here. Who or what is the "I" that somehow stands apart from my whole character? But the philosophic and psychological perplexity aside, there is an ethical problem about the kind of "value commitments" one has when all of one's standards of value are really viewed as provisional. Can one be a morally serious person if even the most basic ethical principles are to be treated as contingent, as susceptible to change and possible obsolescence in an ever-changing world? (Is one supposed to view experimentally such principles as the equal civil rights of citizens, the wrongness of punishing the innocent, the importance of keeping promises, the superiority of loving to sadistic sexuality?) It's hard to see how a thoroughly provisional attitude toward norms and values—a stance of perpetual readiness to change or abandon them—is compatible with moral commitment at all.

Some communitarian critics see at the foundation of the liberal outlook an unattractive conception of the "unencumbered self," an empty self distanced from all substantive ends and belonging to no community.[79] While this self might opt for allegiance to social norms or associations, it cannot be "constituted" by them, its relation to all possible objects of devotion is wholly instrumental or improvisational. Hence, according to these critics, the crucial defect of liberal personality is that it precludes any real belonging of the individual to a community—a belonging whereby the individual would be in some sense *defined* by his or her communal participation or identification. This kind of indictment can be very far-reaching, encompassing not only contemporary liberal thought but classical liberalism as well. "Every man has a property in his own person," says Locke;[80] you belong to yourself first and foremost—and that proposition is at the bottom of all liberalism.

It is safe to say that most Americans will not be persuaded that they ought to become members of the community in the strong or comprehensive sense, with identities "constituted" by such membership. (Most of us want *some* independence from family and church, even when we cherish these institutions.) But the fact that the liberal personality is here to stay doesn't mean that we must pay unqualified homage to it as an unmixed blessing. Even Macedo must acknowledge that the changeable, improvisational liberal personality might well lack depth and that contemporary liberalism promises, or threatens, to make "all the world like California"—a smorgasbord for consumers of lifestyles.[81] Yet Macedo (along with others of this school of thought) seem to regard the prospect of superficiality as a relatively minor disadvantage, clearly outweighed by the "incitement to self-examination" that the dynamic, pluralistic libertarian scene presumably fosters. But it's far from clear how much actual self-examination, how much serious thought, is inspired by a smorgasbord or supermarket of changeable values. We do not expect, and we rarely get, deep thought from superficial personalities or social milieus that promote only ephemeral valuations and attachments.

Yet the liberal view of personality does, I believe, reveal a truth about the human condition. That is the idea, implicit in Western philosophy since its inception, that rationality has a transcendent capacity. We are able to have or acquire some "distance" from ourselves because reason is an active power that transcends, or is capable in some degree of rising above, its genesis in particular environments. If that were not so, then we would be wholly unable to think beyond the conditions—personal or social—from which we have come; the mind, as a mere passive receptacle of those conditions, would be incapable of critical reflection upon them (as some versions of postmodernism suggest). And the injunction to lead an examined life would be meaningless. Liberalism, at its best, believes that an examined life is both possible and desirable, that we need not be and should not be entirely subordinated to the communities and families that have produced us. At this level of the inquiry, the liberals have a valid point, against at least the more pronounced forms of communitarianism.

On the other side of the issue are the following qualifying considerations. Thoughtfulness almost always requires some communal nurturing, and is often stimulated by the presence of norms (civic, moral, religious) that the community takes seriously. In cultural milieus where little is taken seriously (except a contentless "self"), because all is perceived to be in flux, apathy and self-indulgence are more likely results than persistent reflection about what is good or true. Further, as is usually recognized in traditional Western thought on this subject, human beings do not possess equally the ability to lead a fully examined life; great differences exist in our capacities for critical detachment from prevailing norms or opinions—and in the degree of importance we are willing and able to attribute to learning as a goal of life. Very few of us are so Socratic as to be able to live almost wholly for the sake of understanding and who can do so autonomously—in utter independence of what the community believes and expects. In other words, the development of critical reflection is not the only desideratum of a good life or even the most urgent of the human wants that society must try to satisfy. Almost all of us have urgent need of communal bonds and affections, and these depend upon established social beliefs, norms, and commitments. We also need arrangements that sufficiently nurture good character.

We do not owe those communal norms and character-nurturing arrangements that I've been calling public morality primarily to liberalism.

It is hard to maintain that they are imperatives of liberal theory. Historically, they have been accommodated, to an extent, by our liberal institutions—because we have wanted not only a lot of free choice but choice within a framework of decent social relations and moral attitudes. Finally, if, as I am convinced, what we really want is not just a "free society" but also a worthy community, then we must recognize that more is needed than liberalism.

NOTES

1. For a detailed and favorable account of this tendency, see Lawrence M. Friedman, *The Republic of Choice*. For a less-than-favorable account, see Daniel Bell, *The Cultural Contradictions of Capitalism* (New York: Basic Books, 1976).

2. "Legal Paternalism," in *Rights, Justice and the Bounds of Liberty*, p. 116. For an example of a more comprehensive application of the principle of autonomy, see T. M. Scanlon, "A Theory of Freedom of Expression," *Philosophy and Public Affairs* 204 (1977).

3. Fred R. Berger, "Pornography, Sex and Censorship," *Social Theory and Practice*, 4, no. 2 (1977): p. 99. Italics in the original.

4. Some proponents of this "dignity" concept might say that I have misconceived the main point, which is that every adult person has, on account of the dignity of personhood, an inviolable *right* to make such lifestyle choices. Insofar as that is the claim, the argument and its implications are best explored in connection with egalitarian liberalism and the conception of dignity or respect underlying it.

5. *On Liberty*, p. 71.

6. *Areopagitica and Of Education* (New York: Appleton-Century-Crofts, 1951), p. 18.

7. Ibid., p. 25.

8. The immediate target of *Areopagitica* was a comprehensive system of licensing, or as we call it now, prior restraint, for all books and pamphlets.

9. *Utilitarianism, On Liberty and Representative Government*, pp. 7-10.

10. See the discussion of Sartre in the previous chapter. As an indication that his case against censorship has outer limits, Milton said: "That also which is impious or evil absolutely no law can permit that intends not to unlaw itself" (*Areopagitica*, p. 52).

11. Speaking of the inevitability of "dogmatic beliefs," de Tocqueville said: "For society to exist and, even more, for society to prosper, it is essential that all the minds of the citizens should be rallied and held together by some leading ideas, and that could never happen unless each of them sometimes came to draw

his own opinions from the same source and was ready to accept some beliefs already made" (*Democracy in America,* vol. 2, first book, ch. 2, p. 9).

12. *On Liberty,* p. 71.

13. Ibid., p. 82.

14. Ibid., p. 69.

15. Ibid., p. 79.

16. Ibid., p. 76.

17. Elsewhere I have maintained that the doctrine of Mill's *Utilitarianism* would condemn de Sade's way of life and all low hedonism. Yet it's much harder to find grounds for such a judgment in the doctrine of *On Liberty.* In other words, there is a disparity of some magnitude between the two doctrines. See Harry M. Clor, "Mill and Millians on Liberty and Morality," *The Review of Politics,* 47, no. 1 (January 1985), pp. 10–12.

18. For an example of Nietzsche's way of making this point, see *Beyond Good and Evil* in *The Philosophy of Nietzsche* (New York: Random House, 1966), pp. 476–78.

19. Aristotle, in whose definition of a virtuous life the act of choosing is vital, also acknowledged a crucial role for habituation. See *Ethics,* book 2. Apparently Aristotle's theory is able to accommodate both choice and habituation because it does not magnify the status of the former as Mill and Millians do. Aristotle would surely disagree with Stephen Macedo's blanket observation that "the capacity to choose is more basic than what is chosen" (*Liberal Virtues,* p. 239). Yet, I'm not sure that Aristotelianism fully provides the systematic theory of personality that is needed.

20. F. A. Hayek, *The Constitution of Liberty* (Chicago: Henry Regnery Co., 1960), pp. 30–31.

21. Ibid., p. 36.

22. Ibid., ch. 9.

23. Ibid., p. 61.

24. Ibid., p. 62.

25. Ibid., p. 63.

26. Hayek is renowned as a defender of free-market individualism and property rights against egalitarian welfare state redistributionism. So is Robert Nozick. It's most interesting to compare the two rationales. Hayek's rationale is "utilitarian" in that it justifies individual liberty (primarily) with a view to its consequences for the social welfare. Nozick's rationale rests upon the (putatively) inviolable claim of every individual to be treated as a separate, independent being, and hence not to be used as a means to satisfy the needs of others. This argument seeks scrupulously to avoid reliance upon consequentialist considerations such as contingent judgments about the social welfare. Indeed, Nozick goes very far toward the denial that there is any such thing as "an overall social good." See Robert Nozick, *Anarchy, State and Utopia* (New York: Basic Books, 1974), pp.

32–33. To put it simply, Hayek's type of argument is concerned with the sum total of human satisfactions, while Nozick's is concerned with categorical individual rights. Do these two "conservative" individualistic orientations bear at all differently upon public morality? I suspect that they do somewhat but will not pursue the question here.

27. Dewey, *Living Thoughts of Thomas Jefferson*, p. 88.

28. Summarizing Jefferson's view of the pursuit of happiness, Ursula von Eckardt says: "Because happiness is not a minimum condition of existence but the maximum human achievement, and because, moreover, virtue is essential to it, the pursuit of happiness is a social rather than a solitary activity. . . . Government must not only secure for all men the condition of existence and freedom they were able to enjoy prior to its institution; it must establish and further all those conditions that make for the highest possible fulfillment of human excellence. Above all, the task of government is to encourage virtue, because without virtue there is no excellence or happiness" (Ursula M. von Eckardt, *The Pursuit of Happiness in the Democratic Creed* [New York: Frederick A. Praeger, 1959], p. 120). No doubt this exaggerates the point; the liberal Jefferson could not have thought, like Aristotle, that the function of government, "above all" is to promote virtue. But von Eckardt correctly calls attention to a linkage in Jeffersonian thought between happiness and virtue of a certain kind. And that is one crucial difference between Jefferson and the contemporary egalitarians I will discuss.

29. *Taking Rights Seriously*, pp. 272–73.

30. Ibid., pp. 198–201. The specific referent of Dworkin's argument here is the kind of expression characteristic of radical dissenters in the 1960s, and legal efforts to restrain it.

31. If evidence is needed, a fair sampling can be found in Jerry Rubin's *Do It!* (New York: Simon and Schuster, 1970).

32. *Taking Rights Seriously*, p. 201.

33. Ibid., p. 269.

34. For Rawls's initial presentation of the distinction see *A Theory of Justice*, pp. 24–25, 30–32.

35. John Finnis, *Natural Law and Natural Rights*, p. 222.

36. *A Matter of Principle*, p. 353.

37. Ibid., p. 354.

38. *Taking Rights Seriously*, pp. 272–73.

39. *A Matter of Principle*, pp. 262–64.

40. *Taking Rights Seriously*, pp 272–73.

41. Americans in large numbers obviously disagree with the Dworkinian (and Rawlsian) proposition that "those who have less talent, as the [economic] market judges talent, have a *right* to some form of redistribution in the name of justice" (*A Matter of Principle*, p. 199). Emphasis mine.

42. See the chapter "Liberalism" in *A Matter of Principle*.

43. *Taking Rights Seriously*, p. 176. Italics in the original.

44. Ibid., p. 181. Dworkin is quoting Rawls.

45. Chapter 77, "The Basis of Equality," p. 505. Rawls has subsequently elaborated this idea and revised some of the related notions I discuss in the following pages. The elaborations and revisions will be noted, but it's quite important to begin with Rawls's (very influential) original ideas.

46. *A Theory of Justice*, p. 510.

47. Ibid., p. 432.

48. Ibid., p. 509.

49. Ibid., p. 506.

50. Ibid., p. 442.

51. Ibid., p. 104.

52. This is an appropriate point in the analysis to note that Rawlsian "moral personality" can be seen as a revised version of the Kantian idea of human dignity. In Kant's thought, dignity attaches to rational beings as autonomous authors of the moral law to which they subject themselves. On this basis every human being has the right to be treated as an end and never merely as a means (and the duty so to treat himself). This conception of dignity necessarily presupposes freedom of the will and moral responsibility for one's conduct. It also makes very heavy demands upon the individual as moral agent. Kant appears to attribute dignity to all human beings simply on account of their *capacity* to be moral legislators, but he does not (as far as I can tell) emphasize equal dignity whether or not the capacity is actualized. Although philosophizing in the Kantian tradition, Rawls affirms a more far-reaching egalitarianism than Kant does. See Immanuel Kant, "Foundations of the Metaphysics of Morals" (New York: Liberal Arts Press, 1949).

53. "Kantian Constructivism in Moral Theory," *Journal of Philosophy* 77 (September, 1980), pp. 515–72, at p. 525.

54. The subject is very much a matter of interpretation, since Rawls's abandonment of the stance is tacit rather than explicit. On this point my interpretation is in accord with William Galston's in *Liberal Purposes*, p. 124.

55. *Political Liberalism* (New York: Columbia Univ. Press, 1993), pp. 103–4.

56. Ibid., p. 320.

57. *Democracy in America*, vol. 2, second book, Ch. 8.

58. John Rawls, "Justice As Fairness: Political Not Metaphysical," *Philosophy and Public Affairs* (Summer 1985), pp. 223–51, at p. 225.

59. Ibid., p. 234.

60. Refer to my discussion of Ronald Dworkin earlier in this chapter.

61. The simplest source of these ideas is Locke's *Second Treatise of Government*.

62. *A Letter Concerning Toleration* (New York: The Liberal Arts Press, 1950), p. 47.

63. *John Locke on Education*, p. 76.

64. Some versions of the *libertarian* perspective are in a position to give these realities more attention—insofar as their arguments are consequentialist or concerned with the facts of human development. Mill confronts the less-attractive features of human nature more than most contemporary libertarians (not to mention egalitarians) do. But he does so in *Utilitarianism* rather than in *On Liberty*. Finally though, it's hard to disagree with Mill's first great critic, James Fitzjames Stephens, in saying: "The great defect of Mr. Mill's later writings seems to me to be that he has formed too favorable an estimate of human nature" (*Liberty, Equality, Fraternity* [Cambridge: Cambridge Univ. Press, 1967], p. 81).

65. *A Letter Concerning Toleration,* p. 50.

66. See Locke's epistle dedicatory to *Some Thoughts Concerning Education,* and Robert H. Horwitz, "John Locke and the Preservation of Liberty: A Perennial Problem of Civic Education," in *Moral Foundations of the American Republic.*

67. *Second Treatise of Government,* p. 15.

68. This is a question I raised and left somewhat open in chapter 1.

69. *Letter Concerning Toleration,* p. 17.

70. Thomas Paine, *The Rights of Man, Reflections on the Revolution in France and the Rights of Man,* p. 353.

71. *Liberal Virtues,* p. 213. In the following pages, I focus on Macedo's ideas because they formulate the position in an unusually clear and forceful way.

72. Ibid., p. 72.

73. Ibid.

74. See Robert Bellah et al., *Habits of the Heart.*

75. William Galston, who, along with Macedo, presents the most thoughtful exposition of this outlook, seems aware of the problem. "The liberal virtues," he says, "are traits of character liberalism needs, not necessarily the ones it has." But he goes on to say, "Yet these virtues need not be imported from the outside, for they are imminent in liberal practices and theory" (*Liberal Purposes,* p. 217). I cannot quite see in Galston's argument how they are "imminent," except as needs or prerequisites (i.e., the need for a healthy family and the ethic of fidelity [p. 222]).

76. I commend to the reader's attention James Q. Wilson's recent book *The Moral Sense* (New York: Free Press, 1993), which became available after this chapter was written. Wilson suggests that, of the four virtues he discusses, "communalistic" societies tend to promote duty and self-control, while "individualistic" societies tend to promote sympathy and fairness—slighting duty and self-control (Ibid., pp. 154-55). As far as I can tell, Wilson's analysis is generally supportive of mine though differs from it in some important ways.

77. *Liberal Virtues,* p. 236.

78. *The Republic of Plato,* pp. 123, 271–72.

79. See Michael J. Sandel, *Liberalism and the Limits of Justice* (Cambridge: Cambridge Univ. Press, 1982). Also see Bellah et al., *Habits of the Heart*, ch. 3, "Finding Oneself."

80. *Second Treatise of Government*, p. 70.

81. Lawrence Friedman says the same thing. In the current "republic of choice," he notes, many people aim "to go through life like shoppers in some cosmic department store. . . . The metaphor applies . . . even to choices in such crucial and personal matters as sex, religion and mode of life." (*The Republic of Choice*, p. 192.) One might think that Friedman should be bothered by this prospect, but, if he is, he hardly shows it.

5

Pornography: Feminism, Sexuality, and Freedom of Expression

Some years ago I had the opportunity to lead a seminar discussion in an academic institution with persons who had just seen the feminist antipornography film *Not a Love Story*. The film depicts things that go on in pornographic motion pictures, peep shows, pictorial magazines, and the like. The following is a reconstructed version of that portion of our discussion most memorable to me because it highlights a critical issue that is not often clearly confronted.

CLOR: If you think there is something morally wrong with the scenes this movie depicts, what exactly is it? What, in other words, is most fundamentally the matter with pornography?"

DISCUSSANT A: "It's the blatant and obnoxious depreciation of women; we're treated like pieces of meat and dominated as though we were chattel! What's wrong here is the glorification of gross inequality."

DISCUSSANT B: "That's true; women are depreciated in these performances. But something else is depreciated too; I was disgusted at this way of portraying a human relationship that is supposed to be precious or loving."

CLOR: "One of you seems to be primarily concerned with equality and the other with love. Tell us, "A," if such detailed close-ups of sexual acts and responses could be presented without any elements of domination and inferiority, would you criticize them?"

DISCUSSANT A: "If no one is being treated as an inferior, there's no reason to object to any portrayal of sexual encounters."

DISCUSSANT B: "I can't quite go along with that. The scenes you refer to might be less objectionable, but they would still be degrading something of great value.

DISCUSSANT C: "You are both engaged in puritanical moralism. I can't see how this stuff really does any harm—certainly not nearly as much as censorship. If you dislike explicit sexual materials you are free to avoid them. Others find them enjoyable. And they could even be useful in helping to liberate people from oppressive taboos and inhibitions about sexuality."

All of these people had something to say. But if this chapter were to be dedicated to anyone, it would be dedicated to discussant B—a young woman who, in the existing academic milieu, had to defend almost alone an important idea.

Of course the scenario just sketched is not an account of the way the three-cornered debate over pornography has developed historically. In the beginning there was the conflict between traditional moralists and libertarians. The former maintained that large-scale proliferation of obscene literature, films, public performances, and advertising debases the cultural environment and threatens indispensable communal values or standards of civilized living. And, the argument continued, society is entitled to use its law, in accordance with the wishes of a sizable majority, to protect its cherished norms from this corruption. Libertarians replied with a variety of arguments: That "obscenity" is harmless entertainment; that it is indefinable (being "in the eye of the beholder"); that the law has no business enforcing mere moral opinions, and, above all, that freedom of expression—guaranteed by the First Amendment—is what truly matters. The sexual liberationist would weigh in with the claim that the opposition to obscenity or pornography represents a reactionary resistance to the enlightened sexual revolution—on behalf of obsolete, repressive, Victorian views of sexuality.

In recent decades the entry of a new contestant into the arena has heated up the conflict still more. A substantial feminist critique of pornography has emerged to take issue with both of the historic positions. On this view the real theme of pornography is not sexuality but hostility and power: the hostility of men toward and lust for power over women. The feminist is inclined to indict the traditional moralist as a puritanical conservative who seeks to control pornography for the wrong reasons. On the other hand, she castigates the libertarians for gross insensitivity to the damage pornography does to women and for representing the interests of a dominant male establishment. The charge of patriarchalism is also brought against the moralist. But there are practical complications. Regarding questions of personal sexual liberty, these feminists are generally found on the libertarian side. Yet they have, from time to time, joined forces with conservatives in political assaults on pornography, despite their sharp disagreement, if not disdain, for what they take to be the suppositions of any antipornography position alternative to theirs.

The reader won't be surprised to find that I am going to take the side of the traditional moral perspective on pornography (or at least a certain version thereof) as against the other two perspectives. But I'm not undertaking, in this concluding chapter, to do the whole job or to say everything that would be necessary to make a complete case; I want to emphasize the issues most closely related to the broad themes of this book. In the overviews of the pornography debate that I've just provided, one can discern three basic themes. First, there is an issue of ethical judgment; that is, the moral orientation from which pornography is to be judged. Second, there are issues concerning the nature of human sexuality and sexual well-being. Third, of course, the pornography debate involves controversy about freedom of speech and hence the application of the First Amendment. The following sections are organized so as to focus on these themes, more or less in that order. We begin with the disparity between the moralist and feminist outlooks, especially as to the nature of the pornographic and the ethical assessment of it. Then we consider the libertarian viewpoints, with an emphasis upon their conceptions of sexuality. The last section focuses on the relevant legal and constitutional issues.

I. Traditional Moralists and Feminist Moralists

Of course there are differences to be found within each of these two camps of traditional and feminist moralists; neither perspective is simply monolithic. Yet each one has its distinctive theme that is not hard to discern. The quickest way I know of to illustrate the two themes is by means of two quotations. The first is from a rather prominent essay against pornography by political science professor Walter Berns. Says Berns:

> Until recently propriety required the use of the verb "to make love," and this delicacy was not without purpose. It was meant to remind us . . . that, whereas human copulation can be indistinguishable from animal copulation generally, it ought to be marked by the presence of a passion of which other animals are incapable.[1]

The idea implicit here is that the pornographic (and related vulgarity) obliterates the distinction between human and subhuman sexuality—and that essentially is what's wrong with it. This, in one form or another, is a pervasive element in the traditional indictment of pornography. Quite a different indictment is advanced by Catherine MacKinnon, law professor and coauthor of feminist antipornography legislation. Says MacKinnon:

> What pornography *does* goes beyond its content: it eroticizes hierarchy, it sexualizes inequality. It makes domination and submission sex. Inequality is its central dynamic. . . . It institutionalizes the sexuality of male supremacy.[2]

There is nothing in the MacKinnon outlook about "propriety" in the conduct or representation of sexual relations. And there is nothing explicitly in Berns's argument about equality and inequality. The morality informing this kind of argument looks much like what I've been calling an "ethic of decency." And the morality pervading the feminist case (whatever else might be involved in the case) is an emphatic "ethic of equality." When formulated pointedly, the disparity between these two prominent antipornography positions seems wholly intractable.[3]

The Supreme Court has articulated its criteria for the identification of censurable pornography in terms that accommodate somewhat the traditional moral concern. The state may prohibit explicit portrayals of sexual activity when the following three conditions are met:

(1) That the work as a whole "appeals to prurient interest" (i.e., its dominant effect is simply to arouse lust); (2) that it depicts sexual conduct in a manner "patently offensive" in view of contemporary community standards; and (3) that "the work, taken as a whole, lacks serious literary, artistic, political or scientific value."[4] These three criteria are meant to protect from censorship anything that can reasonably be thought to qualify as serious literature or an exchange of ideas about public affairs. Yet the first two criteria may also function to identify what is regarded as objectionable in pornographic representation—the arousal of lust for its own sake and in such a manner as to violate flagrantly the community's beliefs about decency and indecency in the treatment of sexual relations. It is a compromise.

Feminist writers are uniformly hostile to these concepts. Says Susan Brownmiller: "The feminist objection to pornography is not based on prurience. . . . We are not opposed to sex and desire . . . and we certainly believe that explicit sexual material has its place in literature, art, science and education. Here we part company rather swiftly with old-line conservatives."[5] Feminist writers are bent upon distancing themselves from the "conservative" justification for restriction of pornography, which they are inclined to dismiss as nothing more than a reactionary, antisexual moralism. Hence, feminists have drafted their own antipornography statute, a version of which was enacted by the Indianapolis city council in 1984.

The statute, presented as a civil rights law, declared "pornography" to be a "discriminatory practice" based on sex that denies women equal opportunities in society. Pornography was defined as "the graphic sexually explicit subordination of women, whether in pictures or words," which, for example, portrays women "as sexual objects for domination, conquest, violation, exploitation, possession or use."[6] The Federal courts struck down this statute as an effort to establish an officially approved and disapproved view of women, contrary to the First Amendment principle that government may not "ordain preferred viewpoints."[7] In essence what happened in this case is that the Court accepted the feminist understanding of pornography as antifemale propaganda, and they replied in effect that propaganda (be it fascist, communist, racist, or sexist) is protected speech.

Whatever one might think of that proposition, and of the First Amendment considerations as such, one should face the moral and intellectual challenge presented by the feminist position. For one thing, if that position is thought to be sound, then other versions of their statute could be devised that might pass constitutional muster. Such is apparently the objective of Professor Cass Sunstein in his arguments that "the antipornography approach," which focuses on the concerns of women, is superior to the antiobscenity approach because the former addresses actual injuries—"concrete, real-world harms."[8] For now, however, I want to concentrate on the questions of definition and evaluation as they bear upon our public ethos (if not our public law). Would we do well as a society to abandon the older understanding rooted in ideas of propriety or decency in favor of the recent understanding rooted in ideas of equal rights or antidiscrimination? Since much current pornography does in fact portray women in an abusive manner, why not accept the feminist view of what pornography really is and means? Why not settle for the definition offered by philosophy professor Helen Longino: "explicit representations of sexual behavior" whose distinguishing characteristic is "the degrading and demeaning portrayal of the role and status of the human female ... as a mere sexual object to be exploited and manipulated sexually"?[9] Sexual representations that fall short of this definition in any way would not then be considered pornography and presumably would not be appropriately subject to moral censure, no matter how graphically "prurient" they might be.

Among the considerations weighing against that orientation, I wish to stress the desideratum of *ethical clarity*. Moral confusion is no small thing at any time but especially in our time. Our inquiry will need some concrete illustration and points of reference. Several years ago I did a kind of content analysis of a typical general circulation magazine called *Swank*, which was by no means the extreme case among the numerous sex publications generally available. The issue of *Swank* that I have specifically in mind is somewhat less crudely salacious than *Hustler* magazine and somewhat more so than *Playboy* or *Penthouse*. There is no overt violence or sadism in its major pictorials and stories, and none of the most extreme aberrations, such as incest or sex between human beings and animals, is featured. The "intermediate" character of this publication, and the probability that readers will be aware of the type, are the reasons I have chosen it. In what follows there is a bit of self-censorship.

To peruse the contents of the magazine is, in some sense, like entering a world unto itself; one gets an introduction to the world of pornography. First of all, we encounter a number of what the trade calls "spreader" or "beaver" pictorials: close-up shots of nude women with their legs spread wide apart and sexual organs prominently displayed. A series of page-size photographs portrays a man and woman, both completely naked, simulating intercourse, in some scenes oral sex is simulated by both partners. (In the caption the woman is saying "Gimme D . . ., you F . . . machine!) One set of pictures depicts group sex. In still greater detail, a short story depicts the multifarious orgies of a sex club; nothing in the physical act of intercourse is left undescribed. The women in the story are represented as fully voluntary participants, and the only character subjected to evident humiliation is the arrogant male president of the club. The magazine contains over ten pages of advertisements for (apparently) hard-core publications, films, videocassettes, and telephone sex. A few of these promise sadomasochistic experiences ("ask to be Mistress Maria's special sex slave"; Mistress Maria has a whip and leather boots), and a couple of them purport to be featuring rather young girls.

How should we characterize the world depicted in *Swank*? (The phrase "explicit sexual materials" seems comically antiseptic and quite inadequate.) I believe most people would agree with the following tripartite characterization. First, this is an arena of wholly loveless, affectionless sex.

The sexuality it portrays and invites is thoroughly depersonalized; the passion it appeals to is the desire for the possession of someone's body without any interest in the personality to which, in ordinary life, a body belongs. Strictly speaking, this is what is meant by "lust," isn't it? Second, there is an invasion of privacy; physical intimacies and reactions normally protected from public observation are placed conspicuously on display. This "invasion," this aggressive intrusion upon the intimately private, is by no means incidental to *Swank*'s pornographic intent and effect; it is an integral element in the experience that *Swank* is designed to give us, and it is one of the features that make the magazine recognizable as pornography. Third, the magazine presents a pervasive "objectification" of the erotic experience and the female in particular. The erotic activity is reduced, in graphic detail, to its physical components, and the participants are viewed as instruments for the production of pleasurable sensations.

Now, if our judgment of *Swank* were to be governed rigorously by Longino's definition, we could find pornographic only the last of its three basic attributes. So to speak, the magazine would be found innocent on the first two counts and guilty on the third. Indeed, the third attribute would be pornographic only with regard to its portrayal of women. I am far from suggesting that this factor is unimportant; the blatant reduction of a woman to her bodily parts for the entertainment of a leering audience is morally objectionable. My initial point here is that the degradation of women is not all that is happening in this magazine and in pornography in general.

It is observable that men do not altogether escape treatment as mere sex objects in the pages of *Swank*. (Who exactly is the most demeaned by the caption "Gimme D . . . you F . . . machine"?) And the sadomasochistic advertisements offer the male reader materials featuring dominant women who will punish and torture him. Must we classify these materials as nonpornographic? Or, in order to classify them as pornographic must we accept a psychodynamic interpretation that says the dominating woman really (symbolically) represents a male and the dominated male a female? The fact is that in the manifest contents of *Swank* and its ilk *everyone* treated as an object of sexual exploitation and little else.

Of course, given the character of the audience for these publications, women are usually getting the worst of it. But it's important to see that the treatment of women in pornography is an aspect of the pornographic treatment of the erotic life and human beings as such. The purpose—to arouse an elemental passion for other people's bodies independently of any affection or regard for a particular person—virtually guarantees that human beings will be represented as instruments. And the intention to violate, maximally, those conventional proprieties or delicacies that guard the privacy of the erotic act leads to the graphic focus upon bodily functions, parts, and reactions. Pornography caters to the craving for sexual excitation per se and to the voyeuristic interest in viewing people's intimacies. The inevitable consequence of catering to these two inclinations is the phenomenon we are calling objectification: a heavy emphasis on the observable externals, hence the animal and mechanical dimensions, of sexuality, and the depiction of its subjects as *things* to be used for the gratification of the user. These factors—lust, voyeuristic intrusion on the intimate, and objectification characterize productions deserving to be called pornographic. Considered together (as they should be) *these are the prurient interests.*

Ethically speaking, and most briefly, what is wrong with all this is that it dehumanizes in an area of great human importance and some sensitivity. The feminist indictment of pornography grasps a part of this reality and ignores the rest of it. To put it differently, the feminist effort to draw the moral line where they want to draw it results in two sorts of ambiguities—those arising when one seeks to condemn pornography for its mistreatment of women only, and those arising when one seeks to condemn "objectification" while exonerating (in some cases celebrating) pruriently explicit depictions of sex in literature and the arts. As it turns out upon analysis, both ambiguities are related to the disposition of contemporary feminism to see the whole subject as a problem of equality and inequality.

The first difficulty is the easiest to illustrate; to an extent I have already done so. If the point needs more illustration, consider the following short story featured in an old issue of *Hustler* magazine. A syndicate hit man is having intercourse with the woman he has been contracted to kill, while ruminating upon her impending death. His impassioned lover, however, turns out to be a hit woman who triumphantly shoots him three times in the face. The events, both sexual and bloody, are depicted in the usual detail. What judgment are we to make of this story? By Longino's formal definition it isn't even pornography. Nor does it seem to be indictable under the Indianapolis ordinance, since it doesn't portray the subordination of women. One could try to fit it under the terms of the ordinance by claiming that the hit man is really a surrogate woman and vice versa, but that would be unconvincing in this case. And anyway, is that the point one would really want to make? Now some feminists might wish to amend their standard definition of pornography to make it accord with a general principle of equality censuring the denigration of *any* group or gender as inferior. In fact, feminist writings periodically suggest such a definition (inconsistently perhaps). The trouble is, however, that the story under consideration doesn't denigrate or label as inferior any group or gender; *Hustler*'s readers are hardly meant to conclude that men are inferior. If the story is morally blamable, it cannot be on account of any *inequalities* in it but on account of its gross *indecency*. The essential indecency consists in the violation of the act of love by turning it, most strikingly and destructively, into its opposite, thereby depreciating our humanity in a sphere of life that is vital thereto.

The judgment I've just made belongs to an ethical perspective that has the following advantage: it doesn't require moral judgment to depend upon the claim that some particular group or class of persons has been discriminated against. It allows us to recognize that, while a great deal of pornography is virulently antifemale, and wrong for that reason, all of it is dehumanizing, and wrong for that reason. The trouble with relying upon an "antidiscrimination" approach to the judgment of pornography is that it renders this crucial consideration invisible. More broadly, the ethic that is concerned only with discrimination eclipses universal desiderata, qualities important for the well-being of our species as such, in favor of a focus upon particularistic group interests and allegiances. And, often enough, it requires one to go through intellectual contortions in order to turn what could have been a straightforward indictment of indecency into a (strained) claim of victimhood.

The second ambiguity infecting the feminist approach is somewhat harder to articulate with brevity. Many of us are interested in distinguishing valuable or acceptable erotic literature from blamable pornography. Feminist writers regularly undertake to make that distinction on a basis that would exonerate as erotica any representation of sexuality that is consensual or egalitarian. Some of these efforts might well be characterized as "anything goes except domination." But in fact they do not, and perhaps cannot, maintain this position coherently. What follows is Longino's formulation of how the line should be drawn.

> A representation of a sexual encounter between adult persons which is characterized by mutual respect is, once we have disentangled sexuality and morality, not morally objectionable. Such a representation would be

one in which the desires and experiences of each participant were regarded by the other participants as having a validity and a subjective importance equal to those of the individual's own desires and experiences. In such an encounter each participant acknowledges the other participant's basic human dignity and personhood.[10]

Are we to suppose that this model of acceptable erotica is meant to encompass those highly detailed lust-arousing portrayals that are conventionally called pornographic (except those denigrating women)? One would think so; after all, the function of the model is to exempt from moral criticism things that traditional moralists usually criticize. Yet, it's quite unclear how such portrayals, concentrating as they do on the corporeal details of coitus, could be designed to convey anyone's "basic human dignity and personhood." As we've noted, the figures depicted are hardly persons at all, and the passions regularly solicited by these portrayals have nothing to do with an idea of dignity as that is ordinarily understood. The viewer can scarcely regard these "characters" as anything more than pleasure producing objects that he (or she) would like to possess. As a justification of such prurient appeals (if that's what her model is), Longino's terminology is strikingly (preposterously?) high-minded. You might even wonder how many ordinary, nonpornographic sexual acts can measure up to Longino's remarkably elevated standard of mutual respect: you must have an *equal* regard for your own and your partner's experience! (Arguably, that is what occurs only at the summit of genuine love). It should be evident why that standard is out of the question when one is in the business of viewing very explicit scenes of other people's sexual activities; to say the least, the inevitable appeal is to *self-centered* appetites. Now, perhaps Longino's model is not really meant to condone the grossly explicit. Maybe what it really means to condone are erotic literary and artistic works in which corporeal details and prurient appeals are subordinate to the portrayal of personalities who are capable of respecting and being respected. (Such as Constance and Mellors in *Lady Chatterly's Lover*.) If that is so, however, her standard would not be readily distinguishable—as one may assume she intends it to be—from the norms embraced by many traditional moral thinkers and by the Supreme Court.

If Logino adheres to the school of "anything goes except domination," she does so ambiguously, since she is concerned with respect, dignity, and personhood. This kind of obscurity is pervasive. Feminist philosophy professor Ann Garry is in a similar plight in her effort to distinguish morally objectionable pornography from a "non-sexist pornography" that is acceptable, even educationally desirable. To exemplify the latter, Garry suggests a model pornographic film in which men and women are shown "in roles equally valued by society" and in which the "characters would customarily treat each other with respect and consideration," and even "warmly and tenderly."[11] Now, consideration and tenderness are affections most unlikely to be conveyed by a real pornographic production, that is, where the attention of the audience is directed to genitalia, bodily reactions, orgasms, and the like. Tenderness is an affection pertaining to a whole human being and not to body parts, and it is an affection at variance with the impersonal lust to which pornography characteristically appeals. This line of argument can be taken a step further: insofar as tenderness is a kind of loving, it cannot be conveyed at all by "explicit sexual materials." By itself, a picture or detailed description of people copulating cannot possibly represent love (even if it says it does), because love is a subjective experience inaccessible to an outsider who is in a position to observe only the external physical properties and processes. What the observer sees is something far removed from what a loving couple would be experiencing; the emotional meanings that the act has for them are, in his eyes, reduced to an aggregate of physiological organs and animal functions. (That is why most people don't want to make love under the gaze of strangers, isn't it?) Elsewhere I have argued that such a *reduction*— and the experience of it—is what we usually mean by the "obscene."[12]

Great writers of the past, who have been intent upon exploring the meaning of the erotic life (Stendahl, for example), have avoided obscene dehumanizations by avoiding highly detailed depictions of its physical side. Others who have sought to deal with the physical side artistically (such as Lawrence) have found ways to "distance" the reader from it sufficiently—so that one won't become totally absorbed in it at the expense of the larger human context. These literary devices and avoidances have not been in the service of moral purposes only; often they are primarily in the service of aesthetic purposes: the author wants to give the reader an experience of human erotic life, which is the erotic life of personalities. And that intention is incompatible with the pornographic fragmentation of lovemaking and lovemakers.

The writings of antipornography feminists pay little attention to such literary and psychological complexities. Insofar as these problems of pornography and sexuality we've been considering are recognized at all, the assumption seems to be that all is resolved by *equalization*—in art and in life. That assumption is implicit in the oft-repeated claim that "pornography is not about sex; it is about power." Take away the male power—equalize the status of women and men in sexual representations and in society—and there is no problem remaining. But it's hard to believe that equality of status or power is a conclusive guarantee against dehumanization, and even harder to believe that such equality is the sufficient condition of truly respectful, dignified, considerate, and tender sexuality. Surely social inequality is not the only cause of loveless and exploitative sex. To suppose that it is would require one to entertain a most optimistic view of the underlying, natural sexuality of human beings and of human nature as such? Pleasingly optimistic assumptions aside, in the world of pornography, equality might actually mean nothing more than the even-handed objectification of everyone.

A disposition to regard equality as the all-resolving desideratum (a disposition that feminists share with a certain brand of recent liberalism) can serve to conceal or obscure contradictions in one's outlook. The feminists' inclination to celebrate liberated sexuality (and to be ultramodern) impels them to an emphatic rejection of traditional standards of decency regarding prurient productions and activities. On the other hand, when in the business of distinguishing the good erotic from the bad pornographic, they often find it necessary to insist upon "dignity" and to employ (in however muffled a fashion) language associating sex with affection or mutual caring. They condemn "objectification" while apparently validating representations of a sort that inevitably objectify. Self-contradictory inclinations might be unavoidable in today's sexual scene, but isn't it better to face such tensions than to deny or remain unaware of them?

In my view the ethic of decency has two significant advantages over the ethic of equality. The former can (with regard to our subject) speak more coherently about matters of dignity, respect, and affection. Moreover, at its best, the ethic of decency can accommodate reasonable elements in the feminist indictment of pornography; it can address evils against which women can rightly complain.

What do we mean by dignity? For those unwilling simply to equate dignity with equality, or simply with not being told what to do, I offer these three ordinary concepts of it along with their bearing upon pornography. Our dignity is often said to derive from our possession of higher and rational faculties having primacy over the lower or merely animal appetites. It is endemic to pornography that in its portrayals the lower appetites are rendered supreme. The more distinctively human part of us is represented, when it is represented at all, as the slave of the passions. And social conventions that can function to help reason control those passions are relentlessly violated. Our dignity is often said to derive from our capacity for individuality or freedom of choice. The characters in pornographic productions are without dignity of this sort because they are totally at the mercy of physiological reactions. Much of hard-core pornography is devoted to the graphic portrayal of conditions in which human freedom of choice is overwhelmed by elementary deterministic processes. That is most obvious in cases of blatantly coercive or manipulative pornography where the victim has been reduced to a collection of helpless reactions instigated by the dominator. But this factor is present, in varying degrees, in almost all pornography. From another perspective dignity is thought to reside in our capacity for love or, more comprehensively, for solidarity with others of our species. The characters in a pornographic novel or film cannot be loved for the same reason that they cannot have individuality, they are not personalities (or, as in certain sadomasochistic productions, they lose their personalities and become property.) As for solidarity among human beings, pornography disunites us by dramatizing a world in which nothing matters but elementary, self-centered gratification.

The ethic of decency supports proprieties that are calculated to deter, by providing a customary (and sometimes legal) basis for censuring, the grosser forms of derogation from our status as respectably rational, choosing, and loving beings. In the context of this chapter, the ethic of decency pointedly condemns the systematic degradation of human, interpersonal sexuality to a subhuman, merely animal or mechanistic sexuality.

Feminists are quite rightly outraged by the pornography of violence that so often makes women the targets of sensualized aggression and cruelty. But this kind of portrayal is denounced by an ethic of decency every bit as much as it is by an ethic of equality. Moreover, an ethic of decency is quite capable of recognizing the greater degree of evil in violent pornography. A (nonviolent) "spreader pictorial" is morally censurable for graphically reducing a rational personality to a usable *thing* for the gratification of the viewer; scenes of eroticized torture and mutilation are deserving of more censure for carrying the process of dehumanization still further. If the woman in the *Hustler*-type centerfold has been made into a depersonalized instrument, still more so has the helpless victim of coercive abuse and domination. Such things are clear violations of the egalitarian ethic, but they are also clear violations of an ethic that requires that sex have some association with affection or mutual regard. While equality is not its central principle, the ethic of decency will condemn gross inequalities found in these scenes, because they desecrate lovemaking and are incompatible with the dignity of a rational being. More precisely, what is morally censured as indecent is the seductive invitation to find one's enjoyment in such scenes of systematic inhumanity. And where this prurient appeal is sufficiently explicit and lacking in serious literary or artistic worth, it is within the reach of existing obscenity laws as well.

I have been arguing that an ethic of decency can take into account the evils of pornography more comprehensively and more profoundly than an ethic of equal rights. The egalitarian principle by itself cannot adequately account for moral considerations with which even feminist writers periodically evidence a concern. An ethic of decency is able to accommodate egalitarian concerns because it provides the basis for a criticism of vices which are, among other things, causes of inequality. After all, unleashing of animalistic sexuality, uncontrolled and unrefined, can be as destructive of equal as it is of loving, erotic relations.

None of this is meant as an argument that the ethic of decency, as I've treated it here, can be embodied in the *law* of censurable obscenity directly and in its entirety. (For one thing, it is not susceptible of sufficiently precise definition; that is the downside of its superior comprehensiveness.) Yet, as I've suggested, the Supreme Court's rationale and definition of censorable obscenity already incorporates aspects of it (or can easily be understood as doing so). And I hope it is clear enough why the traditional antiobscenity rationale, supported by the ethic of decency, cannot be dismissed for failing to address any "real-world harms."

The ethical and legal orientation I support can accommodate Professor Sunstein's central concerns: that women employed in the pornography industry (consensually or not) are often abused; that the proliferation of pornography probably contributes to violence against women; and that pornography tends to "promote attitudes toward women that are degrading and dehumanizing," thereby promoting harms such as sexual harrassment.[13] However, it is not only the pornography of outright violence (to which Professor Sunstein wishes to confine legal restrictions) that can be said to play a part in the generation of these deleterious conditions. Moreover, these are hardly the only deleterious conditions to which, we may reasonably suppose, a pervasive pornography industry contributes.[14]

From the traditional viewpoint, it is every bit as harmful that pornography (widely proliferated) systematically desecrates all those values or norms that I've associated with the ethic of decency. Pornography is antisocial in its gross assaults on norms designed to maintain the family and on the conditions, moral and psychological, of a loving or affectionate sexuality and, in general, on suppositions about human beings that are premises of mutual respect among us. Insofar as it appeals to strong primitive impulses that civilization seeks (with difficulty) to control or refine, pornography is anticivilization.

If you want to deny that these are real harms, there are two different ways to do it. You can dismiss the standards of value that pornography denigrates as mere "conventional moral standards," as if we could do just as well without them.[15] Or you could acknowledge that these are socially important ethical desiderata but deny that they could be threatened by a pornography industry, however extensive. In refutation of the former claim, I must rely on things already said and cited in this volume—and on reflective common sense. As to the latter claim, one's view of it will depend, ultimately, upon one's view of mass media and human nature, as well as one's observation of the contemporary cultural scene.

In the last two decades a body of experimental research has been generated that tends to indicate that intensive laboratory exposure to "aggressive" pornographic films increases somewhat the subjects' inclinations to aggressiveness, hostile attitudes toward women and "sex callousness."[16] These studies are welcome as reinforcements of the common sense perspective that what people regularly encounter in the arts and mass media can affect minds and character. It is unlikely, however, that controversy over the consequences of pornography can ever be resolved conclusively by scientific methodology. There is no way to be absolutely sure that reactions obtained in (artificial) laboratory situations are wholly accurate measures of reactions in ordinary life. And even the most sophisticated research projects could not give us scientifically certifiable proof about *the long-term effects*. The basic judgment that social policy has to make is about the likely effects, upon mind and character, of growing up and living in a cultural milieu in which obscene productions of every sort were prevalent, accessible, and wholly tolerated by the law. (The society of "anything goes" that the market will render profitable.) While a "culture" cannot be subjected to controlled laboratory investigations, almost everyone believes (and acts upon the belief in one way or another) that the

cultural milieu is a factor in the shaping of attitudes and moral sensibilities—an educator or miseducator.

There is, it seems to me, a heavy burden of proof on anyone who
wishes to contradict the point I've just made. And the burden of argument
is just as great for anyone who would wish to acknowledge that this is
true—that the media can corrupt—but only with regard to sexist attitudes.
It would be an anomalous argument that pornographic media can surely
generate degrading or harmful attitudes toward women but surely cannot
generate degrading attitudes toward men or harmful attitudes in other
areas of moral concern. With regard to the consideration of significant
harms warranting legislative action, the core of the feminist case is a
judgment about probable effects upon *attitudes*. And that also is the core
of the traditional case.

II. Sexual Liberationism

I am employing the terminology "sexual liberationism" to designate an
ideological stance that condemns the social restraint of pornography not
primarily on behalf of "free speech" but primarily on behalf of "free
sexuality." Liberationists (unlike some liberals) do not see the proliferation
of pornography as a problematic by-product of the enlightened sexual
revolution; for them pornography is no problem and it might even be
good for us. It is important to explore this perspective on its own terms.

Liberationism comes in various sizes and shapes, some more radical
than others and some deeper (or less superficial). Initially, perhaps the
best way to classify forms of liberationism is to note the difference between
a claim that pornography is innocuous entertainment and a claim that it
is positively beneficial. Yet, examination of the "pornography is good for
you" school will reveal that it too is divided. There are those who contend
that pornography can promote a better sex life; others specialize in the
contention that it (or some of it) has educational value as a revealer of
harsh discomforting truths about sexual and human reality that most
people would rather not face. As we shall see, these three lines of argument
are not entirely compatible.

I have already discussed the claim that pornography is harmless entertainment. A particular version of it, having to do with the (negligible)
effects of "fantasizing," is worth a brief additional reference here. One
writer, observing that people go to pornographic theaters to enjoy "fanta-
sized sex," concludes: "The patrons know that what they are watching is

an illusion, that real sex involves responsibilities, respect for others and emotional and intellectual involvement. They have fled these bonds in coming to the theaters, and they know they will return to them."[17] The statement apparently concedes that the sexuality portrayed in these films is irresponsible and disrespectful—and that irresponsible and disrespectful sexuality is not a good thing in real life. Yet, the statement is wholly optimistic; it exudes a cheerful confidence. In what exactly are we being invited to place our confidence? Human nature? The maturity of persons who frequent pornographic theaters? The safety-valve theory? (That salacious pictures and stories provide substitute gratification for impulses that would otherwise be acted out in undesirable ways.)

One could manage to sustain all this cheerful confidence by managing to believe that sexual responsibility is an innate propensity sufficiently compelling to immunize the great majority of us from incitements to irresponsibility. Believers of this sort should be asked to explicate and defend the theory of human nature or psychology upon which they rely. Or they might be asked to explain the large amount of casual, if not disrespectful, sexual activities that an observer of the current scene can scarcely avoid noticing. As for the safety-valve theory, there is no research or statistical evidence for it that I'm aware of, and its supposition—that stimulation of a passion is more likely to reduce than inflame it—is rather strange.[18]

The proposition that pornographic fantasizing, stimulated by motion pictures or other media, is just innocuous amusement would be unassailable if we could simply assume that a fantasy is something harmless by definition. A standard dictionary definition includes the following entries: "imagination or fancy; especially wild, visionary fancy . . . a mental image." There is no reason whatever to suppose that because something is a product of the imagination, or is a visionary image, it is wholly innocent. We have common knowledge that there are such things as harmful political and religious fantasies. (Racists, Maoists, and the Jamestown suicide cult come to mind.) Perhaps what is meant is that *sexual* images can't really be injurious. If that's the assumption, why take it seriously?

Nowadays it is often necessary to reach by laborious argument a conclusion virtually self-evident: that man, the image-making and image-using animal, can be influenced for good and ill by images. (If for good, as everyone acknowledges in the educational world, then why not for ill as well?) As a prominent modern jurist has said, "We live by symbols."[19] To be sure, we do not live only by symbols, but they are influential enough to make it a matter of concern what kind of images of human beings and erotic life are regularly presented to us by *mass media*.

We have yet to consider the "pornography is good for you" school of thought, whose proponents are not merely sanguine but positively enthusiastic. One version of this outlook welcomes pornography as a kind of hygiene. In a typical statement of the point, literary critic Stanley Edgar Hyman opines that what the law calls "obscenity" actually helps "to free child and adult from fear, inhibition and guilt. As such it is life-giving; a stimulus for joy."[20] One doesn't know whether the obscenity that Hyman has in mind includes sadomasochistic films and the likes of *Swank* magazine. Maybe not, but one wishing to argue that pornography is a liberator from fear, inhibition, and guilt might be expected to begin by distinguishing between different kinds of pornography (as feminists try to do). A considerable credulity is required to sustain the belief that someone would have his (to say nothing of *her*), fears and guilt relieved by scenes of brutality, torture, and domination. Almost as much credulity would be needed for acceptance of the idea that people with substantial inhibitions would be freed from them by rumination on the contents of *Swank*. (Sensitive folks might find their inhibitions reinforced by the ugliness of it.)

Hyman, and those sharing his view, often see fit to remind moralists that "sexual intercourse is not a depraved and shameful vice. It is a normal bodily function."[21] And this, apparently, is the life-giving message that we are supposed to receive from pornography. Whatever we might think of the message that sex is (only?) a normal bodily function, clearly that is not what is conveyed by *Swank* and its ilk. If it were, productions of that sort would enjoy much less patronage than they do now; prurient interests are rarely aroused by hygienic portrayals of ordinary biological processes.

Let us turn to a more serious presentation of this libertarian perspective. The argument would begin with the (plausible) observation that one's view of pornography is related to one's view of sexuality. Unfortunately, the argument continues, for centuries sexuality has been enveloped in an idealized mystique (conservative or romantic) that places heavy demands upon it as a vehicle of love, commitment, and tender concern. People laboring under these psychic burdens find it difficult to experience real pleasure; they have been made to feel that they are obliged to be loving or caring and will suffer guilt when they are not. Pornography of the right kind (devoid of cruelty and sexism) can help us to break out of these crippling constraints and experience one of the vital human satisfactions—the joy of sex for its own sake.

Fred Berger, a philosophy professor and exponent of the above mentioned viewpoint puts it this way: "[T]he radical-liberal does not reject physical sex for its own sake as something debased or wicked, or shorn of human qualities. Indeed he or she may insist that greater concern with the physical aspects of sexuality is needed to break down those emotional connections with sex which stand as barriers to its enjoyment."[22] We need a freer, less constrained, less idealized sexuality. To provide an example of appropriately liberated sexuality, Berger quotes approvingly from Erica Jong's (notorious) depiction of an ideal sex act.

> For the true, ultimate zipless A-1 fuck, it was necessary that you never get to know the man very well. I had noticed, for example, how all my infatuation dissolved as soon as I really became friends with a man, became sympathetic to his problems. . . . After that I would like him, perhaps even love him—but without passion. And it was passion that I wanted. . . . The incident has all the swift compression of a dream and is seemingly free of all remorse and guilt; because there is no talk of her late husband or of his fiancee; because there is no rationalizing; because there is no talk at all. The zipless fuck is absolutely pure.[23]

The desire for this kind of purity is not difficult to understand. As adolescents we have all dreamt of a world without obligations or bonds in which we could simply run and play. Jong's dream, in essence, is of a sexual fulfillment unencumbered by any demands of social or even personal relations, a sexuality wholly beyond the reach of civilization. It is an invitation to enter a kind of sexual "state of nature," and that is not without its appeal to many of us. But, as thinkers from Hobbes and Locke to Freud have indicated, the state of nature isn't really a safe place. And even if it were safe, how much happiness would there be in the restless search for an absolute and unconstrained gratification, the precondition of which is its isolation from the remainder of human experience? After much of this, one might even dream of a return to civilization—where sex is with persons and relations with persons ordinarily entail obligations and obligations sometimes result in guilt.

Let us come back to Professor Berger's argument, which is of interest as a kind of prototype of the orientation under consideration (when it is presented in the form of an argument). The liberation of sex-for-its-own-sake from moral and emotional commitments is said to be a desideratum on account of the *pleasure* that, thereby, is to be obtained. So far so good. As long as liberationists are willing to rest their case on the hedonistic justification alone, they could have a coherent case, one that could be consistently (if not persuasively) asserted. Professor Berger, however, doesn't leave it at that; he expects from sexual liberation something more than an increase of physically pleasurable sensations. He envisions sex-for-its-own-sake (and hence pornography) as an overcoming of barriers to "free open communication with others," and as a beneficent aid to individuals seeking "the unique development of their personalities" and "human communion."[24] If we are to take this rather elevated language literally (as more than rhetoric), we need an explanation of how these desiderata are expected to result from sexual acts of the kind that Erica Jong depicts. Certainly, human communion is a far cry from what Jong had in mind; indeed escape from the need to communicate is what she had in mind. We may even wonder why that zipless intercourse should require the presence of another human being at all. (Wouldn't a mechanical contrivance or just plain masturbation do the job even better?) Equally perplexing is how personality might be developed (uniquely or otherwise) by sexual encounters whose *raison d' être* is sensual gratification without any engagement of personalities. Perhaps we are in the presence of a kind of romantic materialism that simply equates the pleasurable contact of bodies with interpersonal communion, or a kind of mystical dialectic in which low aspirations spontaneously give rise to higher ones (once the oppressive forces of traditional morality have been thoroughly vanquished). Alternatively, the whole argument could just come down to the claim that sex for recreation only is a great deal of fun because it satisfies a natural impulse, and, after all, pleasure is what everyone wants. But then elementary consistency would require the abandonment of grand expectations or high-sounding talk (whichever it is) about human communion and development.

Berger's viewpoint, however, does give rise to an interesting challenge to what he calls the "conservative" view. The challenge can be articulated as follows. The conservative is not entitled to suppose that it necessarily dehumanizes people to treat them only as sources of pleasure in pornographic or actual sexual intercourse. One can regard sex simply as an animal gratification without emotional involvement, and one's partners in it as sources of such gratification, with no implication that persons as such are mere instruments or objects to be used. One's sexual relations need not have any bearing on one's relations in other areas of life or one's attitude toward human beings in general. That is how I have to read Berger's satirical observation that he has never "met a conservative who thought that, correspondingly, if people are permitted to make profits from others in business dealings, they will come to view them as mere sources of profits."[25] So why not take the same view of sexuality; if people can be made use of for profit without degradation, why not for fun?

Just for the record, I have met conservatives (as well as radicals) who were concerned about the effects of an unrestrained profit-oriented economy upon mutual respect and social bonds. That aside, what are we to think of the apparent assumption that there's no essential difference between treating a person only as an instrument in sexual relations and doing so in the buying and selling of material goods? That equation can be accepted by someone who thinks that, as a matter of fact, sex is just a simple biological gratification, like eating a good meal. It cannot be accepted by anyone who thinks that, ordinarily or by nature, our sexuality is something more far-reaching or complex—engaging the psyche as well as the body. If someone is going to sell you a piece of furniture, no doubt you would rather not be regarded as nothing but an occasion for profit (as good salesmen know); but you would probably care less about that than about someone preparing to use your body for (unaffectionate) self-gratification. Why? Part of the answer is that the body and psyche are not two separate entities in the way that your furniture and you are separate entities. You are more intimately related to your body than to your material possessions; to have your body treated simply as an instrument for someone else's enjoyment is, in a psychological as well as a moral sense, to have *yourself* treated that way. The other part of the answer has to do with the special character of sexuality. For almost everyone everywhere, sexual activity engages the personality, involves one's sense of identity or an investment of the self, far more than eating a good meal does. Therefore, what happens to you sexually is likely to have a psychological impact. (Who really regards rape as just a case of painful assault and battery?) And therefore one's relations and attitudes in the erotic realm are quite likely to have a larger bearing upon one's relations and attitudes in the other areas of life. It is not readily compartmentalized. More about the erotic subsequently.

We have examined two variations of the liberationist outlook, one claiming that pornography is innocuous amusement and the other claiming that it is a force for the amelioration of undesirable sexual inhibitions. It is doubtful that one could, with consistency, fully endorse both of these conclusions at the same time. The former suggests that modes of entertainment have little enduring effect upon attitudes or inclinations, while the latter supposes that pornographic entertainment can have significant effects (albeit only healthy ones).

There is a third variation, without some attention to which our analysis would be incomplete. From this viewpoint, pornography is defended not as an agent of sexual hygiene but as an avenue to knowledge, especially knowledge of realities ordinarily ignored or denied. And, as shall soon be evident, these are realities of a rather unhygienic sort.

Simply stated, the idea is that pornography can function as the revealer of ominous and unpalatable truths (about our sexuality and humanity) that are normally concealed by deceptive social conventions or myths. As English Professor Peter Michelson puts it: "Pornography is part of [a] contemporaneous urgency to pursue the true. It too explores the unknown and therefore fearful in us; our glimpses into that world refute our private and public lies."[26] Now, the vast majority of the productions ordinarily called pornographic are in pursuit of no truth whatever. *Swank* magazine and its cinematic and novelistic analogues do not "explore" anything; nor do they invite us to reflect upon some aspect of reality. Prurient interests are not interests in reflective inquiry. What Professor Michelson and others of his persuasion are really concerned with is the more sophisticated pornography that can lay claim to some artistic or literary purpose. As examples of the genre, we may have in mind writings such as those of the Marquis de Sade, Henry Miller, Genet and the much-discussed novel about masochism called *Story of O*. Writings of this kind are the primary (though by no means the only) intended beneficiaries of the claim that pornography is good for us as truth-teller and challenger of society's falsehoods.

Perhaps the most thoughtful statement of the position is Susan Sontag's "The Pornographic Imagination." Sontag is bent upon showing that some pornographic productions, like *Story of O*, are serious literary works because they illuminate "the most extreme forms of consciousness that transcend social personality or psychological individuality."[27] *Story of O* portrays, in vivid detail, the progressive enslavement of a woman to a group of sadistic men, to the point where she has lost all will of her own and all personality. The woman, "O," has voluntarily submitted herself to a series of escalating sexual humiliations (bondage, beatings, mutilations, and worse), for the sake of becoming an object and nothing but an object. In the end she has been so transformed into a passive thing, with her humanity so extinguished, that no one in the story even thinks of her as a person. Arguably this is a literary work; the quality of the writing is much superior to *Swank*, and, unlike most ordinary pornography, it devotes some attention to the subjective or psychological dimensions of the dehumanization it depicts. What do we learn, what valuable understanding are we supposed to gain from literary confrontation with such extreme states of consciousness? According to Sontag, the message of this pornographic imagination is that: "[T]amed as it may be sexuality remains one of the demonic forces in human consciousness—pushing us at intervals close to taboo and dangerous desires, which range from the impulse to commit sudden arbitrary violence upon another person to the voluptuous yearning for the extinction of one's consciousness, for death itself."[28]

However we might wish to judge the validity of this outlook on sexuality as demonic, one thing is evident: it is thoroughly incompatible with the view that sexuality is just a healthy, pleasant, "normal bodily function." And, on Sontag's understanding, one is hard put to see how pornography could be "life-giving" and a "stimulus to joy" and an antidote to guilt-ridden inhibitions and a bringer of psychic good health. Apparently, the justification of pornography as hygiene and its justification as insight into threatening realities derive from rather divergent views of sexual life.

Sontag is aware that the extreme states of consciousness are not particularly wholesome. "In daily life, to be sure, we may acknowledge a moral obligation to inhibit such states of consciousness in ourselves. The obligation seems pragmatically sound. Such inhibition on the part of most seems necessary for social order in the widest sense, and seems necessary on the part of each in order to establish and maintain a humane contact with other persons (though that contact can be renounced for shorter or longer periods). It is well known that, when people venture into the extremities of consciousness, they do so at the perils of their sanity, that is to say, their humanity."[29]

Sontag is quick to exempt art and the artist from these inhibitions; the task of the artist is to risk the exploration of spiritual dangers and report back to us her or his fascinating discoveries. Arguably, that is a risk worth taking for a widening of one's horizons and deeper insight into reality. But Sontag doesn't sufficiently grapple with the fact that the artists aren't the only ones at risk. In an age of mass media, multitudes—the old and the young, the mature and the immature—can be exposed to these dramatized assaults upon the conditions of "social order" and "humane contact." If the artist is in danger, why not audiences who, insofar as they are proper audiences of a work of art, must enter imaginatively into the action portrayed? To read *Story of O* (on the assumption that it is, in some degree, a work of art) one must identify with the character, experience the dehumanization and *enjoyment* of dehumanization, and, in a sense, live in the world that the novel creates. (Imagine the emotional impact of a film really portraying, dramatically and with thoroughgoing explicitness, what that novel describes!) If, as Sontag says, the radical artist is "a broker in madness," how can she be so confident that the madness will be contained within a small circle of earnest literati who are prepared to deal with it? After all, Sontag is not of the opinion that the "fantasies" inspired by imaginative literature are only harmless amusements!

Before joining the celebration of the pornographic imagination as an enlargement of horizons, the reasonably cautious person will want to ask some questions. What is the value or the magnitude of the insight that literary pornography is supposed to offer us? What are the prospects that some insights, or some understandings, will be lost on this trip? Immersion in literature like *Story of O* can expose us to realities concerning the dark side of sexual life, the precariousness of personality, and the chilling possibilities—even attractions—of dehumanization. But insights of that sort do not harmonize very well with those understandings serving daily life and ordinary consciousness. What if the former undermine or replace the latter? This is no far-fetched supposition; ordinary realities or commitments are sometimes obscured by dazzlingly extreme ones (among intelligentsia and nonintelligentsia alike). In that case are you wiser or more ignorant? Has your consciousness been enlarged or narrowed?

Susan Sontag's endorsement of the pornographic imagination is not unqualified, her analysis retains some contact with a morally or socially responsible view of human affairs. That can hardly be said of all who are influential in the contemporary (ultramodern or postmodern) artistic scene and related media. Among many in this milieu, one discerns a certain contempt for what Sontag calls "daily life" and for the ordinary (bourgeois?) people who continue to believe in a moral order of some kind. There is among us a literary movement for whom the pornographic is to be extolled precisely because it assaults the attitudes of those people and undermines the moral opinions of ordinary social life. Are we not in need of more literati and artists and critics who will come to the defense of those decent conventions?

In an essay written over twenty-five years ago, the critic George P.

Elliott referred to "the use of pornography as a weapon of nihilistic destruction."[30] In the writings of Henry Miller (to whom, among others, Elliott was referring) sex is employed as the prime instrument in the assault upon social values. *Story of O* travels a considerable distance further down the road of literary nihilism, stripping away all vestiges and supports for the idea of personal dignity. The reader's sexual appetites are aroused by the graphic transformation of an attractive individual into a depersonalized thing; dehumanization is intensely eroticized. On behalf of what? Probably not on behalf of some vision of a better social order. On behalf of sheer rebellion? Or the opinion that meaning is to be found in the obliteration of self and others?

If the spectacle of erotic desire in the service of nihilism is morally and esthetically disturbing, it is also theoretically perplexing. We are led to wonder why human sexuality would lend itself to such purposes. Do we have to entertain the idea that sex is a demonic force rather than an agent of love or a source of harmlessly pleasurable physical excitation? These apparently are the three alternative understandings of the erotic life under-lying the controversy over pornography.

III.   Eros

The Supreme Court once said: "Sex, a great and mysterious force in human life, has indisputably been a subject of absorbing interest to mankind throughout the ages; it is one of the vital problems of human interest and public concern."[31] The statement echoes several old ideas: that sexuality is something *mysterious*, that it is something *problematic*, and that it is a matter of *public* (as well as private) interest. In traditional thought the subject has been viewed with a measure of awe or wonder, as a powerful passion that has its heights and depths and its capacity to pose problems for society and the individual.

This body of ideas has been under relentless assault since the inception of what is called the sexual revolution. The contemporary science of sexology, most prominently exemplified in the work of Alfred Kinsey and his successors, analyzes "sexual behavior" and "sexual release" in a manner calculated to undermine any conception that the subject is wondrous or mysterious. Sex is treated clinically as one of several physiological urges that the human animal must satisfy. In his book *The Modernization of Sex*, the historian Paul Robinson says: "The most striking example of Kinsey's materialism—or, more precisely, his behaviorism—was his decision to evaluate sexual experience strictly in terms of orgasms, and orgasms themselves strictly in terms of numbers."[32] That is, what matters is how many orgasms one has had in a given time period; it doesn't matter how the orgasms were attained—with whom or with what (with a loved one or a stranger, by masturbation, with animals, etc.). Robinson observes, more or less approvingly, that "Kinsey . . . is this century's foremost sexual demystifier."[33] On such a view of things, there is nothing very special about sexuality and nothing problematic about it. The difficulties that mankind has had with this aspect of life result from the imposition of conventional proprieties and delicacies upon it. What is necessary for our well-being is not that we learn to control or refine this passion but that we can learn how to free it from controls and refinements. Obviously, the supporters of the pornography-as-hygiene theory are, among others, inheritors of this outlook.

The erotic side of life has hardly proved impervious to those eviscerating tendencies of modernity that Max Weber has memorably called "the disenchantment of the world." Yet for multitudes of people the subject still has its enchantments (or is disappointing when it doesn't). Let us briefly consider why this is so. For my purpose I'm using the terms *eros* and *erotic* (as have Plato, Rousseau, Freud, and many poets), because this terminology connotes a range of human experience more comprehensive than genital orgasm or, in the current vernacular, "having sex." And it can serve to remind us of elements of our own experience that are neglected or obscured by the scientific "modernization of sex."

What is it that erotic desire actually desires? Ordinarily when we think of erotic life a pleasurable sensation located in a particular part of the body is scarcely all that we have in mind. As Roger Scruton notes, "it is undeniably paradoxical to regard the localized pleasures of the sexual act as the aim or object of desire: so to regard them is to ignore the drama of sexual feeling, and in particular to ignore the fact of the other who is desired."[34] What one desires is not simply a physical pleasure (or "sexual release") but also *a person*; that is, one seeks, at least, a pleasure derived from intimate contact with another human being who is perceived as attractive. The first observation to be made, then, is that eros, unlike other sensual appetites (eating, for example), is an appetite oriented to and involving another person. Secondly, it is an intense desire, intensified by the fact that it engages the psyche as well as the body; it is not readily satisfied, or satisfied for long, by mere physiological contacts and organic relief. (If it were, satisfying it would be quite an easy matter.) Third, it can culminate in an affectionate communion overcoming the isolation of our individuality. In an erotic poem called "The Extasie," John Donne writes:

> When love, with one another so
> Interanimates two soules,
> That abler soule, which thence doth flow,
> Defects of lonelinesse controules.[35]

One could, then, regard such a union—a union of two beings inadequate when alone—as the natural end or consummation of sexual aspiration. And, as in both Donne's poem and Scruton's book on sexuality, the interpersonal union depends upon, though it isn't limited to, the physical arousal and interaction of bodies. Of course, if the bodies are not aroused and engaged, there will be no erotic uniting of "two soules" (or, as Scruton has it, "mutual embodiment" of two persons).[36] Yet, it is finally the joining of "soules" that truly matters; hence, one can refer to sexual love.

I'm assuming that a reader, who has been willing to stay with the argument to this point, can take seriously the idea that an interpersonal union is the ultimate object and fulfillment of normal sexual desire. Yet, to a realistic observer of the sexual scene (to say nothing of the pornographic) this picture will seem incomplete. By itself it will appear as an unduly benign vision of sexual life as we know it. Consider these famous lines from William Butler Yeats:

> Fair and foul are near of kin
> And fair needs foul, I cried.
> . . . .
> A woman can be proud and stiff
> When on Love intent;
> But Love has pitched his mansion in
> the place of excrement.[37]

The poem suggests that in sexual life the beautiful often keeps company with the ugly. Why should that be so? I cannot determine with certitude what Yeats intends for us to think about it, but I have been presenting from time to time a number of indications why it might be so.

Are we not all aware, at some level of consciousness, that in the sexual act there is an inevitable element of "objectification"—treating another as an object for self-gratification and submitting to be so treated? That isn't all there is to it; if it were, pornography would be telling the whole truth. Nevertheless, objectification is an inescapable part of the story, even of the love story. Candor seems to require an acknowledgment that sexual desire is not simply a matter of affection and love; there is in it an inevitable element of the possessive. One wishes, among other things, to *possess* the other; "conquest" is a component of erotic excitement for women as well as men. (Isn't it—despite the claims of feminist writers that conquest is a distortion attributable only to oppressive patriarchy?) Sometimes that component can become quite prominent—so much so as to make sex an occasion for the exercise of aggressive and domineering proclivities. The psychoanalyst Robert Stoller goes so far as to suggest that sexuality and hostility are inseparable. Stoller remarks: "One can raise the possibly controversial question whether in humans (especially males) sexual excitement can ever exist without brutality also present (minimal, repressed, distorted by reaction formations, attenuated, or overt in the most pathological cases). . . . If hostility could be totally lifted out of sexual excitement there would be no perversions, but would normal sexuality be possible?"[38] Yet, despite this acknowledgment of unattractive reality, Stoller does not abandon the traditional idea that affectionate sexuality is somehow normative. He does not seem to be in doubt as to the appropriate therapeutic (and educational) objective: to reduce the ingredient of hostility so that "sustained intimacy with another person" is possible.[39]

Almost everyone recognizes (when not under the influence of Kin-seyism) that the erotic is something "sensitive" and that persons intensely engaged in it are often "vulnerable." Vulnerable to what? That is, to be sure, a long question. One might be considered vulnerable to those hostilities to which Stoller refers. Or, one might well be wary of becoming an object of possession, especially an object of loveless possession. One can feel vulnerable to unleashed passions and drives that "take over," threatening to overwhelm the ego or the sense of identity. In the sexual act persons can be "possessed" not just by someone else but by primal impulses and psychological reactions that are involuntary. Perhaps all this erotic fragility is derived from the fact that in the sexual act we are most powerfully reminded of our corporeality—that we are bodies subject to the forces and processes of the material world[40]—at the same time that we are solicited by more sublime interests. At any rate, it is for reasons such as these that respect and disrespect (for self and others) and not only satisfaction and nonsatisfaction, are so frequently at issue in the erotic life.

A reader cognizant of the relevant literature will perceive that I have left open certain questions of theoretical importance. I have not sought to decide conclusively certain issues about the nature of sexual aspiration and fulfillment that would have to be determined, one way or the other, by any theory of the subject laying claim to thoroughness.[41] What I've tried to do is illustrate, sufficiently for our purposes here, this complexity of human sexuality: inevitably it has heights and depths; it can be beautiful or elevating and it can be ugly or destructive. Of course, we find areas of disagreement among thoughtful diagnosticians of the erotic experience (hardly surprising with regard to a subject considered mysterious). Yet, we find many thoughtful diagnoses converging on some realities of great practical importance. There is considerable agreement that the erotic life has vicissitudes—difficulties and dangers that are not simply results of social proprieties arbitrarily imposed upon it. And there is much concurrence as to the humanly desirable outcome: the capability of sustained intimacy, affectionate union with another person.

The achievement or nonachievement of such union is a matter with a great deal of bearing upon personal development, family, moral education, and dignity. Because of the importance of these desiderata, and their relative fragility, society at large has an interest in the subject of sexuality. There has been no society (that I know of) that has failed to take a public interest in this topic, or refused to provide any norms and guidance for its members—on the premise that each individual should decide such things autonomously. And every society has found it necessary to legislate on some aspect of it.

IV. Freedom of Speech

From the analysis pursued in this chapter, two conclusions are to be drawn, one relatively comprehensive and the other more specific. Taken together, the arguments offered here amount to a justification for the maintenance of a public morality regarding sexual matters. And they support antiobscenity or antipornography legislation. But, it will be asserted, pornography belongs to the constitutional "freedom of speech and press." Here we encounter the last of the arguments against legal restriction and the last defenders of pornography—the free speech libertarians.

According to libertarian doctrine, the First Amendment encompasses and protects "the whole area of expression,"[42] that is, all "expression" that doesn't manifestly produce or imminently threaten palpable injury. In the words of Nadine Strossen, President of the American Civil Liberties Union: "Restrictions on speech can be justified only when necessary to prevent actual or imminent harm to compelling interests . . . and the harm can be averted only by suppression."[43] Strossen presents this sweeping proposition—all the more sweeping in that speech and expression are equated—as a basic established principle underlying our First Amendment adjudication (which, I'm quite sure, it isn't). If this principle were rigorously applied, it would follow that a graphic "snuff" film would be constitutionally protected speech, as long as the woman isn't actually dismembered and killed. And, obviously, it would follow that *Swank* magazine and the like are beneficiaries of the First Amendment as much as *Romeo and Juliet*.

For the time being let us leave scenes of extreme violence and brutality aside, focusing instead on the less extreme case. In the interest of concreteness we can have in mind the issue of *Swank* magazine that I've discussed; why should such material be included in the "freedom of speech and press" that government in the United States is solemnly forbidden to abridge? In response, two distinct lines of argument are possible. You could say that *Swank* is something expressive and that expression (as such) is what the First Amendment values. Or you could say that, while the free speech clause does not exist for the sake of productions like *Swank* and doesn't value them, it must protect them in order to secure the serious literature and exchanges of ideas that it does value. In other words, once any restriction of speech (however worthless) is allowed, we are on a slippery slope to censorship of the significant discourse and art with which the Amendment is truly concerned. While this distinction is rarely made or acknowledged with clarity in the libertarian literature, these are in fact two different claims because they are concerned with rather different desiderata. To be ambiguous about this matter is to be ambiguous about the basic purpose and meaning of the constitutional free speech principle. Ultimately, the crucial questions are about the ends to be served by the First Amendment. And, in the light of these ends, I believe it is not hard to show that both of these libertarian positions are problematic.

The former position sometimes presents itself simply as an interpretation of what the Framers of the free speech clause intended, as is indicated by the obvious meaning of the words. Strossen observes that the First

Amendment "refers unqualifiedly to 'the freedom of speech,' indicating that *all* speech should be protected equally."[44] More pointedly against the Supreme Court's obscenity adjudication, she also notes that the First Amendment "contains no exception for sexual expression."[45] Of course it doesn't; the text contains no explicit qualifications at all. It makes no exception for malicious defamation, "fighting words," false advertising, lying to Congress, practicing medicine without a license, trying to persuade your employees not to join the union, and child pornography. These are only some of the uses of language and pictures that, courts have reasonably found, are not the kinds of "speech" with which the First Amendment is concerned. Furthermore, it is incorrect to suggest that the Supreme Court has excluded "sexual expression" from the domain of the First Amendment; what has been excluded is pornography, on the grounds that it is "no part of any exposition of ideas" and is a very slight step, if any, toward truth.[46] With regard to the perspective of those who framed and ratified the free speech clause, it is generally known that they were interested not so much in facilitating personal self-expression as in the promotion of thought and deliberation about matters of public interest— to the end that this shall be an enlightened republic.[47]

Apart from the constitutional text and its original meaning, there is the apparent libertarian claim that the First Amendment *ought* to encompass everything that can be considered an expression or an utterance or a communication (as distinguished, more or less, from an action). But why should this be so; on what basis are we to regard expressions per se (no matter of what) as precious or important? Or, if the word *communication* is preferred, why should there be a special and stringent constitutional solicitude for communications regardless of their content, quality, or objective? Stated in this blunt manner, the question isn't easy to answer, and systematic responses to it are hard to come by. To justify their virtually all-encompassing conceptions of free speech, libertarian theorists often have recourse to the terminology of personal "self-realization" and "self-development." Yet, unless these conceptions are utterly open-ended, signifying little more than doing whatever one desires, it's hard to see how they have much to do with the likes of *Swank* magazine. Development of what? Thomas I. Emerson, a founding father of expressive libertarianism, tells us: "The achievement of self-realization commences with development of the mind";[48] therefore "freedom of expression . . . is a good in itself."[49] But surely not all forms of expression, communication, or utterance are conducive to what one could reasonably consider a development of the mind; as everyone knows, there is much that detracts there-from. Nor do they all facilitate the formulation of "beliefs and opinions" (a desideratum to which Emerson's rationale finds it necessary to refer with some frequency). For example, publications like *Swank* are hardly discourses about beliefs and opinions. And I have yet to see a coherent argument that they deserve the solicitude of the First Amendment simply because they express something. (The closest thing to an effort to make such an argument is the claim that it is good for you to vent whatever is in you, to "get it off your chest." This is the least impressive rationale for a basic free speech principle.) The first libertarian position, then, does not seem to be coherently defensible.

So perhaps the second and alternative position—depending upon the supposition of a "slippery slope"—is the one upon which free speech libertarianism really rests. *Swank* must be deemed protected speech not for its own sake, but because we know that censorship of it would endanger serious literature dealing with sexual matters and ultimately threaten unpopular ideas generally. But do we really know such a thing empiri-cally—or is it largely a matter of doctrinal assumptions? We have visited this subject in chapter 2; here I suggest as a brief answer: Some of each but considerably more of the latter than the former. The notion that legal restriction of (any) "expression" tends to unleash an uncontrollable escalation of censorship is, to say the least, a sizable exaggeration. The kernel of truth in it is that, historically, works of genuine erotic literature like *Lady Chatterly's Lover* and James Joyce's *Ulysses* have been subjected to censorship. But even at the pinnacle of such ("Victorian") censorious-ness in nineteenth- and early twentieth-century England and America, where antipathy to erotica was virtually unmodified by countervailing principles of free speech, we experienced a flourishing of political debate, philosophic and scientific inquiry, and great literature. (Paradoxically, greater literature and art than we've seen in the latter half of this century where almost "anything goes.") Now, with free speech principles at hand, are we really at a loss for criteria by which to make reasonable distinctions between serious literature like *Lady Chatterly's Lover* and prurient appeals like *Swank*? If there were no such criteria at all, then educational curricula (secondary and "higher") would have no basis for preferring, as for the most part they still do, the former to the latter. My point here is not that censorship is an utterly safe enterprise, but that the conception of a "slippery slope" is more rhetoric than reality insofar as it conveys the spector of an inevitable censorious growth, unsusceptible of moderation or rational containment. In more modest form, the conception can function as a prudential cautionary consideration, but not as a conclusive argument against any censorship whatsoever. That is, realistically understood, it cannot serve to sustain the sweeping version of constitutional free speech that strict libertarians advance.

It would seem that *Swank* can't be saved by a First Amendment rationale based on the value of expression per se—or one based on apprehension of the slippery slope. And, of course, that is even more obviously the case with regard to sadomasochistic pornography and "snuff." (Would it make any sense at all to say that once you lay hands on a snuff film, you are on the way to censorship of *Madam Bovary* or even *Carnal Knowledge*?)[50] Nor, I believe, is there any other rationale, distinctively alternative to these two, that would do the job of mandating constitutional protection for all the "speech" that doctrinal libertarians want protected. It should go without saying that the traditional or classical philosophies of free speech will not do that job. John Stuart Mill advocated almost boundless "liberty of thought and discussion" for the sake of the discovery of truth.[51] Alexander Meiklejohn advocated absolute freedom for "political speech," speech requisite for the functions of democratic citizenship.[52] And both of these desiderata were prominent in liberal thinking about free speech when our Bill of Rights was drafted and adopted. But none of these purposes are served by the kinds of productions that one would find on a spectrum from *Swank* to the ultraviolent. Those are neither discussions nor efforts to disclose any truths. And they have nothing to do with opinions or qualities of mind pertinent to the functions of deliberative democracy. (If anything they detract therefrom). Perhaps there are practical reasons for leaving them, or some of them, alone, but I can find no theoretical grounds for a constitutional mandate that they must be free.

But let us not leave the issue to be determined at such a level of theoretical generality. According to recent doctrine, supported not only by libertarians but also by (less extreme) liberal judges, the First Amendment prohibits government from imposing restrictions upon speech that discriminates among points of view or ideas or messages. This proscription of "viewpoint discrimination" is a prominent theme in contemporary First Amendment adjudication; the state may not legislate officially approved and disapproved "viewpoints." But what constitutes a viewpoint and discrimination against one? To put the question a bit more precisely, how stringent or lenient should we be in deciding whether some form of expression qualifies as the assertion or embodiment of a point of view? This is the critical question to which much of recent free speech adjudication gives rise.

As I've suggested, traditional First Amendment doctrine was informed by a more-or-less clear rationale for the free speech principle. The central purpose of the clause was to protect the "exposition of ideas" or "communication of information and opinion" about public affairs. As Justice Brandeis has famously put it, the makers of our Constitution believed that "freedom to think as you will and to speak as you think are means indispensable to the discovery and spread of political truth"; they "believed in the power of reason as applied through public discussion."[53] One may wonder whether the Framers were as optimistic about the power of reasoned discussion in human affairs as was the great liberal Justice. But these oft-quoted remarks of Brandeis can serve to illustrate the extent to which traditional thinking about the free speech principle presupposed a concept of reasoned discourse. Although that principle's protection was sometimes extended to political expression rather more emotional than intellectual, it was generally understood that the desideratum at the core of the First Amendment was freedom for thought, debate, engagements of the mind. Obviously, this perspective has a bearing on the question I've raised above. One deliberating in light of this perspective is inclined to insist that something claiming to be a viewpoint (or for which that claim is made) would have to evidence at least a modicum of rational content, that is, some invocation of thought. To note the outer limits: a sheer emotional outburst wouldn't do, nor would a subliminally delivered propaganda "message."

This rationality concept, as we may call it, has its vicissitudes. It is not always such an easy thing to judge whether the degree of reasoning embodied in some utterance, or the element of thought communicated by some film, is sufficient to get it within the purview of a First Amendment whose core concern is the exposition of ideas. What, after all, qualifies as a genuine *idea*. The difficulty is exacerbated when one has to consider literary or artistic works that are not primarily designed to present discursive analyses. No doubt this problem is one of the factors accounting for ambiguities in free speech adjudication of recent decades, and for the Supreme Court's periodic retreats from the earlier (and more elevated) standards of rationality.

It was essentially on the basis of those standards that the legal control of "obscenity" was upheld in the leading cases of *Roth* v. *United States*, *Miller* v. *California* and *Paris Adult Theatre* v. *Slaton*. The Court decided that obscenity (properly defined—and increasingly defined as hard-core pornography) is not an exchange of ideas; furthermore, laws restricting distribution of "obscene material, which by definition lacks any serious literary, artistic, political or scientific value as communication" do not involve "a control of reason and the intellect."[54] This formulation is in sharp contrast with the dissenting Justice Douglas's far more lenient conception of what constitutes an idea (" 'obscenity' at most is the expression of offensive ideas").[55] The Court majority, unlike Douglas, expects that something deserving to be called an idea will include communication addressing the rational or intellectual faculties.

This rather commonsensical expectation has been eroded in several ways. I have selected three of them for special attention here. First, from time to time the Court has suggested that the First Amendment is as solicitous of the "emotive" as it is of the "cognitive" component of speech. Indeed, according to *Cohen* v. *California*, the "emotive function . . . may often be the more important element of the message sought to be communicated."[56] Insofar as this really means what it says, it certainly tends to undermine the constitutional justification for restrictions upon hard-core pornography. Perhaps the Court can dispel this confusion by indicating that it really means the following: when there is a genuine idea communicated (in the ordinary, not the Douglas, sense of the term), the First Amendment is mindful of the emotive function of language. But it makes little sense to treat a mere expression of one's passion—of anger or of lust, for example—as the kind of "speech" that it is the function of the First Amendment to liberate.

Second, an erosion of the rationality concept is observable in cases involving "expressive conduct." In *Barnes* v. *Glen Theatre* the Court had to decide whether South Bend, Indiana, can proscribe (as indecency) "go-go dancing" in total nudity at the Kitty-Kat Lounge and in the backroom of a pornographic magazine shop. While a fragile majority of the Justices managed to sustain the restriction, what is remarkable here is the claim, subscribed to by at least five Justices, that this sort of "dancing" (the "bumps and grinds") is a performance art entitled to a substantial degree of First Amendment protection. Why? For our purposes the most interesting answer provided is that such expressive activity is designed to convey a "message."[57] Of course, this notion—that peep shows belong to the freedom of speech, as artistic expression conveying an idea of sorts—would virtually demolish the court's long-standing rationale for antipornography laws. (Even more so than *Cohen* v. *California* does.) With such a minimalist conception of what it means to incorporate or communicate messages, one can easily contend that they are incorporated and communicated by hard-core sex orgies, performed with or without music—and by much else.[58] What message is conveyed by the peep show and the bumps and grinds? Justice Souter's concurring opinion suggests that it is an endorsement of erotic activity. (Of course, pornography could be said to do the same.) The four dissenting Justices cite Aristotle's *Poetics* to the effect that the art of dance can function to represent human character. Souter's point fails to distinguish between an endorsement that appeals to the rational faculties and one that simply doesn't, that is, between an idea and a stimulus. As for Aristotle, he apparently did think that the kind of dancing that Greek choruses performed (like poetry and music in general) can serve to represent states of character in an illuminating way. But the man watching the peep show is not reflecting upon human character, nor are the "performances" inviting him to do so. The Justices (unlike Aristotelian poetic theory) are neglecting the crucial difference between an invitation to imaginative reflection upon some erotic reality and a sheer stimulation of lust. That is what happens when one is determined to regard as full-fledged messages stimuli from which rational content, or the provocation of thought, is absent.

The third form of judicial accommodation of the irrational is exemplified in the *Hudnut* case, dealing with the feminist antipornography statute.[59] The Court of Appeals invalidated the statute for establishing an officially approved and disapproved view of women and the appropriate relations between the sexes. In the effort to counteract this judgment, Indianapolis had maintained that pornography (as they defined it) affects attitudes toward women *not* through persuasion answerable by counterargument, but by a kind of subconscious conditioning. The Court, while seeming to acknowledge the validity of this point, was unmoved by it. "[A]lmost all cultural stimuli provoke unconscious responses," they said, and "if the fact that speech plays a role in a process of conditioning were enough to permit governmental regulation, that would be the end of freedom of speech." [60]

No doubt it is true that many cultural stimuli provoke unconscious responses as well as conscious ones. But it would be astonishing to suggest that all things classifiable as cultural stimuli are protected by the First Amendment; some obviously aren't. And proponents of antipornography laws do not have to argue (whatever Indianapolis might in fact have argued) that the presence of a process of conditioning is *enough* to permit governmental regulation of speech. Pure conditioning—as in subliminal or wholly manipulative advertising—is one thing, and a mixed process involving some conditioning and some important ideas—as in a religious or political ceremony—is another. It can be said that in the former case a "viewpoint" has been shaped without addressing the conscious mind, while in the latter case the conscious mind has been addressed at least somewhat—and about matters of central First Amendment import. Arguably the kind of effect that pornography has upon attitudes resembles the former process a lot more than the latter. My point is that people's attitudes or opinions are shaped by influences that involve various degrees of the conscious and the unconscious, the reflective and the manipulative, and that such differences are (often enough) recognizable. Where a "communication" appeals hardly at all to the thinking or deliberative capacities and almost entirely to subconscious motives or primitive impulses, the case for First Amendment protection (the case for regarding this as belonging to "the freedom of speech") is at its weakest. If the communication is apparently about public affairs, perhaps it should get the benefit of the doubt, but pornography and peep shows can hardly claim to deserve such an exemption.

The Court that decided *Hudnut* shows no evidence of having grappled with these and related distinctions; virtually without qualification, it throws the protective mantle of the First Amendment over subconsciously conditioned reactions and expositions of ideas, over the wholly irrational and the rational alike. The judges might believe that these distinctions are illusory, arbitrary, or otherwise impossible to make. But on that basis what is freedom of speech about; why should we cherish and seek to preserve the freedom of speech?[61]

A meaningful concept of free speech will yield meaningful conceptions of what counts as a "viewpoint," and hence as viewpoint discrimination, for First Amendment purposes. To be sure, the problem can't be resolved once and for all by an abstract definition, because the contexts are important and those are various. My effort has been to present, in the form of arguments against the more prevalent modes of free speech irrationalism, some guidelines for distinguishing between "viewpoints" sufficiently thought-related and those insufficiently thought-related in light of the ends of our historic free speech principle. In light of those ends, a viewpoint is a perspective embodying an idea, and an idea is a communication meant to engage the mind—inviting argument or deliberation or contemplation. Where the production in question is a performance or a work of imaginative literature, the existence and nonexistence of "aesthetic distance" is a factor.[62] A sex orgy does not become "speech" simply by being presented on a stage before an audience. Of course, one must be free to publish an argument that sex orgies are good for us and that the morality censuring them is oppressive nonsense. One is even free to make the case in literary form where the orgies would be depicted in such a way as to promote favorable reflection on the idea that they are good for us. (But without an idea or reflection, properly speaking, there is no viewpoint). Likewise, the free speech clause would usually have to protect, regardless of what we think of it, an argument that violence against women is a healthy form of self-expression. What it would not protect is graphic portrayals of such violence with the objective simply of stimulating and gratifying the impulse (for example, some forms of hard rock or "rap" music and videos that emphatically celebrate rape, mutilations, and murder.) Yes, there are borderline cases, some of them troublesome. Does *Story of O* qualify as possessor of a serious viewpoint presented for our reflection—*or* is it primarily an invitation to enjoy violently degrading sexuality? By the criteria I'm seeking to illustrate, it's a close call; hence (though I don't personally like this result), the law is probably obliged to give the novel the benefit of the doubt. A very detailed, "no holds barred" cinematic depiction is another matter.

Do feminist antipornography statutes amount to viewpoint discrimination? I believe this is a closer call than the court in *Hudnut* was willing to acknowledge. On the one hand, the great majority of the materials that Indianapolis sought to reach would not qualify as genuine literature or as any inquiry, discussion, or debate. On the other hand, it is not reassuring that the authors and proponents refused to include in the statutory language an explicit protection for serious literature (as is incorporated in *Miller* v. *California*'s three-part test for censorable obscenity).[63] And, apart from what the statute says, it is clear enough that the authors and proponents intended the law to operate on behalf of an egalitarian principle in relations between the sexes. But, proponents claim, with regard to viewpoint discrimination, the only difference between the feminist antipornography statutes and the ordinary antiobscenity laws that the Supreme Court upholds is that the viewpoint served by the latter is less obvious. Under the "*Miller* test" productions censorable as obscenity must be predominately prurient, patently offensive in light of contemporary community standards, and lacking in serious literary or educational value. On its face the test simply allows for proscription of extremely lust-arousing and obnoxious materials—and then only where the one in question cannot claim to be serious literature. But what is supposed to be the matter with prurient appeals? Could it be that the legislator wants to restrict them for a reason that is utterly viewpoint neutral? It follows from the rationale presented in this book that pornography is appropriately restricted largely because of its long-range effects upon attitudes and feelings in certain sensitive matters of vital social interest. Thus one can say that sexual "viewpoints" are at stake. What we cannot say, however, is that the things to be restricted are such as to encourage thinking about sexual viewpoints. The more likely effect is to encourage the avoidance of thinking or its subordination to passion.

With regard to the question of viewpoint discrimination, the feminist antipornography statutes and the (Court-sanctioned) antiobscenity laws do have some things in common. In the final analysis there is this two-fold difference between them: ideology (feminist) is more evident in the former case, and serious literature regardless of ideology is expressly sought to be protected in the latter.

Thus far I've been making the case that certain restrictions of pornography are compatible with First Amendment principle. This case, however, doesn't settle all questions of public policy on the subject. Among the things that (according to this rationale) the free speech clause leaves unprotected, what should we actually seek to legislate against? This is a realm of practical considerations to which I shall only allude here, depending as it does heavily upon circumstances.

Some commentators would modify existing antiobscenity law so that it encompasses only *violent* pornography, in effect giving up on all the rest of it. Several reasons are advanced for such a policy. Violent pornography more obviously threatens harmful consequences; it poses less difficult problems of definition, and a communal consensus against it is easier to establish. Problems of definition and consensus would still remain, however. How overtly violent? Is sexual coercion without battery violent? What about sadistic acts without mutilation and with consent of the victim acquired by manipulation?[64] But this is a secondary problem. My primary reservation has to do with the aims and desiderata of public morality to which much of this book has been devoted. Most of those aims and values would be abandoned by a policy rigorously limiting anti-pornography law to blatant cases of violence. Of course, productions that make gross brutality erotically arousing, pornography in which sex is systematically intertwined with physical cruelty, is the most obviously destructive kind. There is a good case for elaborating the antiobscenity laws so as to single out such representations as prominent examples of patent offensiveness. (In this way some of the feminist concerns would be accommodated as well.) But it should be recognized that a retreat to the legal control of ultraviolent extremities, giving up on everything else, would give up on a great deal of flagrant indecency. Indeed, such a policy would in fact tolerate (and condone?) a great deal of sexualized brutality and degradation. And it could send the message that, after all, what really counts in our society is not human decency or dignity but avoidance of physical damage. In other words the standard envisioned is too low. We should settle for it as a last resort (not a solution to the problem) if circumstances admit of nothing more elevated. In the absence of that exigency, I think effort should be made to draw the line at the likes of *Swank* magazine. This policy would still leave the greater number of erotic productions untouched, including much that may be considered indecent from a moral point of view. But it would better serve to hold up a standard that society needs to have affirmed in these morally troubled times.

I cannot leave this topic without a brief look at it from a currently very relevant angle. A point periodically made by (not necessarily libertarian) critics is that the focus on pornography is misguided, the real evil is not sexuality in the media but the glorification of violence per se. As I conclude this writing, the country is experiencing yet another debate about media violence; this time the moral indictments are leveled at certain motion pictures and popular music (so-called gangsta rap especially) that feature misogynistic hatred, cruelty for its own sake, and the emphatic celebration of murderous acts. Much of this is catering to the young. As William J. Bennett and C. DeLores Tucker put it, " 'artists' sing about dismemberment and cutting off of women's breasts. This is fair game for an audience of 12 year olds?"[65] The media corporations sponsoring these things reply with the usual claims about creative rights and free expression.

Antipornography laws per se cannot address this kind of depravity, unless the brutality is explicitly associated with appeals to sexual passion. As to the case for such laws (despite that considerable limitation), I would have to stand on the rationale of this and the previous chapters. But, according to the philosophic rationale for public morality, the imposition of restraints on depraved media violence would not be something unthinkable; and legally that might be considered under the rubric of "indecency" (the conception under which the Federal Communications Commission already exercises some mild restraint of radio and television). An argument against doing so is that it is more difficult to define and censor presentations of violence without threatening authentic literature or communication of information than it is to define and censor outright prurient appeals. The argument for doing so is that the corporations making large profits out of these things will not be persuaded to reform themselves (actually, as distinguished from cosmetically or temporarily), nor will the condemnation be sufficiently effective, in the absence of laws "with teeth in them." (Consider the effectiveness of such condemnations in a thoroughly libertarian world where government could not even threaten the corporations with legal restriction.) It seems evident to me that both propositions are valid, that there is a substantial case for such laws, and that careful legislative deliberation should be devoted to the problem. Over twenty-five years ago I tentatively suggested that the legal definition of obscenity might be adjusted so as to include a component addressing productions that predominantly do the following: "Visually portray in detail, or graphically describe in lurid detail, the violent physical destruction, torture or dismemberment of a human being, provided that this is done . . . not for genuine scientific, educational or artistic purposes."[66] No doubt this statement has its difficulties; it would need a lot of work. Probably there are more promising or more meticulous legislative approaches. The larger point to be made is that legislative deliberation need not be crippled by the unexamined assumption that graphic depictions of torture, dismemberment, and massacre necessarily belong to the constitutional "freedom of speech."[67] Murderous "rock" and "rap" are not *ipso facto* expositions of ideas, any more than depictions (on ultra "right wing" radio talk shows) of how to target federal police agents with lethal weapons are expositions of ideas.[68]

The underlying and most enduring issues are about rationality, freedom, and community. There is an important role for a conservative jurisprudence in helping to maintain the connection between constitutional "speech" and reasoned discourse. Why is this connection important? As I've been suggesting, it is a requisite for the respectability, and hence the long-range security, of the free speech principle.[69] Beyond this consideration, the good health of liberal democracy depends in crucial ways upon reason—upon the disposition to engage in thoughtful inquiry and listen to reasoned argument about our public affairs. Such a disposition is vital not only for intelligent responses to our practical problems; it is vital for the maintenance of communal bonds and mutual respect among very diverse people. No service is done to the Republic by the obliteration of distinctions between a thoughtful argument and an outburst of hatred, between an idea and a manipulation of impulses, between articulate speech and (any) "expression"—even if that seems in the short run to expand personal freedom. Where reasoning is not recognized and respected, conflicts of outlook or interest degenerate into immodifiable hostilities and eventual force. And, given the disrespect for it generated in some quarters of our postmodernist culture, reason needs to find support in other quarters, including constitutional law.

Is it reasonable to regard graphic portrayals of grossly depersonalized sex and celebrations of mutilation and slaughter as elements of freedom? It matters how we think about the meaning of freedom. Do we really want to be in the habit of thinking that whenever opportunities for these dehumanizing things are enlarged our freedom has been enlarged, and whenever a restraint is imposed upon them our freedom has been diminished? That attitude makes sense only if there is no connection between freedom, personal or collective, and self-control. But there are such connections.

The libertarian idea, in its unqualified form, is that all such expressions must be tolerated in a free society; restraint is a bad thing and personal option is the good thing. In opposition is the more communitarian idea that the people, in our collective capacity as a citizenry, are entitled to some say-so about the character of the cultural environment in which we live, develop, and have families. The libertarian idea reflects an underlying vision of society as an aggregate of independent and self-determining individuals. Where that vision prevails one is inclined to suppose that there is *no harm* where there is no clear and present danger of palpable material injury to (nonconsenting) individuals. This is a rather simple view of social life and interaction, isn't it? There is a more complex and, I believe, realistic view. Most of us recognize more subtle but nonetheless significant influences and harms, such as the moral and aesthetic degeneration of a neighborhood or a community and the debasement of character. Antipornography and public decency legislation is not simply a matter of letting a majority of individuals have their way only because they happen to be a numerical majority. Well-devised laws or policies can serve an enabling and socializing function: they can support the efforts of citizens to sustain a cultural milieu that reflects shared standards of civility and decency.

I have not maintained that communitarian considerations should always prevail over libertarian ones. Indeed, in a basically liberal society, such as ours, liberty must often take precedence over desiderata of public morality. But, as should be evident, the crucial problem and danger in these times is not a lack of free expression; rather it is an erosion of communal allegiance. Our liberalism needs, as it has always needed, a moral balance.

NOTES

1. Walter Berns, "Beyond the (Garbage) Pale or Democracy, Censorship and the Arts", in *Censorship and Freedom of Expression*, ed. Harry M. Clor (Chicago: Rand McNally, 1971), p. 68.

2. Catherine A. MacKinnon, "Pornography, Civil Rights and Speech," *Harvard Civil Rights—Civil Liberties Law Review* 20 (winter, 1985). p. 18.

3. My discussion of the feminist case against pornography deliberately omits the more extreme or most radical formulations of the case. I do not take up the claim that pornography is an expression of the sexist pathology that characterizes our whole society, that the values in it are the predominant values of the average male (for whom rape is normal sex), and that, as Andrea Dworkin puts it, "the virulent contempt for women . . . is the very foundation of the culture in which we live." (Dworkin, "Pornography and Grief," in *Take Back the Night* [New York: William Morrow & Co., 1980], p. 287. I don't take up these things because I want to focus on the more reasoned and credible claims about matters of principle or standards of judgment. We should also note here that there is a relatively small but vocal school of feminists who oppose legislation against pornography.

4. *Miller* v. *California*, at p. 24.

5. *Take Back the Night*, pp. 253–54.

6. *American Booksellers Association* v. *Hudnut*, 711 Fed. 2nd 323 (1985), at 324.

7. Ibid., at 325.

8. Cass R. Sunstein, "Neutrality in Constitutional Law (with Special References to Pornography, Abortion and Surrogacy)," *Columbia Law Review*, 92, no. 1 (January, 1992) p. 26. Also see Sunstein, *Democracy and the Problem of Free Speech* (New York: The Free Press, 1993), pp. 215–21.

9. Helen E. Longino, "Pornography, Oppression and Freedom: A Closer Look," in *Take Back the Night*, p. 42.

10. Ibid.

11. Ann Garry, "Pornography and Respect for Women," *Pornography and Censorship*, ed. David Copp and Susan Wendell, (Buffalo: Prometheus Books, 1983), p. 77.

12. Harry M. Clor, *Obscenity and Public Morality* (Chicago: Univ. of Chicago Press, 1969), pp. 224–42.

228 FEMINISM, SEXUALITY, EXPRESSION

13. Sunstein, "Neutrality in Constitutional Law," p. 25.

14. Estimates of the actual size of the pornography industry will depend, of course, on one's definition of what is pornographic. Respectable sources have placed the amount as high as 8 billion dollars a year. See *Pornography and Sexual Aggression*, ed. Neil M. Malmuth and Edward Donnerstein (Orlando, Florida: Academic Press, 1984), p. 15, and Attorney General's Commission on Pornography, *Final Report* (Washington, D.C., 1987).

15. Sunstein sometimes appears to engage in such dismissal—for example, see *Democracy and the Problem of Free Speech*, p. 216. Other times, he is not so dismissive—for example, "the debasement of sexuality through distorting influences is a real phenomenon, one that can produce individual and collective harm," ("Neutrality in Constitutional Law," p. 20). This observation seems to concede something to the argument about harm that I've been making.

16. See Malmuth and Donnerstein, *Pornography and Sexual Aggression* and Edward Donnerstein, Daniel Ling, and Steven Penrod, *The Question of Pornography: Research Findings and Policy Implications* (New York: Free Press, 1987). See also Attorney General's *Final Report*, 1987.

17. Joseph P. Slade, "Pornographic Theaters Off Times Square," in *The Pornography Controversy*, ed. Ray C. Rist. (New Brunswick, New Jersey: Transaction Books, 1975), p. 139.

18. As feminist writer Susan Griffin puts it: "What a strange argument the pornographer gives us. He claims his fantasy will relieve the mind from an obsession with violence. And yet his fantasies promise that only violence will give the mind release" (Griffin, *Pornography and Silence* [Glenview, Ill.: HarperCollins, 1982], p. 94).

19. Justice Felix Frankfurter, majority opinion in *Minersville School District v. Goblitis*, 310 US 586 (1940).

20. Hyman, "In Defense of Pornography," in *Perspectives on Pornography*, ed. Douglas A. Hughes (New York: St. Martin's Press, 1970), p. 40.

21. Ibid.

22. Fred R. Berger, "Pornography, Sex and Censorship," *Social Theory and Practice* 4, no. 2 (1977): p. 90.

23. Ibid., pp. 90–91.

24. Ibid.

25. Ibid., p. 89.

26. Michelson, "An Apology for Pornography," in *Perspectives on Pornography*, p. 71.

27. Sontag, "The Pornographic Imagination," in *Perspectives on Pornography*, p. 141.

28. Ibid., p. 154.

29. Ibid., p. 141.

30. Elliott, "Against Pornography," in *Perspectives on Pornography*, p. 89.

31. *Roth* v. *U. S.* at 487.

32. Robinson, *The Modernization of Sex* (Ithaca, N.Y.: Cornell Univ. Press, 1976), p. 57.

33. Ibid., p. 118.

34. Scruton, *Sexual Desire* (New York: Macmillan, 1986), p. 19.

35. *Love Poems of John Donne* (Mount Vernon, N.Y.: Peter Pauper Press), p. 50.

36. *Sexual Desire*, p. 30.

37. "Crazy Jane Talks With the Bishop," in *The Collected Poems of W. B. Yeats* (New York: Macmillan, 1956), p. 255.

38. Robert J. Stoller, "Pornography and Perversion," in *The Case Against Pornography*, ed. David Holbrook (La Salle, Ill.: Library Press, 1972), p. 125.

39. See Robert J. Stoller, *Observing the Erotic Imagination* (New Haven, Conn.: Yale Univ. Press, 1985), p. 8. See also chapters 1–4. Stoller maintains that pornography always expresses hostility by turning persons into "fetishes."

40. This, I believe, is what Simone de Beauvoir must have had in mind when she wrote: "For most women—and men too—it is not a mere matter of satisfying erotic desire, but of maintaining their dignity as human beings while obtaining satisfaction" (*The Second Sex* [New York: Vintage Books, 1974], p. 765). It should not be surprising that dignity is at stake, even in the eyes of an existentialist thinker like Beauvoir. To use the terms of Beauvoir's philosophy, in sex as elsewhere, our "subjectivity" is in danger of submersion in our "objectivity"—that aspect of us that belongs to the realm of *things*. It seems to me that Beauvoir has a less simplistic view of human sexuality and its problems than most of her successors in the feminist movement. She does not regard objectification and possessiveness *merely* as social constructions imposed upon innocent sexuality by bad patriarchy. It seems to me that many contemporary feminist writers are, ultimately, as sanguine about the nature of sexuality as are liberationist writers, differing from them only as to the source of the repression that distorts our (naturally benign) sexuality.

41. For example, it would be hard to maintain a coherent theory of sexuality that would embrace, equally and in their entirety, the viewpoints of both Scruton and Stoller. Scruton's theory is teleological; it envisions a *normal* course of human sexual development reaching its culmination in love. Stoller doesn't seem to see the "normal" or natural in quite the same way, stressing as much as he apparently does the naturalness of sexual hostility. The existential psychotherapist Viktor Frankl has a less pessimistic view than does Stoller. (See Viktor Frankl, *The Doctor and the Soul* [New York: Bantam Books, 1965]). Frankl distinguishes between "physiologically determined sexuality," originally an amorphous urge for objects of gratification, and "the erotic striving" imminent in all of us as a longing for communion or comradship. He envisions a normal and ideal course of psycho-sexual maturation in which the former and the latter have achieved

harmonious synthesis in "monogamous relationship." He notes that the normal course of maturation is subject to inhibition and disruption in a variety of ways, including premature indulgence in sexual intercourse before the erotic disposition is sufficiently developed. This outlook has much in common with the theory Scruton formulated some thirty years later in a more elaborate form. Both outlooks appear to be teleological, and both call attention to the vicissitudes and perversions to which our natural striving toward love is susceptible. However, Scruton would almost certainly reject Frankl's bifurcated picture of two parallel inclinations, a sexual desire for objects and a (nonsexual, though "erotic"?) striving for comradship. I cannot resolve such questions about the sexual telos, questions I believe to be of great philosophic but less practical import. For a most illuminating analysis of eros in Western thought (which also doesn't undertake a final resolution), see Allan Bloom, *Love and Friendship* (New York: Simon and Schuster, 1993).

42. See Thomas I. Emerson, *Toward a General Theory of the First Amendment* (New York: Random House, 1963), p. 61, n. 21.

43. Nadine Strossen, *Defending Pornography: Free Speech, Sex and the Fight for Women's Rights* (New York: Scribner, 1995), p. 42.

44. Ibid., p. 56.

45. Ibid., p. 38.

46. *Roth* v. *U.S.*, *Chaplinski* v. *New Hampshire*, 315 US 568 (1942).

47. In 1774 the Continental Congress wrote a letter to the inhabitants of Quebec explaining their commitment to freedom of speech and press as necessary for "the advancement of truth, science, morality and art in general" and especially "diffusion of liberal sentiments on administration of government" and popular control of officeholders (cited in *Roth* v. *US*, at 484). James Madison regularly associated the free speech clause with the right of "free communication among the people" about public figures and policies. I'm not aware of any assertion, by any major publicist of the time, that personal self-expression is the reason for freedom of speech.

48. *Toward a General Theory of the First Amendment*, pp. 4–6.

49. Ibid., p. 6.

50. In *Jenkins* v. *Georgia*, 418 US 153 (1974), a unanimous Court held that the film "Carnal Knowledge" could not be deemed "patently offensive" under the 3-part "*Miller* test."

51. See Mill's *On Liberty*, ch. 2, "Of the Liberty of Thought and Discussion."

52. Meiklejohn, *Political Freedom: The Constitutional Powers of the People* (New York: Oxford Univ. Press, 1965).

53. *Whitney* v. *California*, 274 U.S. 357 (1927), concurring opinion.

54. *Paris AdultTheater* v. *Slaton*, at 67.

55. Ibid. at 71.

56. *Cohen* v. *California*, 403 U.S. 15 (1971), at 26.

57. *Barnes* v. *Glen Theater*, at 565, 570, 581, 591–93.

58. In the oral argument on *Glen Theatre*, a First Amendment attorney, speaking for the dancers, argued that all performance dancing is communication "inherently expressive of emotions and ideas." Justice Kennedy posed this question: "Suppose the proprietor of a car wash, wishing to attract more customers, hires a woman to take off all her clothes and 'just wander around [naked] to music'; is that a performance dance?" The attorney responded that it is and that it would be within the purview of the First Amendment. See David G. Savage, *Turning Right: The Making of the Rehnquist Supreme Court* (Somerset, N.J.: John Wiley & Sons, 1990), pp. 395–97. A lower standard for the definition of artistic and ideational communication is difficult, though not impossible, to imagine.

59. *American Booksellers Association* v. *Hudnut*.

60. Ibid. at 330.

61. The Supreme Court declined to hear Indianapolis's appeal from the *Hudnut* decision; so the decision stands with regard to that statute. But we don't know how much of *Hudnut*'s reasoning would be accepted by the Supreme Court as authoritative constitutional doctrine on obscenity law. If the whole argument were to be accepted and constitutionalized, the Court would have to abandon the antiobscenity doctrine of *Roth, Miller,* and *Paris*, along with much else. And that might well be the reason the Court declined to hear *Hudnut*, thereby avoiding endorsement of its libertarian rationale.

62. I've discussed the "distancing" factor in serious erotic literature in section 1 of this chapter.

63. I've discussed the *Miller* test in comparison with feminist antipornography attitudes and statutes earlier in this chapter.

64. The most thoughtful effort I know of to define "violent obscenity," and to make the case for limiting legal restrictions thereto, is provided in Donald Alexander Downs, *The New Politics of Pornography* (Chicago: Univ. of Chicago Press, 1989). See Downs's argument in chapter 5 of that book, especially at pp. 195–96. But even Downs doesn't grapple with the problems of definition I've just noted.

65. "Lyrics From the Gutter," *New York Times*, Op Ed, June 2, 1995.

66. *Obscenity and Public Morality*, p. 245.

67. Even such perceptive commentators as Bennett and Tucker seem to be somewhat entangled in an assumption of this sort. Regarding murderous "rap" and the like, they say: "We are not calling for censorship. We are both virtual absolutists on the First Amendment. Our appeal is to a sense of corporate responsibility and simple decency. There are things no one should sell." But as to the recording executives who regularly sell these things, the authors apparently acknowledge that "we cannot expect them to develop normative standards. And we certainly cannot depend on them to end their sponsorship" (Ibid.). So?

68. Apropos of contemporary events, we should note problems posed by new technology that proliferates images of the obscene and the sadistic. Speaking of Internet "Cybersex," journalist Gerard van der Leun observes: "I've had a chance to order whips and chains by the gross, drop in on group sex and download more explicit pictures than are displayed in a decade's worth of *Hustler*," ("Twilight Zone of the Id," *Time* 145, no. 12 [1995]). The author notes that this sort of thing can be addictive. Technically this is not an easy problem to deal with, but it is one to which principles of public morality apply. Apparently there are some legislators who think so; congressional inquiries and efforts have been launched, tentatively so far.

69. Walter Lippman made this point forty years ago: "If there is a dividing line between liberty and licence, it is where freedom of speech is no longer respected as a procedure of the truth and becomes the unrestricted right to exploit the ignorance and excite the passions of the people. Then freedom is such a hullabaloo of sophistry, propaganda, special pleading and salesmanship that it is difficult to remember why freedom of speech is worth the pain and trouble of defending it" Lippman, (*The Public Philosophy* [New York: Mentor Books, 1955], pp. 97–98). Lippman's observation is not a particularly nuanced one; it is, however, worth quoting every now and then against a dogmatic libertarianism that seems to be interested only in the personal liberty to "express" and not at all in the quality or character of what is expressed.

Index

AUTHORS

Aristotle, 25–28, 39–40 n. 37, 47, 66–67, 69, 98 n. 35, 172, 179 n. 19
Arkes, Hadley, 40 n. 39, 130–31 n. 33

Beauvoir, Simone de, 229 n. 40
Beiner, Ronald, 96–97 n. 23
Bellah, Robert, 30, 36, 95 n. 10
Benedict, Ruth, 129 n. 30
Bennett, William, 224, 231 n. 67
Berger, Brigette and Peter, 36, 96 n. 14, 97–98 n. 25
Berger, Fred, 134, 203–5
Berlin, Isaiah, 117, 118, 128–29 nn. 23 and 24
Berns, Walter, 187–88
Bloom, Allan, 128 n. 23, 229–30 n. 41
Brandeis, Louis D., Justice, 218
Brownmiller, Susan, 188–89
Burke, Edmund, 46–47

Clor, Harry M., 14–15, 98 n. 26, 179 n. 17, 195, 225
Committee on Homosexual Offenses. See Wolfenden Report

Davis, Murray, 98 n. 28
De Grazia, Sebastian, 42 n. 64, 52, 95 n. 11
Devlin, Sir Patrick, 48–49, 60, 99–100 n. 48

Dilulio, John J., 72
Donne, John, 211
Donnerstein, Edward, 228 n. 14
Douglas, William O., Justice, 219
Downs, Donald Alexander, 231 n. 64
Dworkin, Andrea, 227 n. 3
Dworkin, Ronald, 103–4, 149–57, 165, 169–70, 180 n. 41

Eckhardt, Ursula von, 180 n. 28
Elliott, George P., 208–9
Emerson, Thomas I., 214, 215–16

Feinberg, Joel, 112–14, 127 n. 3, 134
Finnis, John, 129 n. 31, 153
Frankfurter, Felix, Justice, 201
Frankl, Viktor, 229–30 n. 41
Freud, Sigmund, 65, 98 n. 31
Friedman, Lawrence, 9, 34, 38 n. 18, 183 n. 81
Fuller, Lon L., 99 n. 47

Galston, William, 74, 97 n. 24, 118, 129 n. 31, 182 n. 75
Garry, Ann, 194–95
Geertz, Clifford, 124
Glendon, Mary Ann, 36, 77
Gray, John, 117
Griffin, Susan, 228 n. 18

Harlan, John Marshall, Justice, 111
Hart, H. L. A., 41 n. 49, 49–50, 56, 71,
    76, 99–100 n. 48, 106, 110–11
Hayek, F. A., 144–47, 179–80 n. 19
Herrnstein, Richard J., 100 n. 55
Hobbes, Thomas, 69, 70
Hunter, James Davidson, 41 n. 52
Hyman, Stanley Edgar, 202

Jefferson, Thomas, 10, 148–49, 180 n. 28
Jong, Erica, 203

Kant, Immanuel, 181 n. 52
Kinsey, Alfred, 209–10
Kolakowski, Leszek, 35
Kommers, Donald, 39 n. 35
Kristol, Irving, 40–41 n. 45

Lawrence, D. H., 194, 195
Leun, Gerard van der, 232 n. 68
Levinson, Sanford, 33, 42 n. 56
Lippman, Samuel, 23
Lippman, Walter, 232 n. 69
Locke, John, 28, 29, 65–66, 69–70,
    166–69, 176
Longino, Helen E., 189, 192, 193–94

MacIntyre, Alasdair, 19–21
MacKinnon, Catherine A., 188
Macedo, Stephen, 55, 171–73, 174–75, 176,
    179 n. 19
Madison, James, 10, 54
Malmuth, Neil, 228 n. 14
Marcuse, Herbert, 93
Marx, Karl, 91
Meiklejohn, Alexander, 217
Michelson, Peter, 206
Mill, John Stuart, 10–11, 14, 15, 38 n. 10,
    41 n. 48, 71, 87–89, 92, 137, 140–42,
    147, 179 n. 17, 217
Miller, Henry, 209
Milton, John, 137, 139, 178 nn. 8 and 10

National Commission on Children,
    Report on, 37 n. 6
Nietzsche, Frederick, 143

Nozick, Robert, 179–80 n. 19

Packer, Herbert L., 19, 77, 86, 100 n. 61
Paine, Thomas, 54, 170
Pangle, Thomas, 40–41 n. 45, 99 n. 42
Plato, 115–16, 128 n. 17, 129–30 n. 32,
    172, 175

Randall, Richard S., 38 n. 19
Rawls, John, 128 n. 14, 157–65, 169–70
Robinson, Paul, 209–10
Rorty, Richard, 47, 94 n. 2
Rousseau, Jean-Jacques, 52, 79–80

Sandel, Michael J., 43 n. 65, 76
Sartre, Jean-Paul, 120–22, 129 n. 28
Savage, David G., 231 n. 58
Schauer, Frederick, 101–2 n. 70
Scruton, Roger, 210, 211, 229–30 n. 41
Siegel, Fred, 96 n. 21
Slade, Joseph P., 200–201
Sontag, Susan, 206–8
Stephens, James Fitzjames, 182 n. 64
Stoller, Robert J., 212, 229–30 nn. 39
    and 41
Stout, Jeffrey, 20
Strossen, Nadine, 214–15
Sunstein, Cass, 189, 198, 228 n. 15

Thoreau, Henry David, 42 n. 60
Tocqueville, Alexis de, 31, 163, 178–79
    n. 11
Tucker, C. DeLores, 224, 231 n. 67

van der Leun, Gerard. See Leun, Gerard
    van der

Waldron, Jeremy, 109–10
Warren, Earl, Chief Justice, 29
Weber, Max, 129 n. 30
Wilson, James Q., 72, 74, 100 n. 55, 182
    n. 76
Wolfenden Report, 107

Yeats, William Butler, 211

COURT CASES

California Supreme Court
  Petit v. *State Board of Education*, 23
Illinois Supreme Court
  Jarrett v. *Jarrett*, 23
U.S. Court of Appeals
  American Booksellers v. *Hudnut*, 189,
    220, 221, 231 n. 61
U.S. Supreme Court
  Barnes v. *Glen Theatre*, 16–17, 18, 219–
    20, 213 n. 58
  Cohen v. *California*, 25–27, 33, 39 n.
    34, 219

FCC v. *Pacifica Foundation*, 39 n. 35
Griswold v. *Connecticut*, 101 n. 62
Hoke v. *U.S.*, 41
Miller v. *California*, 24, 39 n. 34, 188,
    218–19, 222–23
Paris Adult Theatre v. *Slaton*, 24–27,
    39 n. 34, 63–64, 218–19
Reynolds v. *United States*, 22, 95 n. 9
Roth v. *U.S.*, 209, 218–19, 230 n. 47
Stanley v. *Georgia*, 101 n. 62